1, 2, AND 3 JOHN

THE NEW TESTAMENT DISCOURSE ANALYSIS COMMENTARIES SERIES

New Testament Discourse Analysis Commentaries (NTDAC) is a new and innovative commentary series on the Greek text of the New Testament. The volumes in the series pay close attention to the New Testament books as individual texts, based upon an explicit discourse analytic model articulated in the commentary and exemplified in the linguistic analysis.

Discourse analysis is an already proven productive method of textual interpretation for New Testament studies. It implies a theory of linguistic description that encompasses the smaller parts of language, such as words and even morphemes, but focuses upon the higher levels, such as the clause, the paragraph, and entire text as a meaningful unit. Discourse analysis—which may have a bottom-up or a top-down approach, or both—is not limited by traditional grammar but analyzes such linguistic features as the information structure, ideas and actions, and participant relations of a text, among other concerns. The interpretation provides both specific commentary supporting larger linguistic observations and broader commentary instantiated in textual particulars. The result is functional commentary useful to scholars for detailed knowledge of the Greek text and to practitioners for textually based information for preaching and teaching.

In the current landscape of commentary writing, in which commentaries have too often become simply comments on other commentaries, the NTDAC stands out by offering something different, compelling, and challenging. This is not to say that previous scholarship and reception history are irrelevant, but rather that the priority in the NTDAC is first and foremost a discourse analysis of the Greek text. In many ways, the series marks a return to what New Testament commentaries were originally designed to do, explicate the Greek text. However, the series seeks to do much more than that by introducing new observations on the Greek text that push interpretive boundaries and support previous findings by providing new linguistic insights.

The contributors to NTDAC approach the Greek text from a range of linguistic backgrounds. Nevertheless, they hold in common their desire to provide fresh interpretations of each book of the New Testament, based upon a specific discourse method.

STANLEY E. PORTER
MCMASTER DIVINITY COLLEGE
HAMILTON, ON, CANADA

1, 2, AND 3 JOHN

MAVIS M. LEUNG

◆PICKWICK *Publications* • Eugene, Oregon

1, 2, AND 3 JOHN

Copyright © 2025 Mavis M. Leung. All rights reserved. Except for brief quotations in critical publications or reviews, no part of this book may be reproduced in any manner without prior written permission from the publisher. Write: Permissions, Wipf and Stock Publishers, 199 W. 8th Ave., Suite 3, Eugene, OR 97401.

Pickwick Publications
An Imprint of Wipf and Stock Publishers
199 W. 8th Ave., Suite 3
Eugene, OR 97401

www.wipfandstock.com

PAPERBACK ISBN: 978-1-5326-8549-1
HARDCOVER ISBN: 978-1-5326-8550-7
EBOOK ISBN: 978-1-5326-8551-4

Cataloguing-in-Publication data:

Names: Leung, Mavis M., author.

Title: 1, 2, and 3 John / Mavis M. Leung

Description: Eugene, OR: Pickwick Publications, 2025 | New Testament Discourse Analysis Commentaries | Includes bibliographical references and index.

Identifiers: ISBN 978-1-5326-8549-1 (paperback) | ISBN 978-1-5326-8550-7 (hardcover) | ISBN 978-1-5326-8551-4 (ebook)

Subjects: LCSH: Bible.—Epistles of John—Commentaries. | Greek language, Biblical—Discourse analysis. | Bible.—New Testament—Language, style.

Classification: BS2805.53 L48 2025 (paperback) | BS2805.53 (ebook)

VERSION NUMBER 08/13/25

CONTENTS

Preface | vii

Abbreviations | ix

Introduction | 1
I. The Participants | 1
II. Occasion and Purpose | 6
III. Systemic Functional Linguistics | 8
IV. Genre, Structure, and Outline | 18

COMMENTARY ON 1 JOHN | 25

1:1–4	**I. Prologue**	27
1:5—5:12	**II. The Body of the Letter**	33
1:5—2:27	A. Adhering to and Behaving in Conformity with the Christian Beliefs	33
	1. 1:5—2:11	33
	2. 2:12–17	51
	3. 2:18–27	59
2:28—4:6	B. Living as God's Children in View of Christ's Future Coming	70
	1. 2:28—3:3	70
	2. 3:4–12	76
	3. 3:13–18	86
	4. 3:19–24	92
	5. 4:1–6	99

4:7—5:12	C. Acting in Conformity with God's Loving Nature | 106
	1. 4:7—5:4 | 106
	2. 5:5–12 | 122
5:13–21	III. Conclusion | 130

COMMENTARY ON 2 JOHN | 141

1–4	I. Opening | 145
5–11	II. Body | 153
12–13	III. Closing | 163

COMMENTARY ON 3 JOHN | 167

1–4	I. Opening | 171
5–12	II. Body | 180
13–15	III. Closing | 194

Bibliography | 197

Modern Authors Index | 203

Ancient Sources Index | 207

PREFACE

I AM HONORED TO BE invited to contribute to the volume on the Johannine epistles for the New Testament Discourse Analysis Commentaries (NTDAC) series. When I received the email invitation to be a contributor, I initially thought it was a promotion for a new commentary. However, when I read the email carefully, I felt honored and thrilled but also worried about my time and ability. About five months ago, I had promised to write a Chinese commentary on Paul's Letter to the Colossians for a commentary series, with a preliminary plan to finish writing the book in a year while on my sabbatical. Thus, I was not sure I would have adequate time to take up another writing project. Nevertheless, I decided to take a step of faith and accept the invitation to be a contributor for NTDAC. The biggest driving force behind my decision was the passion for studying the New Testament Greek and the desire to see the global church benefitting from a commentary series that attends to the original language of the Bible.

In line with the distinctive features of NTDAC, I have endeavored to keep this commentary focused on the text of the Johannine epistles. Discussion on the issues surrounding the history of the production or interpretation of these documents has been kept to a minimum. Given the focus on the use of language and the text itself, there is limited interaction with secondary literature in this commentary and at bottom for the purpose of illuminating the textual interpretation or linguistic analysis. I have adopted Michael A. K. Halliday's model of systemic functional linguistics as a tool to approach the text of 1–3 John, with special interest on how language is used to make meaning and achieve the rhetorical aims of these letters. The basic tenets of the Hallidayan theory of language are elucidated in the Introduction. Despite the adoption of systemic functional linguistics, the use of jargon is avoided in the interpretation of the Johannine epistles and it does not demand from the reader a mastery of this discourse analysis method.

I want to express my gratitude for Dr. Stanley E. Porter's invitation to write the commentary on 1–3 John. Thanks to Dr. Xiaxia Xue for introducing me to Halliday's sociolinguistics. I would like to thank all my former New Testament professors at Trinity Evangelical Divinity School for instilling in me a love of learning Greek. To my students of Evangel Seminary, Hong Kong, I am thankful for the questions that they have asked in class, which have sharpened my teaching of the biblical Greek in the past fifteen years. I am grateful for my husband, Felix, and our son, Ryan, who have been supportive of me throughout the course of this commentary.

Soli Deo gloria.

ABBREVIATIONS

1QS	Serek Hayaḥad (Rule of the Community)
2 Macc	2 Maccabees
Adv. Haer.	Irenaeus, *Adversus haereses* (*Against Heresies*)
BDAG	*A Greek-English Lexicon of the New Testament*
BDF	*A Greek Grammar of the New Testament and Other Early Christian Literature*
CD	Cairo Genizah copy of the Damascus Document
Hist. Eccl.	Eusebius, *Historia ecclesiastica* (*Ecclesiastical History*)
Jub.	*Jubilees*
LCL	Loeb Classical Library
LXX	Septuagint
NA27	*Novum Testamentum Graece*, 27th ed.
NA28	*Novum Testamentum Graece*, 28th ed.
NIV	New International Version
NLT	New Living Translation
NRSV	New Revised Standard Version
NT	New Testament
OT	Old Testament
P.Oxy.	Oxyrhynchus papyri
Pss. Sol.	*Psalms of Solomon*
SFL	Systemic Functional Linguistics

INTRODUCTION

The first, second, and third epistles of John are probably three of the last few books of the New Testament written. Since these three epistles resemble each other in language and thought, it is likely that they have a common source of production and similar social setting. Nevertheless, each of the three Johannine letters has its particular features that are worthy of consideration. This commentary will approach 1, 2, and 3 John as social discourses and seek to provide insights into the use of language in these epistles within their situational contexts. In this introductory chapter, issues regarding the participants (i.e., the author and the audience), occasion, and purpose of the three Johannine letters will be addressed in an effort to map out their social setting. Given our specific interest in language use, a section will be devoted to elucidate the method of discourse analysis adopted to analyze the texts of 1, 2, and 3 John in this commentary. Some preliminary comments concerning the discourse features in the Johannine letters will be provided. The remainder of this chapter will deal with the genre, structure, and outline of 1, 2, and 3 John.

I. THE PARTICIPANTS

A. Author

While the author of 1, 2, or 3 John does not identify himself by name, there is little doubt that the original readers knew his identity. The author of 2 or 3 John refers to himself as "the Elder" in the superscription in the letter opening. Church traditions ascribe authorship of these three epistles to the apostle John, who was the son of Zebedee and the brother of James. The early church historian Eusebius notes that Papias, the bishop of Hierapolis in the second century AD, "used quotations from the first epistle of John"

(*Hist. Eccl.* III.39.17). Irenaeus, writing in the second century AD, makes reference to several passages in 1 and 2 John and ascribes their authorship to John the disciple of the Lord (*Adv. Haer.* I.16.3; III.16.5, 8; cf. 1 John 2:18–22; 4:1–2; 5:1; 2 John 7–8, 10–11). In his *Stromateis* (II.15.66), Clement of Alexandria, a Christian theologian in the second and third centuries AD, speaks of "the longer epistle" of the apostle John and quotes from 1 John 5:16–17. Thus Clement knew of at least two letters written by John. Origen (ca. AD 185–254) refers to all three Johannine epistles and remarks that the authenticity of 2 and 3 John was disputed at his time (*Hist. Eccl.* VI.25.10). In a nutshell, the external evidence supports the view that John the son of Zebedee is the author of 1, 2, and 3 John.[1]

As for the internal evidence, a high degree of similarity in language and ideas between 1 John and the Fourth Gospel suggests that these two documents have the same author. Brooke observes more than fifty thematic parallels between 1 John and the Fourth Gospel, including the following four antitheses: light versus darkness (e.g., John 1:4–7; 3:19–21; 1 John 1:5–7), love versus hatred (e.g., John 3:19–21; 15:9–25; 1 John 3:11–15), God's children versus the devil's children (e.g., John 8:41–44; 1 John 3:10), and truth versus falsehood (e.g., John 8:44–45; 1 John 1:6, 8; 2:4, 21).[2] Furthermore, these two documents share an interest in the subject matters of the love commandment (e.g., John 13:33–34; 15:12, 17; 1 John 3:11; 4:11), Christ's incarnation (e.g., John 1:14; 1 John 4:2), God's gift of the eternal life (e.g., John 20:31; 1 John 5:13), and the believers' mutually abiding relationship with God or Jesus (e.g., John 14:20; 15:1–17; 17:23; 1 John 3:24; 4:13, 15).[3] It merits mention that the lexeme μονογενής is used to denote Jesus Christ as God's unique Son only in 1 John and the Fourth Gospel in the NT (John 1:14, 18; 3:16, 18; 1 John 4:9). Furthermore, all of the five occurrences of the lexeme παράκλητος (John 14:16, 26; 15:26; 16:7; 1 John 2:1) are found in these two writings and nowhere else in the NT.[4] The differences between 1 John and the Fourth Gospel (e.g., the identity of the Paraclete or the meaning of the word λόγος [John 1:1, 14; 1 John 1:1]) can be explained by the fact that they were produced in different circumstances and for varied purposes. Notably, the author of 1 John stresses his privileged status as an eyewitness of Jesus' earthly life and indicates that he has personal experience with what is proclaimed to his audience in 1 John

---

1. For more patristic evidence, see Stott, *Letters of John*, 18–20.
2. Brooke, *Critical and Exegetical Commentary*, ii–ix; cf. Brown, *Epistles of John*, 757–79; Köstenberger, *Theology of John's Gospel and Letters*, 86–87.
3. See the works in the preceding note.
4. Akin, *1, 2, 3 John*, 24.

1:1–5. There is a total of nineteen first-person plural expressions, including altogether twelve verbs (i.e., ἀκηκόαμεν [3x; vv. 1, 3, 5]; ἑωράκαμεν [3x; vv. 1, 2, 3]; ἐθεασάμεθα [v.1]; μαρτυροῦμεν [v. 2]; ἀπαγγέλλομεν [2x; vv. 2, 3]; γράφομεν [v. 4]; ἀναγγέλλομεν [v. 5]), six pronouns (i.e., ἡμῶν [4x; vv. 1c, 1e, 3, 4]; ἡμῖν [v. 2]; ἡμεῖς [v. 4]), and one occurrence of the possessive adjective (i.e., ἡμετέρα [v. 3]) in this passage. Nevertheless, the author often speaks to his audience using the first-person singular, particularly with respect to his reason of corresponding with them in the rest of the letter (e.g., 1 John 2:1, 7, 8, 12, 13, 14, 21, 26; 5:13). Thus the frequent occurrence of the first-person plural does not necessarily imply that 1 John has multiple authorship. It is probable that the author utilizes the exclusive first-person plural expressions (i.e., the audience are not included as part of the "we")[5] to band himself with other eyewitnesses of Jesus' life and ministry and thereby heighten the rhetorical impact of the proclamation in 1 John 1:1–5. Alternatively, the first-person plural expressions can be regarded as the "'we' of authoritative testimony" with respect to the author's self-references.[6] Granted that John the son of Zebedee wrote the Fourth Gospel, it is highly probable that he is the author of 1 John.

The resemblance in the thoughts and vocabulary between 2 John and 1 John suggests common authorship.[7] In both of these two letters, the Christian mandate to love one another is described as that which is not a new commandment but that which the author and his audience have had from the beginning (1 John 2:7; 2 John 5). Another shared feature is that the author's opponents are referred to as the "antichrist(s)" in both of 1 and 2 John (1 John 2:18, 22; 4:3; 2 John 7). Furthermore, the wording of the confession regarding Jesus Christ coming in the flesh in 2 John 7 is similar to that in 1 John 4:2, though there are differences in word order and the verbal tense in the Christological confessions in these two verses.[8] While the author of 2 John identifies himself as "the Elder," this self-reference does not preclude the possibility that he is an apostle. It is worth noting that Peter refers to himself as an apostle and an elder in a single letter (1 Pet 1:1; 5:1). If 2 John and 3 John were written in the first half of the nineties AD, "the Elder" is an appropriate self-designation for the apostle John because of his seniority.

---

5. See commentary on "Prologue."

6. Bauckham, *Jesus and the Eyewitnesses*, 373–75. For the view that the author uses the epistolary plural to refer to himself, see *BDF* 146–47 (§280).

7. Kruse, *Letters of John*, 7; Brooke, *Critical and Exegetical Commentary*, lxxiii–lxxix; Brown, *Epistles of John*, 755–57.

8. While the participle ἐρχόμενον is in the present tense in 2 John 7, the participle ἐληλυθότα is in the perfect tense in 1 John 4:2.

Since John was known to his audience, it is not necessary to introduce himself by name in his correspondences.

Most scholars believe that 3 John was written by the same "Elder" who penned 2 John.[9] The cause of the Elder's joy in regard to the believers' walking in the truth in 3 John 4 is akin to that in 2 John 4. Reminiscent of the closing remark in 2 John 12, the Elder expresses his desire to communicate with his audience face to face rather than with pen and ink in 3 John 13–14. Simply put, it is very likely that John the son of Zebedee is the author of all three Johannine epistles. If John took pen to write these three letters after finishing the Fourth Gospel, they can be dated to AD 90–95 during the time he ministered in Ephesus and other areas in the Roman province Asia according to the traditions (e.g., *Adv. Haer.* III.1.1, 3.4; *Hist. Eccl.* III.1.1, 23.3–4).[10] Therefore, the cultural context in which the meaning of the language in 1, 2, and 3 John should be construed is the Greco-Roman world of the first century AD. Furthermore, as will be pointed out in this commentary, the author's authoritative status over his audience bears on how language is used in these three epistles.

B. Audience

The identity of the audience is not specified in 1 John. There is no named individual or any inkling of the audience's geographical location in this letter. That said, it is evident that 1 John was written for Christians. The audience's spiritual standing and relationship to God are affirmed in 1 John 2:12–14. As indicated in 1 John 5:13, the author writes to those who believe in the name of the Son of God so that they may be certain of their possession of the eternal life. Since the author addresses his audience as "dear children" (τεκνία in 1 John 2:1, 12, 28; 3:18; 4:4; 5:21; παιδία in 1 John 2:14, 18; 3:7), "beloved" (ἀγαπητοί in 1 John 2:7; 3:2, 21; 4:1, 7, 11), and "brothers and sisters" (ἀδελφοί in 1 John 3:13), they probably belong to the congregations that are in his pastoral care and not in close proximity to his current whereabouts. Although the author frequently employs the device of the inclusive "we" to speak to his audience (e.g., 1 John 2:3, 5, 18, 25; 3:1–2, 11, 14, 16, 19–24), there is no evidence that he is corresponding with his home church or physically present with the audience at the time of writing.[11] Lamb shows that the author does not have close contact with his audience on account of

---

9. Kruse, *Letters of John*, 42; Stott, *Letters of John*, 28–29.

10. Jobes, *1, 2, and 3 John*, 29; Köstenberger, *Theology of John's Gospel and Letters*, 93–94.

11. Campbell, *1, 2, and 3 John*, 17.

the relevant linguistic features in 1 John 2:7–17.[12] It has been proposed that 2 John was originally the cover letter of 1 John and provided the author's personal greeting to the recipients.[13] If this is the case, these two epistles might have been sent together as "parts of the same epistolary package" to the same congregation(s) or have an overlap in their intended audiences.[14] Since church traditions affirm that John the son of Zebedee spent his last years of life in and around Ephesus (see above), the audience of 1 John are likely to be the members of the local church(es) located in Asia Minor in the last decade of the first century AD.

Second John was written by the Elder to the "chosen lady and her children" (2 John 1; cf. vv. 4, 5). While it is possible that the "chosen lady" refers to a specific woman, most commentators believe that this feminine designation denotes figuratively a local church in this letter.[15] Thus the "children" of the lady refer to the believers in this church. Moreover, the "children" of the lady's "chosen sister" (2 John 13) denotes the believers of the congregation which the Elder belonged to at the time of his writing. The figurative view above is adopted in this commentary. According to Stott, "the unconscious transition from the second-person singular to the second-person plural" in various places in 2 John suggests that the Elder is addressing a community rather than an individual.[16] While the second-person singular references (5x) are found in v. 4 (σου), v. 5 (σε, σοι), and v. 13 (σε, σου), the second-person plural references (10x) are present in v. 6 (ἠκούσατε, περιπατῆτε), v. 8 (βλέπετε, ἀπολέσητε, ἀπολάβητε), v. 10 (ὑμᾶς, λαμβάνετε, λέγετε), and v. 12 (ὑμῖν, ὑμᾶς) in this letter. It is worth mentioning that the portrayal of God's people as a woman is not uncommon in the biblical traditions (e.g., Isa 54:1, 4–6; Jer 31:32; 2 Cor 11:2; Gal 4:25–26; Eph 5:32; Rev 12:1, 17; 19:7). In particular, Peter employs the feminine nominative singular adjective συνεκλεκτή to depict the Christian community in "Babylon" (1 Pet 5:13), which is likely to be a veiled reference to Rome. By using a feminine form of the lexeme ἐκλεκτός with respect to the lady as the personification of a congregation, the Elder intimates that its members have the status as God's people in the letter opening in 2 John 1.

---

12. Lamb, *Text, Context and the Johannine Community*, 176–83 (182).

13. Jobes, *1, 2, and 3 John*, 28–29, 248–50; cf. Johnson, *Writings of the New Testament*, 497–98.

14. Johnson, *Writings of the New Testament*, 498.

15. See, e.g., Kruse, *Letters of John*, 38; Yarbrough, *1–3 John*, 333–34; Stott, *Letters of John*, 202–4.

16. Stott, *Letters of John*, 203–4; cf. Lamb, *Text, Context and the Johannine Community*, 186–87.

Third John was written to a Christian named Gaius, whom the Elder loves in the truth (3 John 1). Although there are several figures who are called "Gaius" in the NT (Acts 19:29; 20:4; Rom 16:23; 1 Cor 1:14), there is no evidence to identify the recipient of 3 John as any of these figures. Since the Elder praises Gaius for showing hospitality to traveling missionaries and urges him to continue doing so (3 John 5–8), it is likely that Gaius was a wealthy believer belonging to a Christian community in Asia Minor and within the circle of the Elder's influence.

II. OCCASION AND PURPOSE

The occasion for writing 1 John concerns a schism in the church that was caused by the false teachers. The teachers were previously members of the Christian community but have already left (1 John 2:19). These secessionists, whom the author refers to as the antichrists (1 John 2:18, 22; 4:3; cf. 2 John 7) and false prophets (1 John 4:1), seek to undermine the beliefs regarding Jesus—that he is the Christ and the Son of God who has come in the flesh (1 John 2:22–23; 4:1–3, 15; 5:1, 5; cf. 2 John 7–9). Since their erroneous teaching plays down Jesus' messianic status, it has the ramification of diminishing the atoning significance of his death (cf. 1 John 5:6–8).[17] In addition to promulgating the incorrect understanding of the person and work of Jesus Christ, the way in which the secessionists conduct themselves is not exemplary of Christian moral living. They have a distorted view of sin that downplays its importance and perhaps they claim to be sinless (1 John 1:8, 10). They do not obey God's commandments (1 John 2:4), and their behavior is at variance with the truth (1 John 1:6). Importantly, the secessionists do not carry out Jesus' command given to his disciples that they should love one another (cf. 1 John 2:9; 3:23). Rather than practicing righteousness, the false teachers do what is sinful and refuse to love the believers and accordingly showing themselves to be the devil's children (1 John 3:8, 10).[18]

The purpose of 1 John is twofold. First, this letter was written so that its readers are assured of their relationship to God and their possession of eternal life (1 John 5:13). In addition, they know God and are his children (1 John 2:12–14; 3:1–2; 5:19–20). Second, and more crucially, the author attempts to affect his audience to behave in accord with their Christian profession. This attempt is undertaken primarily through covert commands, which are not expressed by the imperative verbs in this epistle (more on this below). While the surface structure of 1 John appears to be expository,

---

17. Streett, *They Went Out from Us*, 358; Marshall, *Epistles of John*, 15.
18. Akin, *1, 2, 3 John*, 29–31.

it was actually produced for a hortatory aim.[19] Despite their departure from the church, the secessionists continue making efforts to influence the believers to adopt the erroneous beliefs and unrighteous behaviors (1 John 2:26; 3:7; cf. 2 John 10). In view of this, the author admonishes his audience to be on their guard against the infiltration of the false teaching into the community. Rather than being led astray by the secessionists, the believers should avoid sin (1 John 2:1) and hold on to the doctrines that are affirmative of Jesus' status as the Messiah and God's Son (1 John 2:23; 4:15; 5:1, 5). Furthermore, they should genuinely love one another in the aftermath of the schism in the church (1 John 3:11, 23; 4:7). It is the author's conviction that Christian love must be put into action and manifest in the believers' willingness to lay down their lives for the welfare of other members in God's family (1 John 3:16–18).

There is not much information in 2 John to draw inferences about the circumstance that led to its production. Yet it is apparent that the audience (i.e., a congregation and its members) are facing the threat of false teachers who err in denying Jesus Christ as coming in the flesh (2 John 7). The opponents of the Elder, whom he denotes as the deceivers and antichrists (2 John 7), do not continue in the teaching of Christ and accordingly do not belong to God (2 John 9). Given the similar descriptions of the false teachers in 1 John and 2 John, it is likely that the Elder's opponents in 2 John are the same as the secessionists being rebuked in the former letter. Upon leaving the church, the false teachers probably travel around to propagate their errant Christology and expand their circle of influence. The Elder wrote 2 John to instruct his audience not to welcome or provide aid to these itinerant teachers, whose teaching is out of line with the Christian faith (2 John 10–11). Another purpose of this letter is to encourage the communal love among the fellow believers (2 John 5–6).[20] If 2 John was sent as the cover letter of 1 John (see above), it serves to provide the author's personal greeting and a concise introduction to the principal matters that are treated in great detail in the latter epistle.

Unlike 1 John or 2 John, no erroneous teaching is mentioned in 3 John. It appears that several traveling missionaries, presumably sent out from the Elder's congregation, visited Gaius and were received by him (3 John 5–6). The Elder encourages Gaius to continue providing hospitality to other Christian workers who come to his place and need his assistance. It is probable that Demetrius is one of these itinerant workers. The Elder took pen

---

19. See Miehle, "Theme in Greek Hortatory Discourse," 178; Longacre, "Exhortation and Mitigation in First John," 3; Longacre, "Towards an Exegesis of 1 John," 277–79; Leung, "Metaphorical Expressions of the Commands in 1 John" (forthcoming).

20. Kruse, *Letters of John*, 39–40.

to write this letter to recommend him to Gaius (3 John 12). Moreover, the Elder calls attention to Diotrephes's wicked deeds in refusing to welcome his envoys and thereby rejecting his authority in 3 John 9–10. By indicating his plan to reproach Diotrephes, the Elder hints that Gaius should behave differently from Diotrephes and show hospitality to the traveling missionaries accordingly.

III. SYSTEMIC FUNCTIONAL LINGUISTICS

The method of discourse analysis employed in this commentary to analyze the texts and linguistic characteristics in 1, 2, and 3 John is based on the model of systemic functional linguistics (SFL) proposed by Michael A. K. Halliday.[21] In this linguistic model, language is conceived of as a system or network of choices available to the speaker or writer to create meanings in a social context.[22] Since people do not simply use language to "mean things" but also "do things," at bottom discourse analysis deals with how language is used to make meanings and achieve goals in different social settings.[23] Rather than focusing on the function of a word or phrase, discourse analysis is concerned with the larger linguistic unit beyond the level of the clause or sentence. However, the small grammatical constituents in the clause or sentence are within the scope of discourse studies.[24] The Hallidayan model of SFL offers a set of powerful tools for the discourse analyst to construe the relationship between text and context and understand how language functions to mean or do things in the text.[25] By adopting the SFL approach to discourse analysis, the interpretative task of this commentary is not simply explicating the content of 1, 2, or 3 John but also the ways in which the author draws on the vast resource of language to convey his ideas to the audience and accomplish the purposes of writing these three letters. From the systemic functional perspective, the language of a text is affected by its specific context of situation and the broader context of culture. As noted above, the latter cultural context of 1, 2, and 3 John is the first-century AD Greco-Roman world. The context of situation of a text is defined by the three variables of "field," "tenor," and "mode," according to the model of SFL.

21. See Halliday and Matthiessen, *Halliday's Introduction to Functional Grammar*.

22. Eggins says that SFL's approach to the use of language can be described succinctly as "functional, semantic, contextual, and semiotic" (*Introduction to Systemic Functional Linguistics*, 3). For the system of choices in SFL model, see pp. 188–205.

23. Gee and Handford, *Routledge Handbook of Discourse Analysis*, 1.

24. Reed, *Discourse Analysis of Philippians*, 28.

25. Graber, "Context in Text," 9.

These three contextual variables are respectively related to the three metafunctions of language (i.e., the ideational, interpersonal, and textual metafunctions) and altogether constitute the "register" of the text. The ideational metafunction is further divided into the experiential and logical functions. The remainder of this section will delineate the tenets of field, tenor, and mode and offer some preliminarily comments in regard to the discourse features of 1, 2, or 3 John.

A. Field

Field deals with "what's going on in the situation" and is related to the ideational metafunction of language for construing human experience in the world.[26] More specifically, field indicates the social activity that the participants are involved in and the activity's circumstance (e.g., time, place, cause, manner). Thus, the field of a text is generally pertinent to its topic. The various experiential meanings in the world are categorized by six "process types" within the system of SFL. By analyzing the different process types of the clauses viewed as representations of human experiences, the interpreter can gain insights into the events being unfolded in the text and the overall flow of topics in it. The six process types are outlined as follows:[27]

i. The "material process" is concerned with the processes of doing and happening. This process type usually involves a performative or dynamic verb with the actor or doer carrying out a physical action.

ii. The "mental process" is concerned with the processes of thinking, perceiving, and feeling.

iii. The "verbal process" is concerned with the processes of saying, showing, and expressing.

iv. The "behavioral process" is concerned with "the processes of physiological and psychological behavior."[28]

v. The "existential process" is concerned with the kind of experience regarding that something exists (i.e., "there was/is something").[29]

vi. The "relational process" is concerned with the processes of being, becoming, and possessing. This process type always involves two

---

26. Halliday and Matthiessen, *Halliday's Introduction to Functional Grammar*, 33.

27. For a succinct summary of the different process types, see Eggins, *Introduction to Systemic Functional Linguistics*, 206–53.

28. Eggins, *Introduction to Systemic Functional Linguistics*, 233.

29. Eggins, *Introduction to Systemic Functional Linguistics*, 238.

participants. There are two major subtypes of the relational process, which are the "attributive" and "identifying" relational processes. The attributive relational process refers to the process of ascribing an "attribute" or characteristic to the "carrier." The identifying relational process refers to the process of defining the identity of the "token" by a "value." Depending on the nature of the participants or participant relationship, the attributive or identifying processes can be classified as "intensive," "circumstantial," or "possessive."[30]

Aside from the experiential function, the logical function is the other aspect of the ideational metafunction of language with respect to field. This latter function is concerned with the logical relation of one event to another as portrayed across the clauses. The two notions concerning the relationship between the conjoined clauses are "taxis" and "logico-semantics." Regarding the notion of taxis, the clausal relation is that of either parataxis (i.e., the two conjoined clauses have equal status and are independent of each other) or hypotaxis (i.e., one clause is the main clause upon which another clause is dependent). Regarding the notion of logico-semantics, the clauses can be related to each other by way of projection (i.e., mental or verbal projection) or expansion (i.e., elaboration, extension, or enhancement).[31]

As for the "field" of 1 John, the relational process type (which concerns the process of being or becoming) predominates and takes up approximately one-third of the altogether 343 ranking clauses that contain a finite verb in this epistle.[32] It is thus evident that there is an emphasis on the process of being in 1 John. For example, the author employs four instances of the first-person plural verbs (i.e., ἐσμέν [2x]; ἐσόμεθα [2x]) to encode the experiential meanings as regards the believers' characteristics or status as God's children in 1 John 3:1–2. All four instances above are relational verbs. The mental process type (which concerns the process of thinking, perceiving, or feeling) has the second highest frequency of occurrences, totaling approximately ninety-four in this epistle.[33] Notably, the author's eyewitness experience is underlined by virtue of several mental process clauses pertaining to the perception of hearing or seeing in 1 John 1:1–4. Generally speaking, the author is fond of utilizing the device of mental projection to convey

---

30. In addition, Eggins mentions the "causative" relational process. See Eggins, *Introduction to Systemic Functional Linguistics*, 248–49.

31. See the discussion in Eggins, *Introduction to Systemic Functional Linguistics*, 258–59.

32. The 343 ranking clauses that contain a finite verb do not include the verbless or embedded clauses in 1 John.

33. The instances in the verbless or embedded clauses are not counted.

the ideas regarding Christian beliefs or reassurance to his audience. There is a total of twenty-one instances of the mental projection that consists of the lexeme γινώσκω (8x), οἶδα (11x), or πιστεύω (2x) in connection with the subordinating conjunction ὅτι in 1 John.[34] The field of 2 John or 3 John is different from that of 1 John. Material process, which deals with the process of doing or happening, is the dominant process type in both of these two epistles. There are altogether seven occurrences (32 percent) of this process type in the ranking clauses in 2 John and fourteen occurrences (41 percent) in the ranking clauses in 3 John.[35] For example, the Elder uses a total of five performative verbs in the third-person singular (i.e., ἐπιδέχεται [vv. 9, 10], ποιεῖ [v. 10], κωλύει [v. 10], ἐκβάλλει [v. 10]) to depict what his opponent Diotrephes has done wickedly in 3 John 9–10. This commentary will address the implications of the various processes and experiential meanings in the three Johannine letters when appropriate.

In addition to the process types or experiential meaning of the clauses, this commentary will attend to the semantic clusters of the related lexemes in order to have a better grasp of what is unfolded in the situational context of 1, 2, or 3 John.[36] For convenience's sake, the semantic domain classification proposed and delineated in Louw's and Nida's lexicon of the NT will be adopted in this commentary.[37] Furthermore, the annotation provided on OpenText.org will be consulted when determining the clausal constructions and the semantic domains that the words are belonged to.[38] To illustrate, there is a total of 118 occurrences of different lexemes from semantic domain 12 ("supernatural beings and powers") in 1 John. These relevant lexemes include θεός (62x), υἱός (22x), πατήρ (12x),[39] πνεῦμα (12x), πονηρός (5x),[40] διάβολος (4x), and εἴδωλον (1x). Aside from semantic domain 12 ("supernatural beings and powers"), the lexical occurrences from semantic

---

34. The lexeme γινώσκω occurs in connection with ὅτι altogether eight times in 1 John 2:3, 5, 28, 29; 3:19, 24; 4:13; 5:2. The lexeme οἶδα occurs in connection with ὅτι altogether eleven times in 1 John 2:29; 3:2, 5, 14, 15; 5:13, 15 (2x), 18, 19, 20. The lexeme πιστεύω occurs in connection with ὅτι twice in in 1 John 5:1 and 5:5.

35. The verbless or embedded clauses are not counted in the total number of the material process clauses in 2 John or 3 John.

36. See Porter, *Letter to the Romans*, 28–29.

37. Louw and Nida, *Greek-English Lexicon of the New Testament*.

38. Porter et al., *OpenText.Org*.

39. Note that the two occurrences of the vocative plural πατέρες (1 John 2:13, 14) do not fall into semantic domain 12 ("supernatural beings and powers").

40. The word πονηρά in 1 John 3:12 is not from semantic domain 12 ("supernatural beings and powers").

domain 33 ("communication"; 89x),[41] semantic domain 25 ("attitudes and emotions"; 74x), and semantic domain 88 ("moral and ethical qualities and related behavior"; 61x) are high in this letter. It is noteworthy that 52 of the total 74 lexical occurrences from semantic domain 25 ("attitudes and emotions") above are various forms of the 3 cognate lexemes ἀγαπάω (28x),[42] ἀγάπη (18x),[43] and ἀγαπητοί (6x).[44] Among the 61 lexical instances from semantic domain 88 ("moral and ethical qualities and related behavior"), there are altogether 27 occurrences of the 2 related lexemes ἁμαρτία (17x) and ἁμαρτάνω (10x).[45] The 2 lexemes Ἰησοῦς (12x) and Χριστός (8x) from semantic domain 93 ("names of people and places") are detected altogether 20 times.[46] In short, the observation from the semantic clusters above suggests that 1 John is primarily concerned with the subject matters regarding God, his Son Jesus Christ, love, and sin, among other topics.

B. Tenor

Tenor, which deals with "who is taking part in the situation," is pertinent to the interpersonal metafunction of language regarding the interactants' statuses and role relationship.[47] Martin and Rose consider "power" and "solidarity" as the vertical and horizontal dimensions of tenor, respectively.[48] According to Halliday and Matthiessen, the different roles played by the participants in a social activity may be "institutional roles," "status roles" (which concern the participants' power relation and social standing), "contact roles" (which concern the participants' familiarity with one another), or "sociometric roles" (which concern the participants' affective involvement

---

41. The majority of the lexical occurrences from semantic domain 33 ("communication") are present in 1 John 1 (14x), 1 John 2 (36x), and 1 John 5 (22x). There are comparably few occurrences of the lexemes from semantic domain 33 in 1 John 3 (9x) and 1 John 4 (8x).

42. 1 John 2:10, 15 (2x); 3:10, 11, 14 (2x), 18, 23; 4:7 (2x), 8, 10 (2x), 11 (2x), 12, 19 (2x), 20 (3x), 21 (2x); 5:1 (2x), 2 (2x).

43. 1 John 2:5, 15; 3:1, 16, 17; 4:7, 8, 9, 10, 12, 16 (3x), 17, 18 (3x); 5:3.

44. 1 John 2:7; 3:2, 21; 4:1, 7, 11.

45. The two related lexemes ἁμαρτία (1 John 1:7, 8, 9 [2x]; 2:2, 12; 3:4 [2x], 5 [2x], 8, 9; 4:10; 5:16 [2x], 17 [2x]) and ἁμαρτάνω (1 John 1:10; 2:1 [2x]; 3:6 [2x], 8, 9; 5:16 [2x], 18) occur seventeen times and ten times respectively.

46. The two lexemes Ἰησοῦς (1 John 1:3, 7; 2:1, 22; 3:23; 4:2, 3, 15; 5:1, 5, 6, 20) and Χριστός (1 John 1:3; 2:1, 22; 3:23; 4:2; 5:1, 6, 20) occur twelve times and eight times respectively.

47. Halliday and Matthiessen, *Halliday's Introduction to Functional Grammar*, 33.

48. Martin and Rose, *Working with Discourse*, 302.

and attitudes towards one another).⁴⁹ One interpersonal resource for the speaker or writer to construct tenor is "appraisal," which deals with how the participants show affect, judgment, or appreciation towards someone or something (e.g., a person's character or action).⁵⁰ For the present purpose, the way in which the author of 1, 2 or 3 John uses language to hint at his approval or disapproval of certain attitudes, deeds, or people to bring the audience into alignment with his position will be observed in this commentary. The participants' relationship may also be encoded through the grammatical persons in the clauses, which are regarded as exchanges pertaining to the tenor of discourse.⁵¹ For example, the author of 2 John or 3 John intimates his authoritative status over the audience by identifying himself as "the Elder" using the nominative case at the beginning of the epistle (2 John 1; 3 John 1). The author of 1 John positions himself as possessing firsthand knowledge and thus having more power than his audience through the use of a number of the exclusive first-person plural pronouns or indicative verbs (i.e., the audience are not included as part of the "we") in the prologue in 1 John 1:1–4. In contrast, he employs the inclusive first-person plural expressions to show commonness with the audience in the body of this letter (e.g., 1 John 2:3, 5, 28; 3:1–2, 14, 16; 5:4, 11, 14, 15, 18–20).

The participants' role relationships can be discerned by analyzing the varied types of speech function or clause in the discourse. There are four basic speech functions in Halliday's model of SFL. They are statement (which gives information), question (which demands information), offer (which gives goods-and-services), and command (which demands goods-and-services).⁵² These four speech functions above find their realizations in different types of mood or clause. In particular, the indicative mood or declarative clause is used for making statement to provide information. The imperative mood or directive clause is used for expressing command to demand goods-and-services. Porter modifies the Hallidayan paradigm of speech functions to befit the Greek attitudinal system and further devises the following Greek speech functions: declarative statement, projective statement, projective contingent statement, command, and question of varied kinds.⁵³ This commentary obtains insights from Porter's reformulated

49. Halliday and Matthiessen, *Halliday's Introduction to Functional Grammar*, 33.
50. Martin and White, *Language of Evaluation*, 1–41.
51. Porter, *Letter to the Romans*, 32.
52. Halliday and Matthiessen, *Halliday's Introduction to Functional Grammar*, 134–39; Eggins, *Introduction to Systemic Functional Linguistics*, 146–48.
53. The "projective statement" involves the use of the subjunctive mood in Greek. The "projective contingent statement" involves the use of the optative mood. See Porter, "Systemic Functional Linguistics," 27–29; *Letter to the Romans*, 33.

network of the types of Greek speech function to approach and construe the tenor of 1, 2, or 3 John. The preliminary comment about the speech function types in 1 John is that declarative statement (82 percent) has the highest frequency. The other speech functions include projective statement (14 percent), command (3 percent), and question (1 percent).[54] There are altogether ten imperative verbs in the whole letter. They are ἀγαπᾶτε (1 John 2:15), μενέτω (2:24), μένετε (2x; 2:27, 28),[55] ἴδετε (3:1), πλανάτω (3:7), θαυμάζετε (3:13), πιστεύετε (4:1), δοκιμάζετε (4:1), and φυλάξατε (5:21).[56] All of the questions are rhetorical questions in 1 John 2:22; 3:1, 12, 17; 5:5. Rather than seeking information, the author employs these rhetorical questions to engage his audience or add emphasis to what is said. The speech functions found in the other two Johannine epistles are declarative statement (70 percent in 2 John; 84 percent in 3 John), projective statement (20 percent in 2 John; 8 percent in 3 John), and command (10 percent in 2 John; 8 percent in 3 John). The speech function of question is not detected in 2 and 3 John. In view of the preponderance of the declarative and projective statements in 1, 2, or 3 John, the author frequently enacts the role of giving information to his audience.

Despite what was said above, it should be stressed that 1 John consists of a considerable amount of the implicit commands.[57] While the author has the power in relation to his audience, he does not propound the ethical exhortations outright or authoritatively.[58] Rather than utilizing the imperative to issue explicit directives to his audience, the author tends to influence them in the subtle manner to practice the communal love or abstain from sinning by virtue of various statements that are realized by the indicative (e.g., the verb of obligation ὀφείλω in 1 John 2:6; 3:16; 4:11), the hortatory subjunctive (e.g., 1 John 3:18; 4:7), or the combination of the lexeme ἐντολή or ἀγγελία with an epexegetical ἵνα-clause (e.g., 1 John 3:11, 23;

---

54. The "projective statement" involves the use of the subjunctive mood in Greek.

55. In this commentary, the predicator μένετε in the present tense is considered as an imperative instead of indicative verb in 1 John 2:27.

56. The two occurrences of the predicator γινώσκετε are probably in the indicative mood in 1 John 2:29 and 4:2. These two instances are not included in the list of the ten imperative verbs in 1 John. Fantin also identifies a total of ten imperative verbs in this letter. Fantin, *Greek Imperative Mood in the New Testament*, 68.

57. For the covert commands in 1 John, see Miehle, "Theme in Greek Hortatory Discourse," 155–56; Longacre, "Exhortation and Mitigation in First John"; Sherman and Tuggy, *Semantic and Structural Analysis*, 2, 6–8; Leung, "Metaphorical Expressions of the Commands in 1 John" (forthcoming).

58. For Lamb, the implicit commands in 1 John "may be regarded as a diminution of the writer's authority" (Lamb, *Text, Context and the Johannine Community*, 178).

4:21).⁵⁹ For instance, in regard to the use of the three occurrences of the lexeme ὀφείλω above, the generic statement functions like a modulated command to exhort the audience to walk as Jesus walked in 1 John 2:6. The first-person plural present active indicative verb ὀφείλομεν is utilized to underscore the believers' obligation to emulate Jesus' self-sacrifice for the sake of others in 1 John 3:16. The third and last occurrence of the lexeme ὀφείλω is pertinent to the Christian duty to love one another in 1 John 4:11.⁶⁰ According to SFL, the construction that involves the employment of an untypical or incongruent mood option (e.g., the indicative or subjunctive mood) for expressing command (which is typically realized by the imperative mood) is considered as the "grammatical metaphor."⁶¹ Generally speaking, the author utilizes the linguistic device of the grammatical metaphor to soften the directives, provide the motivational factors of compliance, or engage the audience for achieving his negotiation goals. The covert commands and their "metaphorical" forms in the Johannine epistles will be indicated throughout this commentary when necessary.

C. Mode

Mode is related to the textual metafunction of language that concerns, specifically, how the clause is organized as a message and, more broadly, the flow of information in the text.⁶² Furthermore, spoken language and written language can be differentiated in general by their textual qualities vis-à-vis the lexical density, grammatical intricacy, and other linguistic features.⁶³ In regard to the mode of 1, 2, or 3 John, these three epistles are written texts produced in the situations where it is impossible for the author to receive immediate feedback from the audience due to their spatial distance from

---

59. For the different degrees of the mitigation pertaining to the exhortations in 1 John, see Miehle, "Theme in Greek Hortatory Discourse," 156; Sherman and Tuggy, *Semantic and Structural Analysis*, 2.

60. See Leung, "Ethics and *Imitatio Christi* in 1 John," 124–26.

61. For the concept of the grammatical metaphor, see Taverniers, "Grammatical Metaphor in SFL," 5–33.

62. Matthiessen et al., *Key Terms in Systemic Functional Linguistics*, 220–23. Halliday and Matthiessen note that mode is concerned with "what role is being played by language." See Halliday and Matthiessen, *Halliday's Introduction to Functional Grammar*, 33.

63. Eggins, *Introduction to Systemic Functional Linguistics*, 92–93. Eggins says that written language tends to have a higher level of lexical density and a lower level of grammatical intricacy (i.e., not many clauses in a sentence) as compared to spoken language (p. 93).

each other.⁶⁴ The two key notions in the analysis of the mode of a text are "cohesion" and "thematic structure." The notion of cohesion deals with "the way the elements within a text bind it together as 'a unified whole.'"⁶⁵ The linguistic devices for creating the textual cohesion include "conjunction" (which concerns how different clauses or paragraphs are connected logically), "reference" (which concerns how the participants are introduced and kept track of), "ellipsis and substitution" (which concerns how a textual element is omitted or replaced by another), and "lexical cohesion" (which concerns how various lexical items are related to each other).⁶⁶ As an example, the prepositional phrase ἐν τούτῳ (14x) occurs frequently to perform the deictic and referential functions in 1 John and thus contributing to its overall cohesion (cf. 1 John 2:3, 4, 5 [2x]; 3:10, 16, 19, 24; 4:2, 9, 10, 13, 17; 5:2). Furthermore, the author employs the two lexemes πνεῦμα (7x) and θεός (8x) that fall into semantic domain 12 ("supernatural beings and powers") and altogether fifteen times to enhance the unity in 1 John 4:1–6. Among the total thirty-two conjunctions in 2 John, there are nineteen conjunctions functioning to link the ranking clauses and indicate their different relations (e.g., elaboration, extension, contrast, condition, comparison, and cause). These altogether nineteen conjunctions joining the ranking clauses in 2 John include καί (5x; vv. 1c, 5a, 6a, 10b, 10d),⁶⁷ ἀλλά (3x; vv. 1d, 8c, 12b), ἵνα (5x; vv. 5b, 6b, 6e, 8b, 12c), καθώς (2x; vv. 4c, 6d), ὅτι (2x; vv. 4b, 7a), εἰ (v. 10a), and γάρ (v. 11a).⁶⁸ As for 3 John, it is noteworthy that there is a total of eleven direct or indirect participant references to Diotrephes in vv. 9–10 (cf. the reference chain: ὁ φιλοπρωτεύων; Διοτρέφης; ἐπιδέχεται; αὐτοῦ; ποιεῖ; φλυαρῶν; ἀρκούμενος; αὐτός; ἐπιδέχεται; κωλύει; ἐκβάλλει).⁶⁹ He is introduced as a person who loves to be first (v. 9) and referred to

---

64. Eggins, *Introduction to Systemic Functional Linguistics*, 91.

65. Eggins, *Introduction to Systemic Functional Linguistics*, 24.

66. For the cohesive devices, see Eggins, *Introduction to Systemic Functional Linguistics*, 31–51; Halliday and Matthiessen, *Halliday's Introduction to Functional Grammar*, 593–657; Porter and O'Donnell, *Discourse Analysis and the Greek New Testament*, 190–223.

67. Following the contrastive conjunction ἀλλά, the conjunction καί (v. 1d) is not considered as linking the two ranking clauses in v. 1c and v. 1d. Therefore, this latter conjunction in v. 1d is not included in the total nineteen instances of the conjunctions that connect the ranking clauses in 2 John.

68. Aside from the nineteen conjunctions that connect the ranking clauses, the remaining thirteen conjunctions are present in different word groups or embedded clauses in 2 John (cf. καί in vv. 1a, 1d, 2, 3 [2x], 7c, 9a, 9c [2x], 12a, 12b; ἀλλά in v. 5a; ὡς in v. 5a).

69. For the idea of participant references or reference chain, see Eggins, *Introduction to Systemic Functional Linguistics*, 37–40.

frequently throughout this unit. To a certain extent, these eleven direct or indirect participant references to Diotrephes above play a part in building the texture of 3 John 9–10 as a cohesive unit in this brief letter.[70]

Aside from the notion of cohesion, the other key notion in regard to "mode" and particularly crucial for construing the clause as message is "thematic structure." In SFL terms, a clause viewed as message is constitutive of a "theme" and a "rheme." According to Halliday and Matthiessen, "the Theme is the element that serves as the point of departure of the message; it is that which locates and orients the clause within its context."[71] Generally speaking, the theme is usually found in the initial position in the clause.[72] The rheme is "the part in which the theme is developed" in the clause and provides the new information about the starting point of the message.[73] The flow of information in the text can be observed by attending to the overall development of the clausal themes in it.[74] At the level of the paragraph, the launching point of the message for the whole paragraph is called the "hyper-theme."[75] Its function is alike the topic sentence of the paragraph. To illustrate, the author announces that "it is the last hour" in 1 John 2:18a and thereby creates an expectation for his audience that the message to be communicated is concerned with the last things in 1 John 2:18–27. In other words, the hyper-theme or overarching topic of this unit is the arrival of the last hour. Notably, the marked topical theme is constitutive of the nominative second-person plural pronoun ὑμεῖς with reference to the audience in all of the three clauses in 1 John 2:20a, 2:24a, and 2:27a. In addition to attracting attention, the three occurrences of this nominative second-person plural pronoun as the clausal themes indicate that what the author has to say about the last hour is pertinent to his audience.

---

70. Porter and O'Donnell note that "reference is one of the most basic grammatical cohesive devices within texts." Porter and O'Donnell, *Discourse Analysis and the Greek New Testament*, 209.

71. Halliday and Matthiessen, *Halliday's Introduction to Functional Grammar*, 89.

72. Halliday and Matthiessen, *Halliday's Introduction to Functional Grammar*, 91; Eggins, *Introduction to Systemic Functional Linguistics*, 296.

73. Halliday and Matthiessen, *Halliday's Introduction to Functional Grammar*, 89; Eggins, *Introduction to Systemic Functional Linguistics*, 296, 300.

74. Martin and Rose use the term "periodicity" to refer to the overall flow of information in the text. See Martin and Rose, *Working with Discourse*, 187.

75. Martin and Rose, *Working with Discourse*, 193–97.

IV. GENRE, STRUCTURE, AND OUTLINE

Genre is "the context of culture in text" and relevant to the author's and the reader's shared expectations and conventions in the Hallidayan theory of language.[76] Martin and Rose note that "a genre is a staged, goal-oriented social process."[77] The identification of the genre of 1, 2, or 3 John is important for analyzing the use of language in these three letters within their cultural context, which is the Roman province Asia in the first century AD. First John has been described as more like a sermon or "paper" than a letter.[78] This document lacks the epistolary components such as the sender's salutation or farewell to the recipient. In fact, the way in which 1 John starts or ends is untypical for the Hellenistic letter. The first word in this document is the nominative neuter singular relative pronoun ὅ, which has no antecedent in 1 John 1:1. The closing of 1 John is also uncustomary. The author unexpectedly issues the directive to his audience to keep themselves from the idols at the end of this writing in 1 John 5:21. Despite the absence of the epistolary convention, the author apparently has a self-consciousness of communicating with his audience through the medium of a written text.[79] The lexeme γράφω appears a total of thirteen times including the twelve occurrences in the first-person singular (1 John 2:1, 7, 8, 12, 13 [2x], 14 [3x], 21, 26; 5:13) and one occurrence in the first-person plural (1 John 1:4). Thus, the author is either the grammatical subject or included as part of "we" in all of these thirteen instances above respecting the action of writing. Moreover, 1 John was evidently composed to address a specific situation of the audience who had undergone an internal schism in the Christian community due to false teaching (see "Occasion and Purpose"). If 2 John actually served as the cover letter for 1 John, the absence of the sender's greeting and other epistolary elements in the latter epistle is understandable. At any rate, this commentary will refer to 1 John as a "letter" in a broad sense while acknowledging that it lacks the genre characteristics of the Hellenistic epistle.

There is a general agreement among scholars that 1 John begins with the prologue in 1 John 1:1–4 and closes with the conclusion in 1 John 5:13–21.[80] Other than the introductory or closing section, scholarly opinions

---

76. Eggins, *Introduction to Systemic Functional Linguistics*, 54–55.

77. Martin and Rose, *Working with Discourse*, 8.

78. See the discussion in Köstenberger, *Theology of John's Gospel and Letters*, 125–26. Smalley describes 1 John as a "paper" (*1, 2, 3 John*, xxx).

79. Lieu, *I, II, & III John*, 5; Kruse, *Letters of John*, 28; Sherman and Tuggy, *Semantic and Structural Analysis*, 6. For Kruse, 1 John is "a circular letter" (*Letters of John*, 28).

80. Köstenberger, *Theology of John's Gospel and Letters*, 171.

diverge widely on the structure of the remaining part of this letter. There have been attempts to divide the body of 1 John into two, three, or more parts or show that this letter has a concentric or chiastic structure.[81] The complexity of delineating the structure of 1 John is partly owing to the fact that its thoughts and arguments are not a linear progression.[82] There are frequent recurrences of various motifs such as loving one another, avoiding sin, confessing Jesus as the Messiah or God's Son, and obeying God's commandments. Nevertheless, the repetitive character of 1 John is not arbitrary but meaningful. According to Watson, the author employs the technique of amplification in Greco-Roman rhetoric to encourage the audience's adherence to the traditional beliefs and admirable values.[83] It is worth mentioning that Longacre's discourse study of 1 John detects the location of the two "double peaks" in 1 John 2:12–27 and 4:1–21. Each of these two double peaks comprises an ethical peak (1 John 2:12–17; 4:7–21) and a doctrinal peak (1 John 2:18–27; 4:1–6).[84] Sherman and Tuggy similarly observe the presence of altogether four peaks or climaxes in the discourse (1 John 2:12–17, 18–27; 4:1–6, 7–11).[85] Yet, they disagree with Longacre on his understanding that this epistle has a long introduction (1 John 1:1—2:21) and the vocative and the verb γράφω function as the markers of paragraph boundary.[86] The outline of 1 John presented at the end of this section takes into consideration the discourse peaks, the shift in topic, the change in participant, and other lexico-grammatical features in this writing. The criteria by which the boundary of each paragraph is determined will be pointed out where necessary in this commentary.

The genre of 2 John or 3 John is not difficult to identify because they contain the standard characteristics of the Hellenistic letter. The three main parts of the Hellenistic epistle are the opening, body, and closing. The function of the opening or closing is to facilitate rapport-building and contact-maintenance between the correspondents. The body of the letter conveys the most important messages and information. Most of the Greek letters written during the period 300 BC–AD 300 open with a prescript, which is

---

81. Köstenberger provides a list of twelve different proposals concerning the structure of 1 John. See Köstenberger, *Theology of John's Gospel and Letters*, 171–72. For a proposal of 1 John's concentric or chiastic structure, see Thomas, "Literary Structure of 1 John," 369–81.

82. Marshall, *Epistles of John*, 22–27; Kruse, *Letters of John*, 31–32.

83. Watson, "Amplification Techniques in 1 John," 119–20.

84. Longacre, "Towards an Exegesis of 1 John," 279–81; "Exhortation and Mitigation in First John," 3.

85. Sherman and Tuggy, *Semantic and Structural Analysis*, 8.

86. Sherman and Tuggy, *Semantic and Structural Analysis*, 8.

commonly made up of three components (i.e., superscription, adscription, and salutation).[87] In the superscription, the sender identifies himself or herself. In the adscription, the sender identifies the recipient. In the salutation, the sender greets the recipient. All of these three epistolary components that are typical of the opening prescript are found in 2 John 1–3. There is a transition between the prescript (2 John 1–3) and the body (2 John 5–11) in 2 John 4, in which the Elder expresses his rejoicing. The subject matters respecting the love commandment and the danger from the false teachers are dealt with in the letter body, which can be divided into two sections (2 John 5–8, 9–11). There are three verbs in the imperative mood (i.e., βλέπετε, λαμβάνετε, λέγετε) in vv. 8a, 10c, and 10d, respectively. In addition to expressing the Elder's commands to the audience, these three imperative verbs serve as the markers of the peak or sub-peak in the discourse. Second John concludes with the Elder's remark about his projected visit and subsequently the final greeting from a congregation and its members (2 John 12–13). Unlike the closing of 3 John (v. 15), there is no peace benediction or second-person type greeting in the closing of 2 John.

Third John is a brief letter written to Gaius. In keeping with the conventionally tripartite division of the Hellenistic epistle, this letter is made up of the opening (3 John 1–4), body (3 John 5–12), and closing (3 John 13–15). Among the three Johannine epistles, 3 John is the most resemblant to the Greek letter, albeit with the lack of the sender's salutation in the prescript. In fact, 3 John is the only NT epistle that contains a health wish (v. 4). Aside from Gaius, two other individuals (i.e., Diotrephes and Demetrius) are mentioned by name in the letter body. There is no explicit reference to Jesus in 3 John, albeit an indirect reference to him present in v. 7. The epistolary elements are also perceptible in the closing of 3 John. The Elder expresses his intention to visit Gaius when this is possible in 3 John 13–14. The final greetings follow the Elder's peace benediction in 3 John 15.

The outlines of 1, 2, and 3 John adopted in this commentary are delineated as follows:

AN OUTLINE OF 1 JOHN:

I. Prologue (1 John 1:1–4)

II. Body (1 John 1:5—5:12)

---

87. Tite, "How to Begin," 60–62; Aune, *New Testament and Its Literary Environment*, 162–64.

A. Adhering to and Behaving in Conformity with the Christian Beliefs (1 John 1:5—2:27)

  1. Walking in the Light (1 John 1:5—2:11)

    a. Acting in Accord with God's Pure Nature (1 John 1:5—2:2)

    b. Doing What God Commands (1 John 2:3-11)

      i. Keeping God's Commandments (1 John 2:3-6)

      ii. Loving the Christian Brothers and Sisters (1 John 2:7-11)

  2. Affirmation of the Believers' Status and Admonition Against Love for the World (1 John 2:12-17)

    a. The Believers' Status (1 John 2:12-14)

    b. Do Not Love the World (1 John 2:15-17)

  3. Warnings Against the Danger of the Antichrists (1 John 2:18-27)

    a. The Last Hour, the Antichrist, and Many Antichrists (1 John 2:18-19)

    b. The Anointing versus the Liar (1 John 2:20-23)

    c. Remain in the Apostolic Teaching (1 John 2:24-26)

    d. The Abiding Anointing (1 John 2:27)

B. Living as God's Children in View of Christ's Future Coming (1 John 2:28—4:6)

  1. The Hope for Jesus' Manifestation (1 John 2:28—3:3)

    a. The Parousia of Jesus (1 John 2:28-29)

    b. The Hope of God's Children (1 John 3:1-3)

  2. The Disparity Between God's Children and the Devil's Children (1 John 3:4-12)

    a. God's Children Should Avoid Sin (1 John 3:4-6)

    b. God's Children versus the Devil's Children (1 John 3:7-12)

  3. Laying Down Our Lives for Others' Sake (1 John 3:13-18)

  4. The Christian Confidence and God's Twofold Commandment (1 John 3:19-24)

  5. Test the Spirits (1 John 4:1-6)

C. Acting in Conformity with God's Loving Nature
      (1 John 4:7—5:12)

      1. Showing Love to the Christian Brothers and Sisters
         (1 John 4:7—5:4)

         a. The Reason to Love (1 John 4:7–10)

         b. Relying on God's Love (1 John 4:11–16b)

         c. Perfect Love Drives Out Fear (1 John 4:16c–18)

         d. Loving God Involves Loving Fellow Believers
            (1 John 4:19–21)

         e. Love, Obedience, and Spiritual Victory (1 John 5:1–4)

      2. The True Faith in Christ as the Basis of Spiritual Victory
         (1 John 5:5–12)

         a. The Three Witnesses of Christ (1 John 5:5–8)

         b. The Testimony of God (1 John 5:9–12)

III. Conclusion (1 John 5:13–21)

   A. Confidence in Prayer (1 John 5:13–17)

   B. Concluding Assurance and Exhortation (1 John 5:18–21)

AN OUTLINE OF 2 JOHN:

I. Opening (2 John 1–4)

   A. The Prescript (2 John 1–3)

      1. The Sender and the Recipient (2 John 1–2)

      2. The Greeting (2 John 3)

   B. An Expression of Rejoicing (2 John 4)

II. Body (2 John 5–11)

   A. Exhortations to Love and Beware (2 John 5–8)

   B. Prohibitions Against Welcoming the Deceivers (2 John 9–11)

III. Closing (2 John 12–13)

   A. Desire to Visit (2 John 12)

   B. Final Greeting (2 John 13)

AN OUTLINE OF 3 JOHN:

I. Opening (3 John 1–4)

    A. The Prescript (3 John 1)

    B. The Health Wish (3 John 2)

    C. An Expression of Rejoicing (3 John 3–4)

II. Body (3 John 5–12)

    A. Gentle Demand for Gaius's Support (3 John 5–8)

    B. Opposition from Diotrephes (3 John 9–10)

    C. Do Not Imitate the Bad Example (3 John 11)

    D. Recommendation of Demetrius (3 John 12)

III. Closing (3 John 13–15)

    A. Desire to Visit (3 John 13–14)

    B. Peace Benediction and Final Greetings (3 John 15)

COMMENTARY ON
1 JOHN

1 JOHN 1:1–4

OUTLINE:

I. Prologue (1:1–4)
II. Body (1:5—5:12)
III. Conclusion (5:13–21)

I. PROLOGUE (1:1–4)

One of the functions of the prologue to 1 John is to orient the audience by setting up the expectation about how this letter will unfold. Furthermore, the author attempts to build rapport with his audience and establish his credentials as an eyewitness qualified to convey the message to them in this prologue. Akin to the prologue to the Fourth Gospel (John 1:1–18), Jesus Christ is referred to implicitly in vv. 1–3b in the early part of 1 John's prologue and subsequently mentioned by name in v. 3c.[1] There is a total of eighty-six words in altogether seventeen ranking clauses in 1 John 1:1–4 (i.e., vv. 1a–f, 2a–f, 3a–c, 4a–b).[2] Most of these ranking clauses are brief, on average containing approximately five words per clause. In contrast, the author employs the longest and verbless clause (which contains sixteen words) to introduce and draw attention to Jesus Christ the Son by slowing down the discourse pace in 1 John 1:3c. The active participant is the "we" throughout the prologue, who are referred to in some way by the altogether

---

1. Culy, *1, 2, 3 John*, 1.
2. In this commentary, the word group περὶ τοῦ λόγου τῆς ζωῆς is considered as an elliptical clause and thus constituting a single ranking clause in 1 John 1:1f. See Porter et al., *OpenText.Org*; cf. Brown, *Epistles of John*, 163.

ten occurrences of first-person plural indicative verbs, six occurrences of first-person plural pronouns, and one occurrence of first-person plural possessive adjective in 1 John 1:1–4.[3] These altogether seventeen "we" expressions can be regarded either as the author's self-references (i.e., using "we" to stand for "I") for accentuating his own testimony or as the exclusive "we" with respect to the author and his group.[4] In any case, the audience being addressed as "you" by the second-person plural (ὑμῖν [vv. 2d, 3a], ὑμεῖς [v. 3b], ἔχητε [v. 3b]) are at large not included as part of the "we" references in the prologue.[5] By creating the "we-you" contrast (cf. v. 5) and underlining his firsthand experiences with the word of life, the author not only distinguishes himself from the audience but also increases his power in their interpersonal relation.

The author draws on the lexico-grammatical resource to create the semantic coherence of the prologue and intimate its emphases. There is a plethora of various sensory verbs (9x) from semantic domain 24 ("sensory events and states"), including the following indicative verbs: ἀκηκόαμεν (vv. 1b, 3a), ἑωράκαμεν (vv. 1c, 2b, 3a), ἐφανερώθη (v. 2a, 2f), ἐθεασάμεθα (v. 1d), ἐψηλάφησαν (v. 1e). A number of these sensory verbs appear in connection with the related lexemes from semantic domain 8 ("body, body parts and body products") that connote the idea of physical sight or touch (e.g., ὀφθαλμοῖς [v. 1c], χεῖρες [v. 1e]). There is a total of five occurrences of different words (i.e., λόγου [v. 1f], μαρτυροῦμεν [v. 2c], ἀπαγγέλλομεν [vv. 2d, 3a], γράφομεν [v. 4a]) falling into semantic domain 33 ("communication") in the prologue. In addition, the two lexemes ζωή (vv. 1f, 2a, 2d) from semantic domain 23 ("physiological processes and states") and κοινωνία (v. 3b, 3c) from semantic domain 34 ("association") are found three times and twice respectively. The semantic or lexical connections above to a certain degree enhance the unity in the prologue. It is noteworthy that the author

---

3. There are ten indicative verbs in the first-person plural in 1 John 1:1–4: ἀκηκόαμεν (2x [vv. 1b, 3a]), ἑωράκαμεν (3x [vv. 1c, 2b, 3a]), ἐθεασάμεθα (v. 1d), μαρτυροῦμεν (v. 2c), ἀπαγγέλλομεν (2x [vv. 2d, 3a]), and γράφομεν (v. 4a). The six first-person plural pronouns are: ἡμῶν (4x [vv. 1c, 1e, 3b, 4b]), ἡμῖν (v. 3a), and ἡμεῖς (v. 4a). In addition, the possessive adjective ἡμετέρα (v. 3c) is a first-person plural expression.

4. For Bauckham, the first-person plural expressions give weight to the "we of authoritative testimony" and refer to the author alone in 1 John 1:1–5. See Bauckham, *Jesus and the Eyewitnesses*, 370–75. Some scholars think that John associates himself with his group or other eyewitnesses by using the first-person plural expressions. See Yarbrough, *1–3 John*, 32–34, 44; Kruse, *Letters of John*, 61; Sherman and Tuggy, *Semantic and Structural Analysis*, 15–17.

5. However, some scholars (e.g., Jobes, Sherman and Tuggy) think that the genitive first-person plural pronoun ἡμῶν is inclusive in 1 John 4b. In other words, the audience are included as part of the referent of this pronoun. See Jobes, *1, 2, and 3 John*, 56; Sherman and Tuggy, *Semantic and Structural Analysis*, 17.

employs the present tense consistently for the verbs of communication (e.g., μαρτυροῦμεν [v. 2c], ἀπαγγέλλομεν [vv. 2d, 3a], γράφομεν [v. 4a]) to foreground his communicative acts.[6] The perfect tense is utilized to give prominence to his personal experience with what is declared to the audience (e.g., ἀκηκόαμεν [vv. 1b, 3a] and ἑωράκαμεν [vv. 1c, 3a]). Simply put, the prologue is pertinent to the author's proclamation regarding the manifestation of the life based on his eyewitness testimony. In regard to the tenor of this prologue, the author avails himself of the sensory lexemes and perfect tense to position himself as an eyewitness authority and underline his privileged status accordingly.

There are four relative clauses beginning with the nominative or accusative neuter singular relative pronoun ὅ that are in apposition to each other in 1 John 1:1. In each instance, the relative pronoun ὅ does not have an antecedent in the preceding co-text (cf. the accusative neuter singular relative pronoun ὅ with no antecedent in v. 3a).[7] All of these four headless relative clauses in v. 1 function as the complements or objects of the ensuing predicator ἀπαγγέλλομεν (v. 3a), which is a saying verb. By starting the letter with a string of free relative clauses as the object clauses, the author puts an emphasis on the message proclaimed to his audience.[8] While the prepositional phrase ἀπ' ἀρχῆς (v. 1a) resonates with the similar phrase ἐν ἀρχῇ at the outset of the Fourth Gospel (John 1:1; cf. Gen 1:1), this prepositional phrase is probably used to refer to the time when God's Son was incarnate and lived in the world (cf. 1 John 2:7, 13, 14, 24 [2x]; 3:8, 11; 2 John 5, 6). If this understanding is accepted, the author alludes to Jesus' earthly life and ministry through the headless relative clauses in the prologue to 1 John.[9] The grammatical relation of the prepositional phrase περὶ τοῦ λόγου τῆς ζωῆς in v. 1f (cf. ζωῆς is an objective genitive) to the surrounding clauses is unclear.[10] Rather than linking with the foregoing clauses in v. 1 (i.e., what we have heard, seen, and touched "concerning the word of life") or the ensuing first-person plural present active indicative verb ἀπαγγέλλομεν in v.

---

6. Culy, 1, 2, 3 John, 2–3.

7. The first occurrence of the relative pronoun ὅ (v. 1a) is the subject of the third-person singular imperfect indicative verb ἦν, which is employed to realize the existential process. The subsequent four occurrences of the relative pronoun ὅ are the objects of various indicative verbs in 1 John 1:1b, 1c, 1d, 3a.

8. Marshall, *Epistles of John*, 100; Jobes, *1, 2, and 3 John*, 42.

9. Brown, *Epistles of John*, 154–58. However, Jobes suggests that the referent of the repeated occurrences of the headless relative pronoun ὅ is "the gospel message centered on Jesus" (*1, 2, and 3 John*, 44).

10. There is a total of thirteen occurrences of the lexeme ζωή in this letter (1 John 1:1, 2 [2x]; 2:25; 3:14, 15; 5:11 [2x], 12 [2x], 13, 16, 20). This lexeme is not found in 2 or 3 John.

2d (i.e., we proclaim "that concerning the word of life"), it is probable that this prepositional phrase above (i.e., περὶ τοῦ λόγου τῆς ζωῆς) stands on its own in v. 1f at the end of this verse and functions to provide an orientation for the parenthesis that will be unfolded in 1 John 1:2.[11] Notice that the two occurrences of the third-person singular aorist passive indicative verb ἐφανερώθη (cf. the subject is ζωή) form an *inclusio* to frame the author's testimony as regards the manifestation of the life at the beginning and end of v. 2. The author further employs the accusative feminine adjective αἰώνιον as the definer of the accusative feminine noun ζωήν (v. 2d) to indicate the eternal nature of the life. The lexeme αἰώνιος occurs a total of six times in this letter (1 John 1:2; 2:25; 3:15; 5:11, 13, 20). It is the author's conviction that his message centered upon Jesus, who is the life, will lead to the audience's enjoyment of spiritual life forever.

The author resumes the topic of eyewitness by employing the word group ὃ ἑωράκαμεν καὶ ἀκηκόαμεν, which functions as the complement of the predicator ἀπαγγέλλομεν that follows in 1 John 1:3 (cf. the free relative clauses in v. 1). Both of the two first-person plural perfect active indicative verbs ἑωράκαμεν and ἀκηκόαμεν have appeared earlier in v. 1, albeit in reverse order. By means of the dependent clause headed by the subordinating conjunction ἵνα (cf. 1 John 1:4; 2:1; 5:13), the author expresses the purpose of his proclamation which is that the audience may have fellowship with him (and his group) in v. 3b. The subject (i.e., ὑμεῖς) of the second-person plural present active subjunctive verb ἔχητε is marked for underlining the audience's participation in this ἵνα-clause. The author also places the accusative singular feminine noun κοινωνίαν (v. 3b) as the complement prior to this subjunctive verb to accentuate the idea of fellowship, which entails "an association involving close mutual relations and involvement."[12] The lexeme κοινωνία is found only four times in this epistle (1 John 1:3 [2x], 6, 7) and absent from the other Johannine writings. In order to encourage his audience to remain in close association with him, the author avers that his fellowship is with the Father and with his Son Jesus Christ in v. 3c.[13] This is the first time the compound name Ἰησοῦς Χριστός (cf. 1 John 1:3; 2:1; 3:23; 4:2; 5:6, 20; 2 John 3, 7) appears in connection with the designation υἱός in this letter (cf. 1 John 1:3; 3:23; 5:20; 2 John 3). Thus, the author's fellowship

---

11. Brown says that the prepositional phrase περὶ τοῦ λόγου τῆς ζωῆς is "an ungrammatical interruption" in 1 John 1:1. See Brown, *Epistles of John*, 163.

12. Louw and Nida, *Greek-English Lexicon of the New Testament*, 1:445 (semantic domain 34.5).

13. The preposition μετά is employed a total of three times to express the associative relations between the author and his audience, the author and the Father, and the author and God's Son in 1 John 1:3 (cf. 1 John 1:6, 7).

with his audience is based on their common identity as the believers in Jesus Christ the Son of God.

The author expresses his reason for writing at the end of the prologue in 1 John 1:4 (cf. 1 John 2:1; 5:13). The accusative neuter plural demonstrative pronoun ταῦτα as the complement is placed in the thematic position of the clause and prior to the predicator γράφομεν and the subject ἡμεῖς to give emphasis to what is written in v. 4a. It is likely that this demonstrative pronoun (i.e., ταῦτα) above refers to 1 John as a whole.[14] As mentioned in the Introduction, the occurrence of the first-person plural present active indicative verb γράφομεν (v. 4a) does not necessarily imply multiple authorship because all of the remaining twelve occurrences of the lexeme γράφω are in the first-person singular in this epistle (1 John 2:1, 7, 8, 12, 13 [2x], 14 [3x], 21, 26; 5:13). The author tells his audience that he writes so that "our joy may be (cf. the third-person singular subjunctive verb ᾖ) complete" in v. 4b (cf. 2 John 12). The textual reading ἡ χαρὰ ἡμῶν adopted in NA28 is supported by codices Sinaiticus (א or 01), Vaticanus (B or 03), and Athous Lavrensis (Ψ or 044), minuscules 436 and 1175, some Byzantine manuscripts, the Syriac Peshitta, the Sahidic versions, and other witnesses. Despite the wide attestation of the variant ἡ χαρὰ ὑμῶν in the manuscript traditions (e.g., codices Alexandrinus [A or 02], Ephraemi Rescriptus [C or 04] and Porphyrianus [P^{apr} or 025], the majority of the minuscules, some Byzantine manuscripts, and the Bohairic versions), it is probable that the scribes would have altered the original first-person plural genitive pronoun ἡμῶν (v. 4b) to the second-person plural genitive pronoun ὑμῶν due to the influence by the similar wording of Jesus' saying in John 16:24.[15] Assuming the authenticity of the textual reading ἡ χαρὰ ἡμῶν (v. 4b), the audience are probably not included as part of the referent of the first-person plural pronoun ἡμῶν (v. 4b) because all of the preceding "we" references are exclusive in 1 John 1:1–4a (see the note in the early part of this chapter above).[16] The word group ᾖ πεπληρωμένη is a perfect periphrastic construction in v. 4b. The author employs the relational verb ᾖ followed by the perfect middle or passive nominative feminine singular participle πεπληρωμένη to ascribe the attribute of completeness or fullness to "our joy." The corollary is that the author focuses attention on the state of completeness of the gladness, which

---

14. Culy, *1, 2, 3 John*, 8.

15. Metzger, *Textual Commentary on the Greek New Testament*, 639. However, Culy thinks that the variant ὑμῶν rather than ἡμῶν is more likely to be original. See Culy, *1, 2, 3 John*, 9.

16. Contra the inclusive view of the first-person plural genitive pronoun ἡμῶν in 1 John 1:4b (cf. NLT) in Jobes, *1, 2, and 3 John*, 56; Sherman and Tuggy, *Semantic and Structural Analysis*, 17.

he anticipates to experience as a result of corresponding with the audience through the present letter.

1 JOHN 1:5—2:11

OUTLINE:

I. Prologue (1:1-4)

II. Body (1:5—5:12)

    A. Adhering to and Behaving in Conformity with the Christian Beliefs (1:5—2:27)

        1. **Walking in the Light (1:5—2:11)**

            a. Acting in Accord with God's Pure Nature (1:5—2:2)

            b. Doing What God Commands (2:3-11)

                i. Keeping God's Commandments (2:3-6)

                ii. Loving the Christian Brothers and Sisters (2:7-11)

II. BODY (1:5—5:12)

A. Adhering to and Behaving in Conformity with the Christian Beliefs (1:5—2:27)

1. Walking in the Light (1:5—2:11)

The letter body (1 John 1:5—5:12) opens with the author's solemn declaration regarding God's morally pure character in 1 John 1:5. This declaration lays the theological foundation for the author's exhortations and admonitions that will follow in 1 John 1:5—2:11. The present unit is framed by the *inclusio* of the antithesis between light and darkness in 1 John 1:5-7 and 2:8–11.[1] This unit can be divided into two sections. The first section is made up of thirty-one ranking clauses in 1 John 1:5—2:2.[2] It deals with the topic of sin, which is incompatible with the admirable qualities of having fellowship with God and living in the light. There are altogether six third-class conditional sentences containing the subordinating conjunction ἐάν in this section (1 John 1:6a, 7a, 8a, 9a, 10a; 2:1c). Most of the protases in these third-class conditional sentences are formulated in the form of the first-person plural, save the sixth protasis in 1 John 2:1c. The second section consists of twenty-six ranking clauses in 1 John 2:3–11.[3] This section can be further divided into the two subsections in 1 John 2:3–6 and 2:7–11 on account of the reference to the old and new commandment in 1 John 2:7. On the whole, the author stresses that an obedience to God's commandments and in particular the commandment to love one another is the token of having a relationship to God in this section. There is a total of thirteen embedded participial, infinitival, or finite clauses that are nested in different ranking clauses throughout 1 John 2:3–11.[4] Most of these embedded clauses are utilized to flesh out the variously generic participants serving as the negative or positive examples for the audience. The implication is that the author is fond of utilizing different embedded clauses to give extra information regarding the variously generic participants in 1 John 2:3–11. To illustrate, the entire construction ὁ λέγων ὅτι ἔγνωκα αὐτὸν καὶ τὰς ἐντολὰς αὐτοῦ μὴ τηρῶν constitutes the generic subject of the predicator ἐστίν in v. 4a, in which the author puts forward the negative example for the audience to avoid. This subject construction above comprises two embedded participial clauses (i.e., ὁ λέγων and καὶ τὰς ἐντολὰς αὐτοῦ μὴ τηρῶν) and an embedded finite clause (i.e., ὅτι ἔγνωκα αὐτὸν). It deserves mention that the author employs the two different word groups ἐὰν εἴπωμεν (3x) and ὁ λέγων

---

1. The lexeme φῶς occurs six times in 1 John 1:5b, 7a, 7b; 2:8b, 9, 10a (cf. the cognate verb φαίνω in 1 John 2:8d) in this letter. The contrastive lexeme σκοτία is found six times in 1 John 1:5c; 2:8c, 9, 11a, b, d. The related lexeme σκότος occurs only once in 1 John 1:6c. These three lexemes above do not recur in the co-text subsequent to 1 John 2:11.

2. The altogether thirty-one ranking clauses are present in 1 John 1:5a–c, 6a–e, 7a–d, 8a–d, 9a–d, 10a–d; 2:1a–d, 2a–c. Note that the embedded clauses are not counted as the ranking clauses in this commentary.

3. The altogether twenty-six ranking clauses are present in 1 John 2:3a–c, 4a–b, 5a–d, 6a–b, 7a–d, 8a–d, 9, 10a–b, 11a–d. Note that the parenthetical clause headed by the subordinating conjunction καθώς is considered as a ranking clause in 1 John 2:6b in this commentary. The embedded clauses are not counted as the ranking clauses.

4. There are altogether thirteen embedded clauses in 1 John 2:3–11 (vv. 4a [3x], 6a [3x], 7d, 9 [3x], 10a, 11a, 11c). In contrast, there are only two embedded clauses in the prior section in 1 John 1:5—2:2 (cf. 1:5).

(3x) to invoke a diversity of "voices" for propounding the altogether six allegations in the present unit in 1 John 1:5—2:11. As an upshot, the nature of the discourse is multi-voiced throughout this unit. The commentary below will address the aforementioned linguistic features in 1 John 1:5—2:11 in greater detail when necessary.

a. Acting in Accord with God's Pure Nature (1:5—2:2)

This section begins with the author's affirmative "message" concerning God's absolutely moral purity in 1 John 1:5. This is the first time the lexeme ἀγγελία from semantic domain 33 ("communication") appears in this letter (cf. 1 John 1:5; 3:11). Aside from this lexeme, the author makes use of a number of words (e.g., ἀναγγέλλομεν [v. 5a], εἴπωμεν [vv. 6a, 8a, 10a], ψευδόμεθα [v. 6d], ὁμολογῶμεν [v. 9a], ψεύστην [v. 10c], λόγος [v. 10d], and γράφω [2:1a]) belonged to semantic domain 33 ("communication") to enhance the coherence in 1 John 1:5—2:2. Following the predicator ἐστίν, the demonstrative pronoun αὕτη (v. 5a) as the complement of this predicator points forward to the ὅτι-clause that follows in v. 5b. The subject of this predicator is the entire construction ἡ ἀγγελία ἣν ἀκηκόαμεν ἀπ' αὐτοῦ καὶ ἀναγγέλλομεν ὑμῖν (v. 5a), which is packed with information due to its long length. The author utilizes this construction to inform his audience that the source of his proclamation is from Jesus Christ. By employing the first-person plural perfect active indicative verb ἀκηκόαμεν for the third time (cf. vv. 1b, 3a), the author evokes the notion of eyewitness testimony in the preceding co-text and thereby transitions from the prologue to the body smoothly in 1 John 1:5a. The author continues to use the positive statement "God is light" to assert his moral purity in v. 5b. The imagery of "light" is often associated with God in the OT (e.g., Exod 13:21–22; Pss 18:28; 27:1; 36:9).[5] The subject θεός and the complement φῶς are juxtaposed to heighten God's association with the notion of light in v. 5b. The assertion of God's moral purity is further bolstered by way of the double negative statement (cf. the two negative polarity adjuncts οὐκ and οὐδεμία) regarding the absence of darkness in him in v. 5c. The two imageries "light" and "darkness" are antithetical to each other and loaded with ethical overtones in Johannine thinking. In brief, God's nature is perfectly pure and holy and without any evilness.

It is the author's conviction that the believers must behave in accordance with God's pure character. The author attempts to expose the faulty

---

5. See Yarbrough, *1–3 John*, 46–51; Thompson, *1–3 John*, 41.

assumptions about sinning and promote holy living by means of the altogether six third-class conditional statements (cf. the conjunction ἐάν with the subjunctive) in 1 John 1:6–2:2. There is a total of twenty-three first-person plural expressions in the relevant conditional clauses in this section.[6] In contrast to the frequent occurrences of the editorial or exclusive "we" (i.e., the audience are not included as the referent) in 1 John 1:1–5, all of these twenty-three first-person plural expressions are inclusive in 1 John 1:6—2:2. The rhetorical effect is that the author's solidarity with his audience is enhanced. Regarding the first, third, and fifth third-class conditional statements, the word group ἐὰν εἴπωμεν occurs to usher in the three lofty claims "we have fellowship with him (i.e., God)" (v. 6), "we do not have sin" (v. 8), and "we have not sinned" (v. 10) in the relevant protases. It is possible that these professions are in some way related to the secessionists,[7] albeit there is no conclusive evidence to ascertain. At any rate, the author evaluates the validity of the three claims above on the basis of the speakers' way of living or God's character and consequently demonstrates that they are false. As for the second, fourth, and sixth third-class conditional statements, the author uses them to elucidate the Christian conduct and seeks to affect his audience to conform to the desired behaviors (1 John 1:7, 9; 2:1–2).

The first instance of the word group ἐὰν εἴπωμεν is present in v. 6a (cf. vv. 8a, 10a). The following subordinating conjunction ὅτι is employed to report what "we" aver in v. 6b (cf. vv. 8b, 10b). The author accentuates the idea of fellowship by fronting the accusative feminine singular noun κοινωνίαν, which functions as the object of the first-person plural present active indicative verb ἔχομεν in v. 6b. In a similar fashion, the author places the adjunctive phrase ἐν τῷ σκότει in the thematic position of the clause to stress the notion of walking "in the sphere of the darkness" in v. 6c. The lexeme περιπατέω occurs a total of five times in this epistle (1 John 1:6, 7; 2:6 [2x], 11; cf. 2 John 4, 6 [2x]; 3 John 3). While this lexeme (i.e., περιπατέω) literally means "walk," the predicator περιπατῶμεν (v. 6c) is utilized to connote the figurative sense of a way of life. Given the preceding premise that God is light with no darkness (v. 5), the claim to have fellowship with him

---

6. There are fifteen first-person plural indicative or subjunctive verbs in 1 John 1:6—2:2: εἴπωμεν (1:6a, 8a, 10a), ἔχομεν (1:6b, 7c, 8b; 2:1d), περιπατῶμεν (1:6c, 7a), ψευδόμεθα (1:6d), ποιοῦμεν (1:6e, 10c), πλανῶμεν (1:8c), ὁμολογῶμεν (1:9a), and ἡμαρτήκαμεν (1:10b). In addition, there are altogether seven first-person plural pronouns (i.e., ἡμᾶς [1:7d, 9d], ἡμῖν [1:8d, 9c, 10d], and ἡμῶν [1:9a; 2:2a]). The first-person plural possessive adjective ἡμετέρων is detected once in 1 John 2:2b.

7. Several scholars (e.g., Wahlde, Smalley, Brown) lay stress on the possible connection between the allegations or statements in 1 John 1:6—2:2 and the false beliefs of the secessionists. See Wahlde, *Three Johannine Letters*, 46–51; Smalley, *1, 2, 3 John*, 16–39; Brown, *Epistles of John*, 241–42.

(v. 6b) and a way of life in the darkness (v. 6c) are apparently incompatible. The logical consequent is that the presumed speakers (i.e., "we") who make this claim above actually "lie" (v. 6d) and do not practice the truth (v. 6e). The lexeme ψεύδομαι is detected only once in 1 John 1:6d. The two cognate nouns ψεῦδος (1 John 2:21, 27) and ψεύστης (1 John 1:10; 2:4, 22; 4:20; 5:10) occur twice and five times, respectively, in the whole letter. In view of the author's negative appraisal of the presumed speakers who walk in the darkness (cf. v. 6c–e), it is apparent that their false claim expressed via the first-person plural (i.e., κοινωνίαν ἔχομεν μετ' αὐτοῦ) does not represent his own standpoint in v. 6b. Rather, the author avails himself of the literary device of the first-person plural to set forth the opposing viewpoint so as to refute it. The feminine noun ἀλήθεια (9x) from semantic domain 72 ("true, false") occurs for the first time in 1 John 1:6e (cf. 1 John 1:8; 2:4, 21 [2x], 27; 3:19; 4:6; 5:6).[8] Whether or not the construction ποιεῖν τὴν ἀλήθειαν originates from the LXX or has a Semitic background,[9] the author's employment of the action verb ποιέω intimates that the notion of the truth bears on a person's behavior in 1 John 1:6 (cf. John 3:21).

The author continues to promote the positive quality of walking in the light in 1 John 1:7 (cf. v. 6). The prepositional phrase ἐν τῷ φωτί is fronted to emphasize in v. 7a, in which the first-person plural present active subjunctive verb περιπατῶμεν recurs (cf. v. 6). It should be noted that the third-class protasis "if you walk in the light" (v. 7a) is likely to be the metaphorical expression of the covert command "walk in the light!" for influencing the audience's action subtly (cf. using the subjunctive mood to realize an implicit directive; see "Tenor" in "Introduction").[10] Upon implicating this covert command via the protasis, the author avers that God's moral purity is the standard and basis of the believers' pure living in v. 7b (cf. 1 John 1:5). The referent of the nominative masculine singular pronoun αὐτός (v. 7b) is God, who is characterized as being in the light. The author encourages his audience to walk in the light as God is in the light by informing them the positive upshot (i.e., "we have fellowship with one another") of doing so in v. 7c. Notice that the accusative feminine singular noun κοινωνίαν (v. 7c), which is

---

8. In relation to the noun ἀλήθεια, the cognate adjective ἀληθινός is found altogether four times in 1 John 2:8 and 5:20 (3x).

9. Brown, *Epistles of John*, 199–200.

10. See Miehle, "Theme in Greek Hortatory Discourse," 155–56; Longacre, "Exhortation and Mitigation in First John," 7; Sherman and Tuggy, *Semantic and Structural Analysis*, 6–7, 26–27; Culy, *1, 2, 3 John*, 16. For the Hallidayan concept of the "interpersonal grammatical metaphor," see Halliday and Matthiessen, *Halliday's Introduction to Functional Grammar*, 698–707; Taverniers, "Grammatical Metaphor in SFL"; "Grammatical Metaphor."

the complement of the following predicator ἔχομεν, is assigned the thematic position of the clause to stress the notion of fellowship. In fact, the believers' fellowship with one another has implications for their fellowship with God and his Son in Johannine thought (cf. v. 3). Since in the Jewish thinking sin has the capacity of producing moral defilement that taints the person who has done the wrongdoing,[11] there are occasions when a believer living in the light becomes morally impure as a result of committing a transgression against God. In case such an occasion happens, the author assures his audience that the blood of Jesus the Son of God (cf. Jesus' blood as a symbol of his death) purifies us from all sin in 1 John 1:7d. The lexeme καθαρίζω encodes the figurative sense of cleansing from the moral impurity owing to sin in the present co-text.[12] This is the first time the lexeme ἁμαρτία (17x) from semantic domain 88 ("moral and ethical qualities and related behavior") is found in this epistle (cf. 1 John 1:7, 8, 9 [2x]; 2:2, 12; 3:4 [2x], 5 [2x], 8, 9; 4:10; 5:16 [2x], 17 [2x]).[13] The author will further discuss the topic of sin in the remainder of this section in 1 John 1:5—2:2.

The author invokes an alternative "voice" to speak for the countering viewpoint ("we have no sin") by using the third-class protasis and the first-person plural again in 1 John 1:8 (cf. vv. 6, 10). The underlying problem of the individual who avows to be without sin is that he or she does not acknowledge the personal need to remove sin, even the spiritual purification effected by Jesus' death (cf. v. 7). To counter this opposing viewpoint, the author utilizes the apodosis to assert that we deceive ourselves and the truth is not in us if we claim to have no sin in v. 8c–d. The accusative plural reflexive pronoun ἑαυτούς, which is the complement of the predicator πλανῶμεν, is fronted to underscore the idea of self-deception in v. 8c.[14] The lexeme πλανάω will recur regarding the danger from the false teachers in the subsequent co-texts in 1 John 2:26 and 3:7 (cf. the related lexemes πλάνη in 1 John 4:6 and πλάνος in 2 John 7).[15] The articular noun ἀλήθεια is the subject of the predicator ἐστίν, which probably functions as an existential verb in v. 8d. In other words, the author indicates that the truth does not exist in the person who alleges to have no sin. The implication is that the

---

11. Klawans, *Impurity and Sin in Ancient Judaism*.

12. In relation to the lexeme καθαρίζω, the cognate adjective καθαρός (John 13:10 [2x], 11; 15:3) and verb καθαίρω (John 15:2) are employed with respect to the purity or purification of Jesus' disciples in the Fourth Gospel.

13. The lexeme ἁμαρτία is absent from 2 and 3 John.

14. The lexeme πλανάω from semantic domain 31.8 carries the connotation of causing someone to "hold a wrong view and thus be mistaken" (Louw and Nida, *Greek-English Lexicon of the New Testament*, 1:366).

15. Yarbrough, *1–3 John*, 61–62.

claim of sinlessness is false and the audience are thus implicitly prohibited to allege to be without sin.

For the fourth time, the author utilizes the third-class conditional construction (cf. vv. 6, 7, 8) to promote the correct Christian behavior that we should confess our sins in 1 John 1:9a. While the indirect object of the first-person plural present active subjunctive verb ὁμολογῶμεν (v. 9a) is not specified, it can be presumed that the believers should confess their sins to God. In fact, God is the implicit subject of the subsequent three indicative or subjunctive verbs in the third-person singular (i.e., ἐστιν, ἀφῇ, and καθαρίσῃ) that are relevant to the removal of the believers' sins in v. 9b–d. The author underlines God's faithful and just character as the basis of his dealing with our sins in v. 9b. The faithfulness of God is particularly emphasized in view of the placement of the adjective πιστός (which is part of the complement πιστός . . . καὶ δίκαιος) at the forefront of the clause.[16] The author employs the two aorist active subjunctive verbs ἀφῇ (v. 9c) and καθαρίσῃ (v. 9d) with the perfective aspect to sum up the whole action of God's forgiving and cleansing our sins. The lexeme ἀφίημι from semantic domain 40 ("reconciliation, forgiveness") occurs only twice vis-à-vis the removal of sins in this epistle (1 John 1:9; 2:12; cf. John 20:23). As mentioned above, the figurative depiction of a person being purified from all unrighteousness is akin to the Jewish thought that sin can cause an individual to be morally defiled.[17] It will be explicated that all unrighteousness is sin in 1 John 5:17 in the closing of this letter. In the present co-text, the incongruence between the two notions of unrighteousness and God's just nature is heightened through the employment of the two lexemes ἀδικία (v. 9d) and δίκαιος (v. 9b) that are antithetical to each other. In a nutshell, the audience are summoned to confess their sins before God in the case that they have done an unrighteous deed because he will forgive their sins and purify them from all moral uncleanness.

The verbal clause ἐὰν εἴπωμεν occurs for the third and last time to usher in the false claim as regards the denial of sin in 1 John 1:10 (cf. vv. 6, 8). This is the fifth instance of the third-class conditional construction in the section in 1 John 1:5—2:2 (cf. 1 John 1:6, 7, 8, 9, 10; 2:1). The author gives prominence to this false claim by employing the perfect tense (cf. ἡμαρτήκαμεν) in the protasis in v. 10b. This is the only time a perfect form of the lexeme ἁμαρτάνω is found in the NT. Both of the two masculine singular accusative or genitive pronouns αὐτόν and αὐτοῦ refer to God in the apodosis in v. 10c–d. Given these two references to the deity and the

---

16. Culy, *1, 2, 3 John*, 18.
17. Klawans, *Impurity and Sin in Ancient Judaism*.

author's foregoing assertion of God's trustworthy and just nature (cf. v. 9b), the grave ramification (i.e., we make God a liar and his word is not in us) of alleging to be sinless is evident. The complement ψεύστην is marked in the clause-initial position in v. 10c. The implication is that the identification of God as a "liar" is underlined. The wording and structure of the negative statement in v. 10d (i.e., καὶ ὁ λόγος αὐτοῦ οὐκ ἔστιν ἐν ἡμῖν) is resemblant to the negative statement that precedes in v. 8d (i.e., ἡ ἀλήθεια οὐκ ἔστιν ἐν ἡμῖν). In both cases, the refusal to acknowledge our sinfulness is related to the lack of the truth (v. 8d) or God's word (v. 10d) in us.[18] Thus it is evident that the believers should not claim to be sinless.

As indicated in 1 John 2:1a–b, the author took pen to write to the audience so that they will not sin. The referent of the accusative neuter plural demonstrative pronoun ταῦτα (v. 1a) is probably the whole letter. The author employs the device of the vocative (i.e., τεκνία μου) to address his audience directly as "my children" to grab their attention at the outset of v. 1a. Furthermore, the author shows affection and positions himself at a higher level of authority in such a way that the audience will respond positively to what he has to say. The neuter plural vocative noun τεκνία (v. 1a), which occurs a total of six times in this letter (1 John 2:1, 12, 28; 3:18; 4:4; 5:21; cf. John 13:33),[19] is a diminutive form of the related lexeme τέκνον. Instead of the predictor γράφομεν in the first-person plural in 1 John 1:4, the author shifts to use the first-person singular present active indicative verb γράφω to intimate that he is the sole author in v. 1a (cf. 1 John 2:7, 8, 12, 13 [2x]). It is likely that the prohibition "do not sin!" is conveyed implicitly by means of the purpose statement in v. 1b (cf. ἵνα μὴ ἁμάρτητε). Thus, the function of this purpose statement is not simply giving information about the author's reason of writing but also attempting to urge the audience to avoid sinning.[20]

The author avails himself of the third-class conditional construction for the sixth and last time to posit the hypothetical situation of anyone committing a sin in 1 John 2:1c–2c (cf. 1 John 1:6, 7, 8, 9, 10). The conjunction καί, which precedes the conditional conjunction ἐάν, is employed to create the textual tie with v. 1a–b and hint at the continuation of the flow of thought at the beginning of v. 1c.[21] While the foregoing five occurrences of

---

18. Sherman and Tuggy, *Semantic and Structural Analysis*, 28.

19. Note that the reading τεκνία in 1 John 3:7 in NA27 has been altered to παιδία in NA28.

20. Longacre, "Exhortation and Mitigation in First John," 9.

21. The conditional conjunction ἐάν is not preceded by the conjunction καί in the preceding five instances of the third-class conditional construction (1 John 1:6, 7, 8, 9, 10).

the third-class conditional construction are formulated in the first-person plural, the author shifts to use the generic participant "anyone" in the protasis of the present instance. The word group ἐάν τις is found four times in this letter (1 John 2:1, 15; 4:20; 5:16). The indefinite pronoun τις is the subject of the third-person singular aorist active subjunctive verb ἁμάρτῃ in v. 1c. That said, the generic participant (v. 1c) is changed to the inclusive "we" (cf. the first-person plural present active indicative verb ἔχομεν) in the apodosis in v. 1d. It is affirmed that we have an advocate, namely Jesus Christ the righteous one (cf. the Spirit as the believers' advocate in John 14:16, 26; 15:26; 16:7),[22] to defend and speak for us in the presence of the Father. The author focuses attention on Jesus' identity as the advocate by fronting the accusative masculine singular noun παράκλητον, which is part of the complement (i.e., παράκλητον . . . Ἰησοῦν Χριστὸν δίκαιον), in the initial position of the clause in v. 1d. Just as God is "just" (the lexeme δίκαιος) and willing to forgive our sins (1 John 1:9), Jesus Christ is "just" (the lexeme δίκαιος) and qualified to defend and offer support to the sinner in 1 John 2:1d (cf. 1 John 3:7).

The author attempts to elaborate God's remedy of our sins through the full or elliptical statements in 1 John 2:2a–c. The full statement is utilized to identify Jesus Christ (cf. the antecedent of the pronoun αὐτός) as the propitiation on behalf of our sins in v. 2a. This is the first time the lexeme ἱλασμός from semantic domain 40 ("reconciliation, forgiveness") appears in this letter (cf. 1 John 2:1; 4:10). In view of the preceding reference to Jesus' "blood" as a symbol of his death in 1 John 1:7, Jesus' sacrificial death is the means by which the believers' sins are atoned for in 1 John 2:2a. The author makes use of the two subsequent elliptical statements, which are contrastive to each other, to stress the far-reaching extent of what Jesus' atoning death has achieved in v. 2b–c. Both of these two elliptical statements are realized by the verbless clauses (i.e., οὐ περὶ τῶν ἡμετέρων δὲ μόνον [v. 2b] and ἀλλὰ καὶ περὶ ὅλου τοῦ κόσμου [v. 2c]). The polarity adjunct οὐ is employed to negate the idea of Jesus being the propitiation only because of our sins in v. 2b.[23] In contrast to this idea (cf. the adversative conjunction ἀλλά), the author says that Jesus offered himself as the atoning sacrifice because of the sins of the whole world in v. 2c. As Culy says, the implicit word group τῶν ἁμαρτιῶν in the genitive case is the presumed head of the preposition περί in 1 John 2:c (i.e., περὶ [τῶν ἁμαρτιῶν] ὅλου τοῦ κόσμου).[24] Furthermore, the

---

22. "Jesus Christ" is mentioned a total of six times in this letter (1 John 1:3; 2:1; 3:23; 4:2; 5:6, 20; cf. 2 John 3, 7).

23. The preposition περί (2x) is probably employed to convey the meaning of "reason" (cf. semantic domain 89.36) in 1 John 2:2b–c.

24. Culy, *1, 2, 3 John*, 24.

construction ὅλου τοῦ κόσμου is likely the subjective genitive (i.e., the whole world [sins]) and the figure of speech for all the people living in the world.[25] Nevertheless, there is no hint of the belief of universal salvation in 1 John. From the author's perspective, Jesus' atoning death is pertinent to all the people in the world because everyone is sinful.

b. Doing What God Commands (2:3–11)

This section is the second part of the discourse that begins from 1 John 1:5 and ends in 1 John 2:11. There is a change of topic from sin in the preceding section in 1 John 1:6—2:2 to obeying what God commands in the present section in 1 John 2:3-11. The author creates the coherence of this section in part by employing the altogether fourteen words from semantic domain 33 ("communication") including the six occurrences of the lexeme ἐντολή (1 John 2:3, 4, 7 [3x], 8), three occurrences of the lexeme λέγω (1 John 2:4, 6, 9), one occurrence of the lexeme ψεύστης (1 John 2:4), two occurrences of the lexeme λόγος (1 John 2:5, 7), and two occurrences of the lexeme γράφω (1 John 2:7, 8). Moreover, the three independent clauses starting with the word group ὁ λέγων (vv. 4a, 6a, 9) contribute to this section's structural unity.[26] The present section can be divided into the two units in 1 John 2:3-6 and 2:7-11. The first unit (1 John 2:3-6) introduces and underlines the notion of obedience to God's commandments. There are repeated occurrences of the two lexemes τηρέω (3x; cf. vv. 3, 4, 5) and γινώσκω (4x; cf. vv. 3 [2x], 4, 5). The second unit focuses on the particular commandment of loving one another in 1 John 2:7-11. The two contrastive lexemes σκοτία and φῶς are detected a total of five times (vv. 8, 9, 11 [3x]) and three times (vv. 8, 9, 10; cf. the cognate lexeme φαίνω in v. 8), respectively. Both of these two lexemes (i.e., σκοτία and φῶς) are absent from the prior unit in 1 John 2:3-6 and do not recur in the discourse after 1 John 2:11 in this letter. It is also worth noting that the author connects the two positive notions of light and love on the one hand and associates the lack of love with the negative notion of darkness on the other hand in 1 John 2:7-11.

---

25. Culy, *1, 2, 3 John*, 24.

26. This commentary considers the word group καθὼς ἐκεῖνος περιεπάτησεν as a parenthetical dependent clause in 1 John 2:6b. The independent clause beginning with ὁ λέγων does not include this word group in 1 John 2:6a.

i. Keeping God's Commandments (2:3–6)

Upon affirming God's forgiveness of our sins through Jesus' atoning death, the author utilizes the third-class conditional construction again to point out that keeping God's commandments is the indicator of knowing him in 1 John 2:3a–c. In this third-class conditional construction, the apodosis (v. 3a–b) is put forward prior to the protasis that is headed by the conditional conjunction ἐάν (v. 3c). The prepositional phrase ἐν τούτῳ, which occurs for the first time in v. 3a, is found a total of fourteen times in this epistle (1 John 2:3, 4, 5 [2x]; 3:10, 16, 19, 24; 4:2, 9, 10, 13, 17; 5:2). In one-half of these fourteen instances including the present instance in v. 3a (cf. ἐν τούτῳ γινώσκομεν), this prepositional phrase appears in connection with a plural form of the lexeme γινώσκω with respect to the knowledge of a certain thing (cf. 1 John 2:3, 5; 3:16, 19, 24; 4:13; 5:2). The author attempts to evoke a sense of solidarity with his audience by using the device of the inclusive "we" repeatedly in 1 John 2:3 (cf. γινώσκομεν [v. 3a], ἐγνώκαμεν [v. 3b], τηρῶμεν [v. 3c]). While the indicative verb γινώσκομεν (v. 3a) and the subjunctive verb τηρῶμεν (v. 3c) are in the present tense, the perfect active indicative verb ἐγνώκαμεν above is employed to give prominence to the idea that we are in the state of knowing God personally in v. 3b (cf. the referent of αὐτόν is probably God).[27] The author further draws attention to God's commandments by assigning the complement τὰς ἐντολὰς αὐτοῦ the thematic position prior to the predicator τηρῶμεν in the clause in v. 3c. This is the first time the lexeme ἐντολή (14x) occurs in the plural with respect to the decrees of God in this letter.[28] On the assumption that the pronoun αὐτοῦ (v. 3c) refers to God and is the subjective genitive,[29] the author avers that doing what God commands is the means by which the believers are sure of knowing him personally. Furthermore, the author implicitly urges his audience to act in accordance with God's commandments through the third-class protasis in 1 John 2:3c.

There is a change of participant from the inclusive "we" in v. 3 to the generic participant in 1 John 2:4a. The author uses this generic participant, which is encoded by the entire participial construction ὁ λέγων ὅτι ἔγνωκα αὐτὸν καὶ τὰς ἐντολὰς αὐτοῦ μὴ τηρῶν,[30] to refer to a whole class of people

---

27. Kruse, *Letters of John*, 78; Schnackenburg, *Johannine Epistles*, 89–90.

28. The total fourteen occurrences of the lexeme ἐντολή are present in 1 John 2:3, 4, 7 (3x), 8; 3:22, 23 (2x), 24; 4:21; 5:2, 3 (2x). This lexeme is found four times in 2 John (vv. 4, 5, 6 [2x]).

29. Culy, *1, 2, 3 John*, 26; Sherman and Tuggy, *Semantic and Structural Analysis*, 32–33.

30. The placement of the complement τὰς ἐντολὰς αὐτοῦ prior to the predicator τηρῶν is emphatic (cf. v. 3c).

whose characteristics are claiming to know God but not keeping his commandments. This is the first occurrence of the word group ὁ λέγων in this unit in 1 John 2:3–6 (vv. 4a, 6a, 9). The two present active nominative masculine singular participles λέγων and τηρῶν share the single nominative masculine singular article ὁ, which is located at the outset of v. 4a. The author utilizes the embedded finite clause ὅτι ἔγνωκα αὐτὸν in this participial construction above to realize the direct and reported speech "I know him (i.e., God)." This utterance concerning knowledge of God is prominent in view of the use of the perfect tense (i.e., ἔγνωκα). In addition to fleshing out the features of the generic participant, the author probably utilizes the long participial construction above to build suspense so as to anticipate the identification of the person purporting to know God but not doing what he commands as "a liar" near the end of v. 4a (cf. 1 John 1:6d). The author further avails himself of the subsequent negative statement to elaborate that the truth is not in such a person in v. 4b. The placement of the prepositional phrase ἐν τούτῳ (v. 4b) prior to the subject (i.e., ἡ ἀλήθεια) and the predicator (i.e., ἐστίν) is emphatic. The demonstrative pronoun τούτῳ (v. 4b) in the dative case above is anaphoric. The author is of the conviction that the profession to have a relationship to God must be evidenced in obedience to carry out his commandments. On the contrary, refusing to do what God commands exposes the invalidity of such a profession and actually shows the speaker to be a liar.

After criticizing the deceitful person as depicted in v. 4, the author turns the focus to the positive portrayal of a different kind of individual through the two generic statements in 1 John 2:5a–b. The elided postpositive conjunction δ' is mildly contrastive in v. 5a. In contrast to the lack of obedience to God's commandments in v. 4, this kind of individual "keeps his word" in v. 5a (cf. 1 John 1:10). The nominative masculine singular relative pronoun ὅς, which does not have an antecedent, is linked with the probability adjunct ἄν (cf. 1 John 3:17; 4:15 [ἐάν]) to realize the subject in v. 5a. Granted that the third-person singular prefect indicative verb τετελείωται is in the middle voice, the author affirms that truly the love of God has reached a state of maturity in the person in v. 5b.[31] Notice that the adverbial adjunct ἀληθῶς (v. 5b) is marked to accentuate the notion of actuality in the clause. Both of the two lexemes ἀγάπη (18x) and τελειόω (4x) occur for the first time in connection with each other in v. 5b in this letter.[32] In fact,

---

31. Alternatively, τετελείωται can be construed as a passive verb ("is made complete").

32. There is a total of eighteen occurrences of the lexeme ἀγάπη in this epistle (1 John 2:5, 15; 3:1, 16, 17; 4:7, 8, 9, 10, 12, 16 [3x], 17, 18 [3x]; 5:3). This lexeme appears twice in 2 John (vv. 3, 6) and once in 3 John 6.

all of the four occurrences of the lexeme τελειόω are in the perfect tense and pertinent to the topic of love (1 John 2:5; 4:12, 17, 18; cf. the cognate adjective τέλειος in 1 John 4:18). Depending on the meaning of the genitive θεοῦ, the subject phrase ἡ ἀγάπη τοῦ θεοῦ can refer to the individual's love for God or God's love for him or her in v. 5b. The former understanding is preferred because the active participants are mostly humans in the immediate co-text.[33] The corollary is that the believer's love for God is inseparable from his or her willingness to obey God's word.

The author uses the inclusive first-person plural expressions again to enhance solidarity with his audience in 1 John 2:5c–d. The mental clause ἐν τούτῳ γινώσκομεν (8x; cf. 1 John 2:3, 5; 3:16, 19, 24; 4:2, 13; 5:2) occurs for the second time with the conjunction ὅτι to usher in the reported thought regarding what we are sure of in v. 5c. The author places the prepositional phrase ἐν αὐτῷ prior to the predicator ἐσμέν to stress the locative idea that we are "in him [i.e., God]" in v. 5d. The prepositional phrase ἐν τούτῳ above (v. 5c), which is of instrumental use, can be regarded as pointing backward to either the notion of obeying God's word (v. 5a) or the perfection of the love of God (v. 5b). Yet, it is possible that this prepositional phrase (i.e., ἐν τούτῳ) in v. 5c points forward to the notion concerning the modulated command of imitating Jesus that will be set forth in 1 John 2:6 (cf. NIV).[34] On this latter understanding, we can be certain of our union with God by virtue of following in Jesus' footsteps. Whether the prepositional phrase ἐν τούτῳ (v. 5c) is anaphoric or cataphoric, on the practical level there is no significant difference between the notions of obeying God's word (v. 5a) and living just as Jesus lived (v. 6) given that the Father and the Son are in perfect unity in Johannine thinking.[35] At any rate, it is conspicuous that the believer's union with God has ethical bearings on his or her everyday conduct.

For the second time, the author utilizes the word group ὁ λέγων to portray the kind of individual who alleges to remain in God in 1 John 2:6a (cf. 1 John 2:4, 9). The construction ὁ λέγων ἐν αὐτῷ μένειν as a whole constitutes the generic subject. This is the first time the lexeme μένω (24x) is employed

---

33. Marshall, *Epistles of John*, 124–25; Culy, *1, 2, 3 John*, 28.

34. For the cataphoric understanding of the prepositional phrase ἐν τούτῳ in 1 John 2:5, see Stott, *Letters of John*, 96; Marshall, *Epistles of John*, 126; Smalley, *1, 2, 3 John*, 47. Aside from this instance, the prepositional phrase ἐν τούτῳ is cataphoric in several places in this letter (e.g., 1 John 2:3; 3:16, 24; 4:2, 9, 10, 13). Brown thinks that the prepositional phrase ἐν τούτῳ "refers to both what precedes and what follows" in 1 John 2:5. See Brown, *Epistles of John*, 249. For the ethical notion of imitating Christ in 1 John, see Leung, "Ethics and *Imitatio Christi* in 1 John"; Bennema, *Mimesis in the Johannine Literature*; Watt, "Reciprocity, Mimesis and Ethics in 1 John."

35. Marshall, *Epistles of John*, 126; Smalley, *1, 2, 3 John*, 47.

in regard to a person's abiding relationship with God in v. 6a in this epistle.[36] The author avails himself of the declarative statement, which is expressed by the third-person singular present active indicative verb ὀφείλει, to implicate the modulated directive for exhorting his audience to walk in the same way in which Jesus walked.[37] Aside from the present instance in 1 John 2:6, the lexeme ὀφείλω occurs twice pertaining to the Christian duty of ethical living on account of what Christ or God has done in 1 John 3:16 and 4:11 (cf. 3 John 8; John 13:14). It merits mention that the parenthetical clause καθὼς ἐκεῖνος περιεπάτησεν (v. 6b) is actually placed inside the main clause in v. 6a. The referent of the nominative masculine singular demonstrative pronoun ἐκεῖνος is "Jesus" (cf. 1 John 2:6; 3:3, 5, 7, 16; 4:17). Notably, the rhetorical effect of this parenthetical clause is that Jesus' exemplary life is underlined as the benchmark of the Christian conduct.[38] In fact, the author establishes the correlation between Jesus' way of living and the believers' way of living by employing the comparative conjunction καθώς at the outset of this parenthetical clause above.[39] Moreover, the lexeme περιπατέω is detected twice in the present or aorist tense in 1 John 2:6. The author utilizes the present active infinitive περιπατεῖν with the imperfective aspect to foreground the believers' ongoing living in the main clause in v. 6a. The third-person singular aorist active indicative verb περιεπάτησεν with the perfective aspect is used to portray Jesus' way of life as a whole in the parenthetical clause in v. 6b, which contains the supporting materials.

ii. Loving the Christian Brothers and Sisters (2:7–11)

Having affirmed that obeying God's commandments and following in Jesus' footsteps are the tokens of one's relationship to God, the author deals with specifically the old and new commandment that the audience have received from the beginning in 1 John 2:7–8. Instead of the inclusive "we" or generic

---

36. The total twenty-four occurrences of the lexeme μένω are found in 1 John 2:6, 10, 14, 17, 19, 24 (3x), 27 (2x), 28; 3:6, 9, 14, 15, 17, 24 (2x); 4:12, 13, 15, 16 (3x). This lexeme occurs a total of three times in 2 John 2; 9 (2x).

37. Sherman and Tuggy, *Semantic and Structural Analysis*, 32–34; Leung, "Metaphorical Expressions of the Commands in 1 John" (forthcoming).

38. The authenticity of the word οὕτως is debatable. The reading οὕτως is attested in 1 John 2:6 in codices Sinaiticus (ℵ or 01), Ephraemi Rescriptus (C or 04), and Athous Lavrensis (Ψ or 044), and other textual witnesses. However, this word is absent from 1 John 2:6 in codices Alexandrinus (A or 02) and Vaticanus (B or 03), minuscules 5 and 33, and a number of other manuscripts. See Metzger, *Textual Commentary on the Greek New Testament*, 639–40.

39. Bennema, *Mimesis in the Johannine Literature*, 60–61, 108–15.

participant (cf. vv. 3–6), he shifts to use the first-person singular for self-reference and speaks to the audience directly in the second-person plural in vv. 7a–8a. The author has previously employed the term of endearment τεκνία in the vocative case and the word group γράφω ὑμῖν to capture his audience's attention in 1 John 2:1. He changes to utilize another vocative plural ἀγαπητοί (6x; 1 John 2:7; 3:2, 21; 4:1, 7, 11; cf. 3 John 2, 5, 11) from semantic domain 25 ("attitudes and emotions") with this word group above to address his audience directly and thereby enhances positive affect in 1 John 2:7a. The two statements are contrastive to each other in v. 7a–b (cf. the adversative conjunction ἀλλά and the two contrastive lexemes καινός and παλαιός). The author tells his audience that what he conveys to them is not a new commandment but rather is an old commandment. The lexeme ἐντολή has occurred in the plural twice with reference to God's commandments in general in the preceding unit in 1 John 2:3–6 (vv. 3, 4). Nevertheless, all of the four occurrences of this lexeme are in the singular and pertaining to specifically the new and old commandment in vv. 7–8 in the present unit.

There is little doubt that the old and new commandment refers to the new commandment that Jesus gave to his disciples after washing their feet in John 13:34–35. At stake in Jesus' directive to his disciples is that they should love one another in the same manner as he has loved them. In fact, Jesus' self-sacrifice for others has set the standard of the believers' mutual love, which should be a hallmark of God's people in the eschatological age.[40] The author expounds that the old commandment is that which the audience has had from the beginning in 1 John 2:7c (cf. 2 John 5). The antecedent of the nominative singular feminine relative pronoun ἥν is ἐντολὴν παλαιάν (v. 7b) at the beginning of this clause in v. 7c. The prepositional phrase ἀπ' ἀρχῆς (v. 7c) is utilized to hint at that the source of the old and new commandment is Jesus' earthly life and ministry (cf. 1 John 1:1; 2:7, 13, 14, 24 [2x]; 3:8, 11; 2 John 5, 6). The author employs the relational verb ἐστίν to identify the old commandment as "the word" that the audience have heard in v. 7d (cf. 1 John 3:11; 2 John 6). The complement of this relational verb (i.e., ἐστίν) is the word group ὁ λόγος ὃν ἠκούσατε (v. 7d), in which the embedded relative clause (i.e., ὃν ἠκούσατε) is used to modify the articular noun λόγος. The implication is that the audience have had the old and new commandment since the time they have heard and received the gospel message centered upon Jesus.

The author makes use of the adverbial adjunct πάλιν to intimate the resumption of the topic of the new commandment at the outset of v. 8a. At first glance, the positive statement that the author is writing a new

---

40. Carson, *Gospel According to John*, 484–85; Keener, *Gospel of John*, 2:924–25.

commandment to the audience (i.e., πάλιν ἐντολὴν καινὴν γράφω ὑμῖν) in v. 8a seems to be contradictory to the foregoing negative statement (i.e., Ἀγαπητοί, οὐκ ἐντολὴν καινὴν γράφω ὑμῖν) that he is not writing a new commandment to them in v. 7a. However, there are nuances in the meaning of the two occurrences of the lexeme καινός in the two clauses above. On the one hand, the lexeme καινός from semantic domain 28 ("know") is employed to express that the commandment is not "previously unknown" to the audience in v. 7a.[41] On the other hand, the author utilizes the lexeme καινός from semantic domain 58 ("nature, class, example") to indicate that the commandment is "new" in nature in v. 8a. As an interpersonal effect, the author uses the positive statement (v. 8a) to round off the preceding negative statement (v. 7a) through contrast so as to increase audience engagement. The nominative neuter singular relative pronoun ὅ (v. 8b) likely refers to the aforementioned idea that what the author conveys to his audience is the new commandment (v. 8a). The antecedent of the dative masculine singular pronoun αὐτῷ (v. 8b) is the nominative masculine singular demonstrative pronoun ἐκεῖνος (v. 6b), whose referent is Jesus. As asserted in v. 8b, this idea is "true" in Jesus and in the audience. The implication is that the realization of the new commandment is exemplified in Jesus' sacrificial life and death and in the Christian community (presumably by way of the believers' loving one another).[42] The author utilizes the causal conjunction ὅτι to introduce the reason to support his assertion in v. 8c. It is said that the darkness is passing (v. 8c) and the true light is already shining (v. 8d).[43] While God is light in 1 John 1:5, "the true light" most likely refers to Jesus in v. 8d (cf. John 1:9; 8:12; 9:5). The author employs the third-person singular present middle indicative verb παράγεται to portray that the darkness as the symbol of evilness is in the process of ceasing to exist in v. 8c (cf. 1 John 2:17). In contrast, the third-person singular present active indicative verb φαίνει is used in connection with the temporal adjunct ἤδη to depict that the process of the shining of the true light has begun. Although evilness has not yet completely disappeared, the believers are assured that the realization of the new commandment given by Jesus is being seen in them in the present.

The author uses the generic participants, who are realized by various embedded participial clauses, to set forth the negative example for the believers to avoid in 1 John 2:9 and 2:11 or the positive example for them to

---

41. Louw and Nida, *Greek-English Lexicon of the New Testament*, 1:337.

42. Kruse, *Letters of John*, 83–84; Jobes, *1, 2, and 3 John*, 95; Brown, *Epistles of John*, 267.

43. Both of the two lexemes σκοτία (1 John 1:5; 2:8, 9, 11 [3x]; cf. σκότος in 1 John 1:6) and φῶς (1 John 1:5, 7 [2x]; 2:8, 9, 10) do not recur in the discourse subsequent to 1 John 2:11.

follow in 1 John 2:10. The author introduces the notion of hatred, which is the antithesis of the notion of love, by employing the lexeme μισέω from semantic domain 88 ("moral and ethical qualities and related behavior") altogether twice in v. 9 and v. 11 (cf. 1 John 3:13, 15; 4:20). Furthermore, he attempts to correlate the contrast of love and hatred with the other contrast of light and darkness in vv. 9–11. As illustrated in v. 9,[44] the person claiming to be in the light but hating his or her Christian brother or sister is still in the darkness. The generic subject is expressed by the entire participial construction ὁ λέγων ἐν τῷ φωτὶ εἶναι καὶ τὸν ἀδελφὸν αὐτοῦ μισῶν, in which the two nominative singular present active participles λέγων and μισῶν share the single article ὁ in this participial construction in v. 9.[45] This is the third and last time the participial clause ὁ λέγων occurs in this epistle (1 John 2:4, 6, 9). The author utilizes the kinship term ἀδελφός (15x) for the first time to denote a Christian brother or sister in God's family in v. 9.[46] By indicating that the person above is actually in the darkness, the author not only exposes the falsity of his or her allegation to be in the light but also intimates a negative appraisal of such a person in 1 John 2:9.

On the positive side, the author uses the generic statement to depict the kind of the individual who loves a Christian brother and sister and is in the light in 1 John 2:10. The embedded participial clause ὁ ἀγαπῶν τὸν ἀδελφὸν αὐτοῦ as a whole is the generic subject of the third-person singular present active indicative verb μένει in v. 10a. Since this individual loves the fellow believers, he or she lives a life in conformity with Jesus' sacrificial love for his followers (cf. 1 John 2:6). There is a progression of ideas from "being in the light" regarding the false claim in v. 9 to "remaining in the light" regarding the exemplar's perpetual union with God or Jesus in v. 10a. The author continues to utilize the negative statement to elaborate that there is no cause for stumbling in such a person above in v. 10b. The dative masculine singular pronoun αὐτῷ (v. 10b) harks back to the person as portrayed in v. 10a. The lexeme σκάνδαλον (v. 10b) is a *hapax legomenon* in the Johannine epistles but is employed to convey the negative idea of committing a transgression or causing someone to sin against God in other NT writings (e.g., Matt 13:41; 16:23; 18:7; Rev 2:14). Simply put, the author avers that

---

44. There are three embedded clauses in 1 John 2:9. They are (i) ὁ λέγων, (ii) ἐν τῷ φωτὶ εἶναι, and (iii) καὶ τὸν ἀδελφὸν αὐτοῦ μισῶν.

45. The embedded infinitival clause ἐν τῷ φωτὶ εἶναι is the complement of the participle λέγων that precedes in v. 9. Note that the prepositional phrase ἐν τῷ φωτί is marked in this embedded infinitival clause.

46. The lexeme ἀδελφός is found a total of fifteen times in 1 John 2:9, 10, 11; 3:10, 12 (2x), 13, 14, 15, 16, 17; 4:20 (2x), 21; 5:16.

the person who loves the fellow believers abides in the light and will not do anything to cause a Christian brother or sister to stumble and fall into sin.[47]

The author avails himself of the four conjoined clauses to elaborate the negative portrait of the individual who hates a Christian brother or sister and is in the darkness in 1 John 2:11 (cf. v. 9). The postpositive conjunction δέ is mildly contrastive and signals the shift of thought from the positive to negative example for the believers in v. 11a. In contrast to the two lexemes ἀγαπάω and φῶς that are positive in meaning in v. 10a, the author employs the two negative lexemes μισέω and σκοτία that are antithetical to ἀγαπάω and φῶς respectively to depict the individual above in v. 11a. Moreover, the parallel structure of the two embedded participial clauses ὁ δὲ μισῶν τὸν ἀδελφὸν αὐτοῦ (v. 11a) and ὁ ἀγαπῶν τὸν ἀδελφὸν αὐτοῦ (v. 10b) in effect heightens the contrast between hating and loving the fellow believers. The author describes that the person who hates his or her Christian brother or sister is in the darkness in v. 11a. Then he provides further information to affirm that this person lives in the darkness in v. 11b (cf. the progression of ideas from "being in the darkness" to "walking in the darkness"). In addition, such a person does not know where he or she is going in v. 11c.[48] Notice that the author places the prepositional phrase ἐν τῇ σκοτίᾳ in the emphatic position prior to the third-person singular present active indicative verb περιπατεῖ to underline the sphere (i.e., "in the darkness") in which the individual is walking in v.11b (cf. vv. 9, 11a). There is a change of the subject or active participant from the person who hates the fellow believers in v. 11a–c to "the darkness" (i.e., ἡ σκοτία) in the dependent clause beginning with the causal conjunction ὅτι in v. 11d. It is explained that this individual does not know his or her direction because the darkness has blinded his or her eyes. In view of the employment of the aorist active indicative verb ἐτύφλωσεν with the perfective aspect, the event of the blinding of the individual's eyes is portrayed as complete in v. 11d.

---

47. See the discussion in Jobes, *1, 2, and 3 John*, 97; Yarbrough, *1–3 John*, 108–9; Akin, *1, 2, 3 John*, 99–100.

48. There are altogether fifteen occurrences of the lexeme οἶδα in 1 John 2:11, 20, 21 (2x), 29; 3:2, 5, 14, 15; 5:13, 15 (2x), 18, 19, 20.

1 JOHN 2:12–17

OUTLINE:

I. Prologue (1:1–4)

II. Body (1:5—5:12)

    A. Adhering to and Behaving in Conformity with the Christian Beliefs (1:5—2:27)

        1. Walking in the Light (1:5—2:11)

        2. Affirmation of the Believers' Status and Admonition Against Love for the World (2:12–17)

            a. The Believers' Status (2:12–14)

            b. Do Not Love the World (2:15–17)

2. Affirmation of the Believers' Status and Admonition Against Love for the World (2:12–17)

The present unit in 1 John 2:12–17 is divided into two sections (vv. 12–14 and vv. 15–17), which are connected to each other by way of a logical flow of thought. The author's affirmation of the audience's spiritual status in the former section is the basis for his admonition to them in the latter section. The author makes a smooth transition between these two sections by referring to "the evil one" at the end of v. 14 and, subsequently, "the world" in v. 15 (cf. 1 John 5:19).[1] The first section comprises a total of sixty words in altogether fourteen ranking clauses in 1 John 2:12–14. The main participant is the audience. The author creates the structural coherence of this section

---

1. Brown, *Epistles of John*, 323.

by utilizing the tripartite division twice in vv. 12–13 and v. 14. In each of these two tripartite divisions, there are three independent clauses beginning with either the word group γράφω ὑμῖν with the vocative (vv. 12a, 13a, 13c), or the word group ἔγραψα ὑμῖν with the vocative (vv. 14a, 14c, 14e). Furthermore, there are altogether six dependent clauses that are headed by the causal conjunction ὅτι in this section (vv. 12b, 13b, 13d, 14b, 14d, 14f). It is also noteworthy that the author uses the perfect tense a total of six times to give prominence to the affirmative messages to his audience in 1 John 2:12–14 (cf. ἀφέωνται [v. 12b], ἐγνώκατε [vv. 13b, 14b, d], νενικήκατε [vv. 13d, 14h]). The second section consists of seventy-one words in altogether nine ranking clauses in 1 John 2:15–17. Instead of the audience, the world is the main participant in this latter section. The author enhances the internal unity of this section by employing the lexeme κόσμος for a total of six times (vv. 15 [3x], 16 [2x], 17) and a number of the words from semantic domain 25 ("attitudes and emotions").[2] In contrast to the prior section, none of the finite verbs is in the perfect tense in 1 John 2:15–17. Significantly, the first occurrence of the second-person plural present active imperative verb ἀγαπᾶτε in v. 15a suggests that a discourse peak can be identified in this section in this letter.[3]

a. The Believers' Status (2:12–14)

The author uses the declarative statements to give information pertaining to his audience's Christian identity and their relationship to God in 1 John 2:12–14.[4] There is a change from the mostly generic participants in the preceding co-text in 1 John 2:3–11 to the audience and the author as the primary and secondary participants, respectively, in this section. Among the total fourteen occurrences of the indicative verbs in 1 John 2:12–14, there are six occurrences of the first-person singular indicative with reference to the author (γράφω [3x], ἔγραψα [3x]) and six occurrences of the second-person plural indicative with reference to the audience (ἐγνώκατε [3x], νενικήκατε [2x], ἐστέ [1x]). While the remaining two indicative verbs ἀφέωνται and μένει are in the third-person singular, they are linked with the second-person plural dative pronoun ὑμῖν in v. 12b and v. 14g. Thus, the experiential meanings encoded in these two third-person singular

---

2. The following words fall within semantic domain 25 ("attitudes and emotions"): ἀγαπᾶτε (v. 15a), ἀγαπᾷ (v. 15c), ἀγάπη (v. 15c), ἐπιθυμία (vv. 16a [2x], 17b), θέλημα (v. 17c).

3. Longacre, "Exhortation and Mitigation in First John," 14.

4. Lieu, *I, II, & III John*, 85; Marshall, *Epistles of John*, 134.

indicative verbs are relevant to the audience. In fact, there is a total of eight occurrences of the second-person plural dative pronoun ὑμῖν including the two instances above in 1 John 2:12–14 (vv. 12a, 12b, 13a, 13c, 14a, 14c, 14e, 14g). If the altogether six occurrences of the different vocative plural nouns used for the audience's direct addresses are included (τεκνία [v. 12a], παιδία [v. 14a], πατέρες [vv. 13a, 14c], and νεανίσκοι [vv. 13c, 14e]), there is a total of twenty participant references to the audience in this section. It is apparent that what the author says is chiefly concerned with his audience in the present unit in 1 John 2:12–14.

As noted above, the tripartite structure is detected in the two subsections in 1 John 2:12–13 and 1 John 2:14. The first subsection is constitutive of the three clause complexes beginning with the word group γράφω ὑμῖν (i.e., v. 12a–b, v. 13a–b, v. 13c–d). The second subsection consists of the three clause complexes beginning with the word group ἔγραψα ὑμῖν (i.e., v. 14a–b, v. 14c–d, v. 14e–h). In all of these altogether six clause complexes above, the author gives a direct address to his audience using the vocative plural (see above) to capture their attention. It is likely that the two vocative plural nouns τεκνία (v. 12a) and παιδία (v. 14a) are used to denote the whole audience instead of a certain group in them because the author frequently employs these two vocative plural nouns to speak to his audience elsewhere in this letter (cf. τεκνία in 1 John 2:1, 28; 3:18; 4:4; 5:21; παιδία in 1 John 2:18; 3:7). As for the referent(s) of the other two vocative plural nouns πατέρες (vv. 13a, 14c) and νεανίσκοι (vv. 13c, 14e), it is debatable whether two distinct groups according to age or maturity or only one group (i.e., the whole audience) are in view.[5] Both of these two understandings concerning the referent of the two vocative plural nouns πατέρες and νεανίσκοι are possible. Nevertheless, this commentary adopts the view that the author utilizes these two vocative plural nouns to address rhetorically all the audience members from different perspectives in terms of the various stages in a person's life in 1 John 2:13–14. The reason this view is preferable is that the characteristics of the "fathers" or "young men" are applied to describe the entire audience, not limited to a particular group in them, in other places in this epistle (cf. 1 John 2:3; 3:16; 4:2, 6; 4:4, 7; 5:4).[6]

After addressing all his audience as "dear children," the author says that he writes to them because (cf. the causal conjunction ὅτι) their sins have been forgiven on account of Jesus' name in 1 John 2:12b. The referent of

---

5. For the view that considers the "fathers" and "young men" as representing two different groups, see Kruse, *Letters of John*, 88; Yarbrough, *1–3 John*, 114. For the view that regards the "fathers" and "young men" as denoting all the audience, see Jobes, *1, 2, and 3 John*, 105–6; Lieu, *I, II, & III John*, 86–87; Marshall, *Epistles of John*, 137–38.

6. See the relevant works in the prior note.

the masculine singular genitive pronoun αὐτοῦ in the prepositional phrase διὰ τὸ ὄνομα αὐτοῦ (v. 12b) is likely to be "Jesus" because his blood, which signifies his death, has been associated with the cleansing of sins in 1 John 1:7. Aside from this instance in v. 12b, the author makes reference to Jesus' "name" in 1 John 3:23 and 5:13 (cf. the "name" in 3 John 7). The author employs the third-person plural perfect passive indicative verb ἀφέωνται to underscore the idea regarding the forgiveness of sins in 1 John 2:12b. The unspecified agent who performs the act of forgiving sins is presumably God, who is faithful and just (cf. 1 John 1:9). As noted above, the direct address "fathers" is likely to be a rhetorical designation of the whole audience in 1 John 2:13a (cf. v. 14c). The author writes to the "fathers" because they know him (probably with reference to Jesus) who is from the beginning in v. 13b. While the notion of knowledge of God is mentioned in the preceding co-text in 1 John 2:3–4, the author probably utilizes the masculine singular accusative article τόν to denote Jesus and thereby asserts that the audience knows him in 1 John 2:13b.[7] This understanding of the referent of this article is probable because the following prepositional phrase ἀπ' ἀρχῆς (v. 13b) has been employed to allude to Jesus' earthly life and ministry at the beginning of the prologue in 1 John 1:1a.[8] Therefore, the author affirms the spiritual status of the "fathers" by pointing out their relationship to Jesus in v. 13b. The sixth and last occurrence of the first-person singular present active indicative verb γράφω is present in 1 John 2:13c (cf. 1 John 2:1, 7, 8, 12, 13a), in which the vocative plural noun νεανίσκοι occurs to depict the audience as being in the active stage of life.[9] The author has declared that the darkness is passing and the true light is already shining in 1 John 2:8. Now he further avers that the believers have overcome the evil one (i.e., Satan), who is expressed by the articular masculine singular accusative adjective πονηρόν in 1 John 2:13d.[10] This is the first time the lexeme νικάω (6x) from semantic domain 39 ("hostility, strife") appears in this letter (cf. 1 John 2:13, 14; 4:4; 5:4 [2x], 5). The second-person plural perfect active indicative verb νενικήκατε (v. 13d) is employed to give prominence to the believers' victorious status over the evil one and presumably resulting from Jesus' triumph over the world (cf. John 12:31; 16:33).

Akin to the tripartite structure in 1 John 2:12–13, there is also a three-part division in 1 John 2:14. The author avails himself of the three clause

---

7. The masculine singular accusative article τόν functions to nominalize the ensuing prepositional phrase ἀπ' ἀρχῆς.

8. Culy, *1, 2, 3 John*, 40; Brown, *Epistles of John*, 303.

9. The lexeme νεανίσκος occurs altogether twice in 1 John 2:13 and 2:14. This lexeme is not found in other Johannine writings.

10. See Lieu, *I, II, & III John*, 89; Culy, *1, 2, 3 John*, 40.

complexes containing altogether eight ranking clauses to address his audience from three vantage points in succession regarding the three stages in a man's life (i.e., "children" in v. 14a–b, "fathers" in v. 14c–d, and "young men" in v. 14e–h). Instead of the first-person singular present active indicative verb γράφω (vv. 12a, 13a, c), the author shifts to use the first-person singular aorist active indicative verb ἔγραψα (3x) to usher in his affirmative messages to the "children," "fathers," and "young men" in 1 John 2:14 (v. 14a, v. 14c, v. 14e; cf. 1 John 2:21, 26; 5:13). Since some of the characteristics of these three groups are repeated, the aorist tense (i.e., ἔγραψα) is probably employed to divert attention rhetorically from the action of writing to what the author seeks to convey to his audience in v. 14.[11] It is also worthy of mention that the author changes to employ the vocative plural noun παιδία (which is a diminutive form of παῖς) instead of the vocative plural τεκνία (v. 12a) to speak to the audience as "dear children" in v. 14a (cf. 1 John 2:18; 3:7; John 21:5). By asserting that his "dear children" know the Father, the author indicates his confidence in the audience's relationship to God in v. 14b. The author's reason of writing to the "fathers" in v. 14c–d is similar to that in v. 13a–b (see above). As an outcome of repeating the notion of knowing Jesus, the author in effect reinforces the affirmation of the audience's status as believers in v. 14c–d.

The author expands the third part in the tripartite structure as regards the depiction of the "young men" in v. 14e–h. While only two ranking clauses are employed with respect to "the young men" in the preceding cotext in v. 13c–d, a total of four ranking clauses are utilized to provide extra information to elaborate their spiritual status in v. 14e–h. The author writes to "the young men" because they are strong (v. 14f) and the word of God remains in them (v. 14g) and they have overcome the evil one (v. 14h). The placement of the complement ἰσχυροί prior to the predicator ἐστέ suggests that the author puts emphasis on the young men's feature as being spiritually strong in v. 14f. The lexeme ἰσχυρός occurs only once in 1 John 2:14 and is absent from 2 and 3 John or the Fourth Gospel. The author employs the second-person plural perfect active indicative verb νενικήκατε for the second time in connection with the complement τὸν πονηρόν to reiterate what he has previously said about the young men in 1 John 2:14h (cf. v. 13d). While the young men are the implicit subject of the two predicators ἐστέ (v. 14f) and νενικήκατε (v. 14h) in the second-person plural, the word group ὁ λόγος τοῦ θεοῦ is the subject of the third-person singular present active

---

11. Porter, *Verbal Aspect in the Greek of the New Testament*, 229–30. Yarbrough, Kruse, and Burge consider the three occurrences of the first-person singular aorist active indicative verb ἔγραψα as examples of the epistolary aorist in 1 John 2:14. See Yarbrough, *1–3 John*, 115–16; Kruse, *Letters of John*, 91; Burge, *Letters of John*, 111.

indicative verb μένει in v. 14g (note that v. 14g is sandwiched between v. 14f and v. 14h). The corollary is that the believers' spiritual strength and victory over Satan is not owing to their own vigor. Rather, they must be obedient to and rely on God's word, which remains in them.

b. Do Not Love the World (2:15–17)

Building on what was said of the audience's spiritual standing in 1 John 2:12–14, the author attempts to influence them not to love the world and hold the things in it in high esteem in 1 John 2:15–17. The main participant is changed from the audience in the prior section to the "world" in this section. All of the seven finite verbs are in the present tense in vv. 15–17 (cf. ἀγαπᾶτε [v. 15a], ἀγαπᾷ [v. 15c], ἔστιν [vv. 15d, 16a, b], παράγεται [v. 17a], μένει [v. 17c]). While the author has implicated several covert commands by way of the statements in the preceding co-text (e.g., 1 John 1:7, 9; 2:1, 3), he employs the second-person plural present active imperative verb ἀγαπᾶτε with the negative polarity adjunct μή to issue the prohibition to his audience to abstain from loving the world in 1 John 2:15a. This is the first occurrence of the imperative (10x) in the whole epistle (cf. 1 John 2:15, 24, 27, 28; 3:1, 7, 13; 4:1 [2x]; 5:21; see "Tenor" in "Introduction"). It should be noted that the use of the present tense does not necessarily imply that the audience are currently loving the world in v. 15a.[12] The imperative ἀγαπᾶτε above is also the implicit predicator in the subsequent elliptical verbless clause μηδὲ τὰ ἐν τῷ κόσμῳ in v. 15b, in which the author urges his audience not to love the things in the world. Although the lexeme κόσμος is used to express the neutral meaning in regard to Jesus' atoning death concerning the sins of "the whole world" in 1 John 2:2, the connotation of this lexeme is different in 1 John 2:15. Unlike this neutral meaning, the author employs the lexeme κόσμος to denote figuratively the rebellious system of beliefs and practices that are antagonistic to God in 1 John 2:15 (cf. 1 John 3:1, 13; 4:5; 5:4, 5, 19).[13] In view of this, the author forbids the believers to love "the world" and the things in it so that they will not fall into temptation and sin against God.

The author spells out the reason in support of the prohibition against loving the world in 1 John 2:15c–17. The two mutually exclusive ideas regarding the love for the world and the love for the Father (cf. πατρός is the objective genitive) are expressed by means of the protasis (v. 15c) and the apodosis (v. 15d) in the third-class conditional sentence, respectively.

12. See Huffman, *Verbal Aspect Theory*, 38, 106.

13. Köstenberger, *Theology of John's Gospel and Letters*, 281–82; Campbell, *1, 2, and 3 John*, 81–82.

If anyone loves the world, the love for the Father does not exist in him or her. The nominative masculine singular indefinite pronoun τις functions as the generic subject of the third-person singular present active subjunctive verb ἀγαπᾷ in the protasis in v. 15c. The meaning of the lexeme κόσμος (v. 15c) is in the same wavelength of its prior occurrences in 1 John 2:15a–b and thus pertaining to the system of the rebellious forces opposing God. The author explains why the person loving the world cannot love the Father subsequently through the two contrastive statements in 1 John 2:16a–b. The first negative statement is used to illustrate that everything that is in the world does not originate from the Father in v. 16a, in which the entire word group πᾶν τὸ ἐν τῷ κόσμῳ, ἡ ἐπιθυμία τῆς σαρκὸς καὶ ἡ ἐπιθυμία τῶν ὀφθαλμῶν καὶ ἡ ἀλαζονεία τοῦ βίου constitutes the subject. The nominative neuter singular adjective πᾶν, which occurs at the beginning of this word group, serves to enhance the sense as to the totality of the things in the world. The author utilizes the three articular genitive constructions in this word group above to point out the three categories of the things in the world that the believers should watch out for temptations or illusionary allurements in 1 John 2:16a. Furthermore, the word in the genitive is used to restrict or limit the meaning of the governing noun in each of these three articular genitive constructions.[14] The first genitive construction (i.e., ἡ ἐπιθυμία τῆς σαρκὸς) deals with the human lust for gratification of the sinful desires of the flesh.[15] The second genitive construction (i.e., ἡ ἐπιθυμία τῶν ὀφθαλμῶν) deals with specifically the human lust for gratification of the sinful desires that are engendered by the visual perception or something appealing to the sight.[16] The third genitive construction (i.e., ἡ ἀλαζονεία τοῦ βίου) deals with the false arrogance due to the material possessions or even personal achievements (cf. 1 John 3:17; Luke 15:12, 30; 21:4).[17] Since the things in these three categories above do not come from the Father, the believers should not love them.

Contrary to the notion of originating with the Father, the author uses the clause beginning with the elided adversative conjunction ἀλλ' to indicate that everything that is in the world carries the negative feature of originating with and belonging to the world in 1 John 2:16b. Following this

---

14. Broadly speaking, "the essential semantic feature of the genitive case is restriction" (Porter, *Idioms of the Greek New Testament*, 92).

15. The genitive noun σαρκός is either the subjective genitive or used to qualify the governing noun (i.e., ἐπιθυμία) in 1 John 2:16.

16. The genitive noun ὀφθαλμῶν is either the subjective genitive or used to specify the origin with reference to the governing noun (i.e., ἐπιθυμία) in 1 John 2:16.

17. The genitive noun βίου is likely used to specify the origin with reference to the governing noun (i.e., ἀλαζονεία) in 1 John 2:16.

elided adversative conjunction, the placement of the prepositional phrase ἐκ τοῦ κόσμου is emphatic and draws attention to this negative feature in v. 16b. The author continues to strengthen his case by elaborating the transient nature of the world and its desires in 1 John 2:17a–b. The full declarative clause in v. 17a is followed by the elliptical clause (i.e., καὶ ἡ ἐπιθυμία αὐτοῦ) in v. 17b. Despite the absence of a predicator, the third-person singular present middle or passive indicative verb παράγεται can be inferred from this full declarative clause (v. 17a) to be the implicit predicator in the elliptical clause that follows in v. 17b. The lexeme παράγω has occurred in the author's foregoing assertion that the darkness as a symbol of the evilness is passing in 1 John 2:8. By the same token, the world is in the process of passing away, along with the things that it desires (cf. ἡ ἐπιθυμία αὐτοῦ is probably the subjective genitive) in 1 John 2:17a–b.[18] In view of the transient nature of the world, it is not worth being held in high regard as the object of the believers' love (cf. v. 15). In dualistic contrast to the passing of the world and its desires, the one who does the will of God abides forever in 1 John 2:17c. The embedded participial clause (i.e., ὁ . . . ποιῶν τὸ θέλημα τοῦ θεοῦ) is the generic subject of the predicator μένει in v. 17c. This is the first time the author employs the participial clause ὁ ποιῶν for realizing the generic participant (6x; cf. 1 John 2:17, 29; 3:4, 7, 8, 10) in this letter. On the assumption that the genitive noun θεοῦ is the subjective genitive in the embedded participial clause above (cf. 1 John 5:14), the author concludes his admonition to the audience on the positive note of obeying God and acting in accord with his will in v. 17c. In the Fourth Gospel, Jesus demonstrates the perfect obedience in doing the Father's will (cf. John 4:34; 5:30; 6:38, 40; 7:17; 9:31). Thus, the person who is obedient to God's will actually follows in the footsteps of Jesus, who is the source of life.

---

18. According to Brown, the genitive pronoun αὐτοῦ in the phrase ἡ ἐπιθυμία αὐτοῦ is probably the subjective genitive in 1 John 2:17 in view of the similar genitival phrases in 1 John 2:16. Culy thinks that this genitive pronoun (i.e., αὐτοῦ) could be the subjective or objective genitive in v. 17. See Brown, *Epistles of John*, 313; Culy, *1, 2, 3 John*, 45.

1 JOHN 2:18–27

OUTLINE:

II. Body (1:5—5:12)

    A. Adhering to and Behaving in Conformity with the Christian Beliefs (1:5—2:27)

        1. Walking in the Light (1:5—2:11)

        2. Affirmation of the Believers' Status and Admonition Against Love for the World (2:12–17)

        3. Warnings Against the Danger of the Antichrists (2:18–27)

            a. The Last Hour, the Antichrist, and Many Antichrists (2:18–19)

            b. The Anointing versus the Liar (2:20–23)

            c. Remain in the Apostolic Teaching (2:24–26)

            d. The Abiding Anointing (2:27)

3. Warnings Against the Danger of the Antichrists (2:18–27)

The author attempts to warn his audience concerning the threat posed by the secessionists and facing the community in 1 John 2:18–27. While there is a scholarly consensus on the beginning of this unit in 1 John 2:18, it is debatable whether it ends in v. 27 or v. 28. On the one hand, the author probably employs the vocative plural noun τεκνία to denote his audience directly and speaks of Jesus' parousia to signal the shift of topic at the beginning of a new section in v. 28. Furthermore, there are five lexemes (i.e., παρρησία, αἰσχύνομαι, παρουσία, δικαιοσύνη, and γεννάω) that appear for the first time in 1 John 2:28–29 in this epistle.[1] On the other hand, the occurrence of this vocative plural noun above (i.e., τεκνία) in v. 28 resonates with another vocative plural noun παιδία that precedes in 1 John 2:18. Moreover, it is not impossible that the author's reference to Jesus' parousia (v. 28) harks back to and is contrastive with the prior mention of the coming of the antichrist in v. 18. On this latter understanding, v. 18 and v. 28 constitute an *inclusio* that brackets the unit in 1 John 2:18–28.[2] Both of the two understandings above are possible. In view of the topical shift in v. 28 and the clustering of several new lexemes in vv. 28–29, the former understanding that considers 1 John 2:18–27 as constituting a unit is preferable and adopted in this commentary. This unit can be further divided into four sections (i.e., vv. 18–19, 20–21, 24–26, 27) on account of the three direct references to the audience by the nominative second-person plural pronoun ὑμεῖς (3x) in v. 20a, v. 24a, and v. 27a.[3] These repeated references to the audience are telling of the author's concern or matter of interest in the present unit. In brief, he endeavors to enable his audience to discern the false teaching and exhorts them to adhere to the apostolic teaching in 1 John 2:18–27.

a. The Last Hour, the Antichrist, and Many Antichrists (2:18–19)

The author uses the vocative plural παιδία to address his audience directly and attracts their attention at the outset of 1 John 2:18 (cf. 1 John 2:14; 3:7), in which there are altogether six ranking clauses in v. 18a–f. Following this vocative plural noun above, the author utilizes the subject phrase ἐσχάτη ὥρα in connection with the predicator ἐστίν to introduce the topic of the arrival of the last hour in v. 18a.[4] It is worth noting that the word group ἐσχάτη ὥρα regarding eschatology is found only twice in v. 18a and v. 18f in this epistle and nowhere else in other NT documents. While it is possible to consider the "last hour" as denoting the whole period between Christ's first and second comings (cf. Acts 2:17; 1 Pet 1:20), it is more likely that the two occurrences of the word group ἐσχάτη ὥρα (v. 18a, f) above refer to the

---

1. For the view that considers 1 John 2:18–27 as constituting a unit, see Marshall, *Epistles of John*, 164–65; Brown, *Epistles of John*, 362–63; Sherman and Tuggy, *Semantic and Structural Analysis*, 46–52.

2. For the view that considers 1 John 2:18–28 as constituting a unit, see Jobes, *1, 2, and 3 John*, 118–33; Lieu, *I, II, & III John*, 114.

3. Brown, *Epistles of John*, 341, 363.

4. Brown, *Epistles of John*, 363.

final stage in this period prior to Christ's return on account of the mention of the antichrist as God's eschatological antagonist in v. 18c.[5] The lexeme ἀντίχριστος is found a total of four times in this letter (1 John 2:18c, 18d, 22; 4:3; cf. 2 John 7).[6] The nominative masculine plural noun ἀντίχριστοι is connected with the nominative masculine plural adjective πολλοί to denote "many antichrists" in v. 18d. Aside from this instance, the remaining three occurrences of the lexeme ἀντίχριστος are in the singular (1 John 2:18c, 22; 4:3; cf. 2 John 7). Rather than focusing attention on the future coming of God's final enemy, the author employs the perfect tense (i.e., the third-person plural perfect active indicative verb γεγόνασιν) to give prominence to the existence of "many antichrists" with respect to the false teachers at his time in 1 John 2:18d. The audience can be sure that this is the last hour in view of the appearance of the antichrists now in v. 18e-f. Jesus warned his disciples that false Christs and false prophets will arise and perform great miracles to attempt deceiving God's people in the last days (cf. Mark 13:22; Matt 24:5, 11, 24). Although there is no hint that the antichrists in the author's time are miracle-workers or claim to be the Messiah, they apparently try to lead the believers astray by promulgating their errant view on Jesus' status (cf. 1 John 2:22, 26).

The author uses the statements to provide the information that the false teachers were members of the community but have left the church in 1 John 2:19a-f. The implied subject of all of the six finite verbs (i.e., ἐξῆλθαν, ἦσαν [2x], μεμενήκεισαν, φανερωθῶσιν, εἰσίν) in v. 19a-f is the nominative noun phrase ἀντίχριστοι πολλοί that precedes and with reference to the false teachers in v. 18d. The prepositional phrase ἐξ ἡμῶν is found a total of four times in this verse (v. 19a, b, c, f).[7] The first occurrence of this prepositional phrase implicates the idea of dissociation apropos the false teachers' departure from the community in v. 19a. The author accentuates this idea by placing the prepositional phrase ἐξ ἡμῶν prior to the predicator ἐξῆλθαν and in the clause-initial position. In this instance, the preposition ἐκ (v. 19a) functions as a marker of "dissociation in the sense of being 'independent from' someone or something."[8] In regard to the subsequent three occurrences of the prepositional phrase ἐξ ἡμῶν (v. 19b, c, f), they are

---

5. Cf. the relevant phrases τῇ ἐσχάτῃ ἡμέρα (2x) in John 6:39-40, ἐσχάταις ἡμέραις in 2 Tim 3:1, and ἐσχάτου χρόνου in Jude 18. See Marshall, *Epistles of John*, 148-51.

6. Aside from 1 and 2 John, the lexeme ἀντίχριστος is not detected in other NT writings.

7. Aside from 1 John 2:19, the prepositional phrase ἐξ ἡμῶν does not occur elsewhere in this epistle or other Johannine writings.

8. Louw and Nida, *Greek-English Lexicon of the New Testament*, 1:793 (semantic domain 89.121).

utilized to express the counter-expectation (cf. the adversative conjunction ἀλλά in v. 19b or v. 19e) concerning that the false teachers actually did not belong to the Christian community. Moreover, the preposition ἐκ (v. 19b, c, f) probably functions as a marker of "a part of a whole."[9] The author avails himself of the second-class or contrary-to-fact conditional construction to propound the reason in support of his assertion that the false teachers were not really part of the community in v. 19c–d.[10] The false premise that the secessionists belonged to the community is set forth through the protasis in v. 19c. On the assumption of this false premise, the author subsequently uses the apodosis to express the inference that the false teachers would have remained with the community in v. 19d. Notably, this apodosis contains the only occurrence of the pluperfect tense (cf. the third-person plural pluperfect active indicative verb μεμενήκεισαν) in 1 John 2:19d in the whole letter. Following the elided adversative conjunction ἀλλ', the implicit predicator ἐξῆλθαν is assumed and modified by the ἵνα-clause in v. 19e.[11] Contrary to staying with the believers, the false teachers' secession from the church is telling that none of them really belonged to the community in v. 19e–f. Rather than linking with the nominal adjective πάντες that functions as the subject, the negative polarity adjunct οὐκ is probably related to the predicator εἰσίν in v. 19f.[12] The implication is that the whole idea "all of them are of us" is negated. As a corollary, the author avows and concludes that none of the antichrists (i.e., the false teachers) is part of the Christian community.

b. The Anointing Versus the Liar (2:20–23)

Following the initial conjunction καί, the author utilizes the nominative second-person plural pronoun ὑμεῖς as the subject (v. 20a) to intimate a change of topic from the secessionists in the prior section (vv. 18–19) to the audience in the present section in 1 John 2:20–23 (especially vv. 20–21). There is also a shift from the negative criticism of the antichrists to the positive tone for affirming the audience's possession of an anointing from the Holy One and a knowledge of the truth in v. 20. The author draws attention to the notion of the anointing by placing the accusative neuter singular noun χρῖσμα, which functions as the complement, prior to the predicator ἔχετε in v. 20a.

---

9. Louw and Nida, *Greek-English Lexicon of the New Testament*, 1:613 (semantic domain 63.20).

10. For the second-class conditional construction, see Mathewson and Emig, *Intermediate Greek Grammar*, 238–39.

11. Culy, *1, 2, 3 John*, 50.

12. Jobes, *1, 2, and 3 John*, 124; Brown, *Epistles of John*, 341.

This is the first time the lexeme χρῖσμα appears in this epistle (3x; 1 John 2:20, 27 [2x]). The prepositional phrase ἀπὸ τοῦ ἁγίου,[13] which most likely refers to Jesus Christ (cf. John 6:69; Rev 3:7), is used to indicate the source of the anointing.[14] The author uses the statement to elaborate that all of his audience (cf. the nominal adjective πάντες as the subject) know in 1 John 2:20b. The reading πάντες adopted in NA28 is attested in codices Sinaiticus (א or 01), Vaticanus (B or 03), Porphyrianus (P[apr] or 025), and Athous Lavrensis (Ψ or 044), the minuscule 1852, the Syriac and Sahidic versions, and other textual witnesses. Instead of this reading, the accusative neuter plural adjective πάντα is found in a number of the manuscripts including codices Alexandrinus (A or 02) and Ephraemi Rescriptus (C or 04), minuscules 5, 33, 81, 614, and 1739, and the Latin and Bohairic versions. It is probable that the latter variant (i.e., πάντα) was introduced into the text by the scribes who might have felt a need to supply the object of the predicator οἴδατε in 1 John 2:20b.[15] Granted that the nominative masculine plural adjective πάντες (v. 20b) is original, the author utilizes the two occurrences of this word to hint at the contrast between the secessionists (who is referred to by the nominal adjective πάντες in v. 19f) and the audience (who is referred to by the nominal adjective πάντες in v. 20b) in 1 John 2:19–20.[16]

Rather than communicating his message to the audience straightforward, the author attempts engaging them by using the device of litotes in the two negative clauses in 1 John 2:21a–b. It is said that he does not write to his audience (v. 21a) because they do not know the truth (v. 21b). The subordinating conjunction ὅτι is found altogether three times in v. 21b, v, 21c, and v. 21d. It is probable that the first and second occurrences of this conjunction are utilized to introduce a cause or reason (v. 21b, c) and its third occurrence is used epexegetically in v. 21d.[17] Contrary to being ignorant of the truth, the author declares that the reason (cf. the causal conjunction ὅτι) of his writing is that the audience know the truth in 1 John 2:21c. It is presumed that the implicit word group ἔγραψα ὑμῖν follows the elided adversative

---

13. The lexeme ἅγιος occurs only once in 1 John 2:20 in this epistle.

14. Akin, *1, 2, 3 John*, 118–19.

15. Metzger, *Textual Commentary on the Greek New Testament*, 641; Kruse, *Letters of John*, 103.

16. For the connection between 1 John 2:20 and Jer 31:34 (Jer 38:34 LXX), see Carson, "You Have No Need," 274.

17. Kruse, *Letters of John*, 97, 104; Culy, *1, 2, 3 John*, 53–54. Contra Brown, who translates all of the three occurrences of the conjunction ὅτι as "that" in 1 John 2:21. In contrast, Jobes thinks that all of the three occurrences of ὅτι are causal conjunctions in v. 21.

conjunction ἀλλ' in v. 21c.[18] The author employs the epexegetical conjunction ὅτι with the implicit predicator οἴδατε to usher in the idea that his audience know that no lie is of the truth in 1 John 2:21d. Since the subject is made up of the nominative singular neuter noun ψεῦδος with the definer πᾶν, the author in effect expresses that every lie does not carry the attribute of being of the truth. As an upshot, lies and truth are incompatible with each other.

The author creates the lexical link with the preceding co-text by employing the articular nominative singular masculine noun ψεύστης in 1 John 2:22a. This word is lexically related to the nominative singular neuter noun ψεῦδος that has occurred in v. 21d. Among the total five occurrences of the lexeme ψεύστης in this epistle, this lexeme is modified by the nominative singular masculine article ὁ only once in v. 22a. The other four occurrences of the lexeme ψεύστης are anarthrous (1 John 1:10; 2:4; 4:20; 5:10). The author utilizes the interrogative pronoun τίς (v. 22a) and the subsequent word group εἰ μή (v. 22b) to realize the negative rhetorical question to indicate the liar's identifying feature,[19] which is the denial of Jesus as the Christ. Rather than seeking information from the audience, the author avails himself of this negative rhetorical question to make the point, add emphasis, and increase audience engagement in 1 John 2:22a–b. It is evident that the liar's denial of Jesus as the Christ is erroneous and at variance with the apostolic teaching, which upholds Jesus' messianic status. The author provides additional information to describe the liar in v. 22c, in which the demonstrative pronoun οὗτος points backward to the person who denies Jesus as the Christ (v. 22b). Furthermore, the anaphoric article ὁ with the nominative masculine singular noun ἀντίχριστος (v. 22c) harks back to the foregoing reference to this evil figure in 1 John 2:18. The embedded participial clause ὁ ἀρνούμενος τὸν πατέρα καὶ τὸν υἱόν is appositional to the articular noun ὁ ἀντίχριστος in the nominative masculine singular that precedes in v. 22c. As a corollary, the antichrist is depicted as the person who denies the Father and the Son. Given the Son's perfect unity with the Father, the denial of the Son and the denial of the Father are interrelated and cannot be neatly separated. Therefore, it is impossible for anyone who denies that Jesus is the Christ to have a relationship to God.

The author portrays two contrastive classes of people by the two generic participants in 1 John 2:23, who are realized by the two embedded

---

18. Kruse, *Letters of John*, 104.

19. The interrogative pronoun τίς and the word group εἰ μή are also utilized to express the rhetorical question in 1 John 5:5. The word group εἰ μή functions as "a marker of contrast by designating an exception" in 1 John 2:22. See Louw and Nida, *Greek-English Lexicon of the New Testament*, 1:794 (semantic domain 89.131).

participial clauses πᾶς ὁ ἀρνούμενος τὸν υἱόν (v. 23a) and ὁ ὁμολογῶν τὸν υἱόν (v. 23b). In each of these two embedded participial clauses, the accusative masculine singular noun υἱόν functions as the object of the participle ἀρνούμενος (v. 23a) or ὁμολογῶν (v. 23b). In view of the liar's depiction in v. 22, it can be presumed that the denial or confession of the Son is concerned with Jesus' identity as the Christ in 1 John 2:23. The author firstly uses the negative statement to indicate that everyone who denies the Son does not have the Father either in v. 23a. The employment of the adjective πᾶς in connection with the embedded participial clause ὁ ἀρνούμενος τὸν υἱόν (v. 23a) has the effect of stressing the assertion that no one who denies the Son has the Father.[20] In contrast to this negative statement (v. 23a), the author uses the subsequent positive statement to indicate that the person who confesses the Son has the Father also in 1 John 2:23b. The lexeme ὁμολογέω (5x) from semantic domain 33 ("communication") occurs for the second time in v. 23b in this letter (cf. 1 John 1:9; 2:23; 4:2, 3, 15). In the present instance, this lexeme is not simply employed to express the idea of a public declaration but rather "one's allegiance to a proposition or person."[21] It should also be mentioned that the author emphasizes the notion of having "the Father" by placing τὸν πατέρα (which functions as the complement) prior to the third-person singular present active indicative verb ἔχει in both of the two clauses in v. 23a and v. 23b. The implication is that one's denial or confession of the Son has the solemn ramification as to his or her relationship to the Father.

c. Remain in the Apostolic Teaching (2:24–26)

Having fleshed out the characteristic of the liar or antichrist, the author utilizes the second-person plural nominative pronoun ὑμεῖς to signal the shift of topic and capture the audience's interest at the beginning of 1 John 2:24a (cf. v. 20a). This pronoun is grammatically independent from the rest of the sentence but is logically related to the following second-person plural pronoun ὑμῖν (v. 24b) in the dative case. While the traditional label for the use of the pronoun ὑμεῖς (v. 24a) is the "hanging nominative," this pronoun alone is considered as a minor clause and thus constituting a ranking clause in this commentary. The author focuses attention on the audience by making altogether seven references to them in 1 John 2:24. These seven references to the audience include the total four occurrences of the second-person plural pronouns ὑμεῖς (2x) and ὑμῖν (2x), the two occurrences of the

---

20. Brown, *Epistles of John*, 353.
21. Louw and Nida, *Greek-English Lexicon of the New Testament*, 1:417 (semantic domain 33.274).

second-person plural aorist active verb ἠκούσατε, and the second-person plural future active verb μενεῖτε.

The author underlines the idea of remaining "in you (i.e., the audience)" by placing the prepositional phrase ἐν ὑμῖν prior to the predicator μενέτω in v. 24b or μείνῃ in v. 24c. While the antecedent of the two occurrences of the accusative neuter singular relative pronoun ὅ (v. 24b, c) is unspecified, there is little doubt that what the audience heard from the beginning is concerned with the gospel message centered upon Jesus Christ. The author employs the third-person singular present active imperative verb μενέτω for the second time (cf. 1 John 2:15) to express the explicit command to the audience to let what is heard from the beginning abide in them in v. 24b. While this imperative verb (i.e., μενέτω) is in the third-person singular, it is connected with the dative second-person plural pronoun ὑμῖν (v. 24b) and thus this command is directed towards the audience. The author exhorts them to hold firmly to the apostolic teaching, which they have received at the time of their conversion and originates with Jesus' life and ministry. The author spells out the positive outcome to attempt increasing the audience's motivation to comply with his exhortation through the use of the third-class conditional sentence in v. 24c-d. Proceeding from the premise that the audience remain in the Christian teaching in the protasis (v. 24c), it is inferred that they will remain in both the Son and the Father in the apodosis (v. 24d). The author gives emphasis to the sphere of being "in the Son and the Father" by placing the adjunctive phrase ἐν τῷ υἱῷ καὶ ἐν τῷ πατρί between the subject (i.e., ὑμεῖς) and the predicator (i.e., μενεῖτε) in this apodosis in v. 24d. Furthermore, the future verb μενεῖτε in the second-person plural is employed to evoke the sense of expectation for abiding in the Son and the Father and thereby heighten the believers' necessity to adhere to the apostolic teaching.[22]

The author speaks of Jesus' promise of the eternal life to encourage his audience in 1 John 2:25 (cf. 1 John 5:12; John 17:3). The entire construction ἡ ἐπαγγελία ἣν αὐτὸς ἐπηγγείλατο ἡμῖν is the subject of the predicator ἐστίν in v. 25a, in which the demonstrative pronoun αὕτη in the nominative case functions as the complement.[23] Notice that the author employs the two lexically related words ἐπαγγελία and ἐπαγγέλλομαι in this construction above to accentuate the idea of "promise." Although the word πατρί in the

---

22. The future form is employed a total of eight times in 1 John 2:24; 3:2 (3x), 19 (2x); 5:16 (2x).

23. The articular nominative feminine singular noun ἐπαγγελία is modified by the embedded relative clause (i.e., ἣν αὐτὸς ἐπηγγείλατο ἡμῖν) that follows in 1 John 2:25a. The antecedent of the accusative feminine singular relative pronoun ἥν is this noun (i.e., ἐπαγγελία).

dative case (v. 24d) is the nearest noun preceding the pronoun αὐτός in this construction (v. 25a), this pronoun probably refers to the Son instead of the Father in view of the Christological focus within the immediate co-text.[24] In other words, the author refers to Jesus' promise rather than the Father's promise in v. 25a. It is likely that the demonstrative pronoun αὕτη as the complement in v. 25a points forward to the accusative noun phrase τὴν ζωὴν τὴν αἰώνιον, which is presumably the complement of the implicit predicator ἐστίν in the elliptical clause in 1 John 2:25b.[25] Since the complement of the relational verb ἐστίν is normally in the nominative case, there is a grammatical incongruence because the phrase τὴν ζωὴν τὴν αἰώνιον is in the accusative case in v. 25b. Nevertheless, it is possible that the aforementioned grammatical incongruence is meaningful and serves to heighten the connection between the notions of the eternal life and Christ's promise. This connection is heightened by making the accusative noun phrase τὴν ζωὴν τὴν αἰώνιον (v. 25b) appear to be appositional to the preceding accusative relative pronoun ἥν, whose antecedent is the noun ἐπαγγελία in regard to Jesus' promise in v. 25a.[26] At any rate, the author indicates that his present correspondence with the audience arises from his concern about the danger posed by those who seek to lead them astray in 1 John 2:26. The first-person singular aorist active indicative verb ἔγραψα occurs for the fifth time in this epistle (cf. 1 John 2:14 [3x], 21, 26; 5:13). The author employs the lexeme πλανάω from semantic domain 31 ("hold a view, believe, trust") to portray the false teachers attempting to lead the believers astray by spreading an incorrect understanding of Jesus' messianic status. In the subsequent co-text, he will utilize this lexeme again to urge his audience not to let anyone lead them astray in 1 John 3:7.

d. The Abiding Anointing (2:27)

There is a total of nine ranking clauses in v. 27a–i. For the third time, the author utilizes the nominative second-person plural pronoun ὑμεῖς to orient his audience and intimate that what will be unfolded is relevant to them in 1 John 2:27a (cf. vv. 20a, 24a).[27] It is said that the anointing which the audience received from Jesus (cf. the genitive masculine singular pronoun

---

24. Brown, *Epistles of John*, 358; Smalley, *1, 2, 3 John*, 115.

25. In this commentary, the accusative noun phrase τὴν ζωὴν τὴν αἰώνιον is considered as an elliptical verbless clause in 1 John 2:25b.

26. Culy, *1, 2, 3 John*, 58.

27. In this commentary, καὶ ὑμεῖς is considered as a minor clause and thus constituting a ranking clause in 1 John 2:27a.

αὐτοῦ in v. 27b and v. 27e) abides in them and teaches them all things that they need to know. The reappearance of the lexeme χρῖσμα (2x; v. 27b, e) harks back to the preceding assertion regarding the believers' reception of the anointing from the Holy One, who is probably Jesus in 1 John 2:20a. As an upshot of the repeated references to the anointing in v. 20 and v. 27, the author creates an *inclusio* to frame his admonition to the audience concerning the false teachers' deception.[28] On the one hand, it is probable to construe the anointing as signifying God's word or the apostolic teaching, which was handed down from Jesus.[29] On the other hand, there are significant parallels between the description of the anointing in 1 John 2:20 and 2:27 and the Spirit's ministry in Jesus' farewell discourse to his disciples in the Fourth Gospel (cf. John 14:16–17, 26; 15:26; 16:7).[30] In fact, there is an emphasis on the anointing's abiding presence with the believers and the anointing's teaching role in the Christian community in this epistle. In line with this emphasis regarding the anointing, Jesus says that the Spirit of truth will be sent to abide with the disciples and teach them everything upon his departure to the Father in the Fourth Gospel (John 14:16–17, 26). Thus, it is likely that the anointing in 1 John refers to the Holy Spirit, who has been sent by the Father and the Son to indwell the believers.[31]

The author elucidates the implication of the anointing's abiding presence with the believers through the statements in v. 27c–d. Since the anointing remains in the audience, they have no need that anyone "might teach" (cf. the third-person singular present active subjunctive verb διδάσκῃ) them. The negative polarity adjunct οὐ is used in connection with the accusative singular feminine noun χρείαν (v. 27c), whose content is spelt out by means of the ἵνα-clause in 1 John 2:27d. It is probable that the author employs the generic subject τις (v. 27d) to level criticism against any false teacher or specifically those who are trying to deceive his audience to wander away from the orthodox beliefs about Jesus Christ. Contrary to having a need for the false teachers' wrong beliefs, the author affirms the sufficiency of the anointing's teaching with respect to all things that the believers need to know in v. 27e (cf. v. 20). The notion of the believers' knowledge probably resonates with the covenantal promise concerning all of God's people possessing a direct knowledge of him as envisaged in Jeremiah 31:34 (Jer 38:34 LXX).[32] The referent of the genitive masculine singular pronoun αὐτοῦ (v.

---

28. Jobes, *1, 2, and 3 John*, 120.
29. Yarbrough, *1–3 John*, 149; Painter, *1, 2, and 3 John*, 198.
30. Akin, *1, 2, 3 John*, 118; Kruse, *Letters of John*, 109–10; Thompson, *1–3 John*, 77.
31. See the works in the prior note.
32. Carson, "You Have No Need."

27e), which is sandwiched between the nominative neuter singular article τό and noun χρῖσμα in the subject phrase (i.e., τὸ αὐτοῦ χρῖσμα), is likely to be Jesus. The author further uses the two positive or negative statements to elaborate the nature of the anointing in v. 27f–g. In both of these two clauses in v. 27f–g, the implicit subject of the predicator ἐστίν is in all likelihood the noun χρῖσμα that precedes in v. 27e. The positive statement is utilized to affirm that the anointing is true in v. 27f, in which the adjective ἀληθές is marked to underline this attribute of the anointing. The negative statement is used to add the information that the anointing is without any characteristic of a lie in v. 27g.

The author exhorts his audience that just as the anointing has taught them (v. 27h), they should abide in Jesus (v. 27i). Since there is no hint of a change of the subject, the implicit subject of the third-person singular aorist active indicative verb ἐδίδαξεν should be the anointing in v. 27h. While the predicator μένετε in the present tense can be in the imperative or indicative mood in v. 27i, this predicator should be an imperative in view of the subsequent command to remain in Jesus in 1 John 2:28.[33] It follows that the dative singular pronoun αὐτῷ (v. 27i) is masculine, not neuter, and with reference to Jesus. Summing up, the author concludes the present section with the exhortation to his audience to abide in Jesus, just as the anointing (i.e., the Spirit) has taught them to do so.

---

33. Smalley, *1, 2, 3 John*, 121; cf. Brown, *Epistles of John*, 361.

1 JOHN 2:28—3:3

OUTLINE:

I. Body (1:5—5:12)

    A. Adhering to and Behaving in Conformity with the Christian Beliefs (1:5—2:27)

    B. Living as God's Children in View of Christ's Future Coming (2:28—4:6)

        1. The Hope for Jesus' Manifestation (2:28—3:3)

            a. The Parousia of Jesus (2:28-29)

            b. The Hope of God's Children (3:1-3)

B. Living as God's Children in View of Christ's Future Coming (2:28–4:6)

1. The Hope for Jesus' Manifestation (2:28—3:3)

Having admonished his audience not to succumb to the false teachers' doctrinal error but to obey the anointing's teaching to remain in Jesus, the author summons them to live as God's children in light of Jesus' future coming in 1 John 2:28—3:3. There are altogether four occurrences of different lexemes (i.e., δίκαιος and δικαιοσύνη in 1 John 2:29 and ἁγνίζω and ἁγνός in 1 John 3:3) from semantic domain 88 ("moral and ethical qualities and related behavior") in this unit. Thus, it is apparent that eschatology has an ethical bearing on the Christian conduct. Some of the reasons for starting the present unit in 1 John 2:28 have been laid out in the commentary on 1 John 2:18-27 and are not repeated here. The present unit is divided into two sections, which are 1 John 2:28–29 and 1 John 3:1–3. The author introduces the idea of the divine begetting by employing the lexeme γεννάω at the end of the first section in 1 John 2:29. He develops this idea with respect to the believers' status or characteristics as God's children in 1 John 3:1–2 in the second section. It is underlined that the nature of God or Jesus is the basis and model of the ethical living of the believers as God's children.

a. The Parousia of Jesus (2:28–29)

The author makes the transition to the new section by dint of the initial conjunction καί with the adverb νῦν,[1] which is followed by the vocative plural noun τεκνία functioning as a direct address to the audience in v. 28a (cf. 1 John 2:1, 12; 3:18; 4:4; 5:21).[2] The author also builds bridges with the prior unit by reiterating the preceding command to abide in Jesus (v. 27), who is the referent of the masculine dative singular pronoun αὐτῷ in v. 28a. It is likely that the predicator μένετε (v. 28a) in the present tense is in the imperative instead of the indicative mood because this predicator is linked with the subsequent purpose clause beginning with the conjunction ἵνα in v. 28b.[3] The author uses the three statements to speak of the future hope of Jesus' appearance so as to encourage the audience to comply with the aforesaid command to remain in him (cf. v. 28a) in the present in 1 John 2:28b–d. This is the only time the lexeme παρουσία occurs with reference to Jesus' future coming in 1 John 2:28 in the Johannine writings. The lexeme φανερόω has occurred twice regarding the manifestation of God's Son in his earthly life and ministry in 1 John 1:2 in the prologue to this letter (cf. 1 John 3:5, 8). Yet, the author employs the third-person singular aorist passive subjunctive verb φανερωθῇ (v. 28b) in connection with the conjunction ἐάν to portray Jesus' appearance at the end of time in 1 John 2:28b. In this instance, the conjunction ἐάν is not used to implicate an uncertainty as to the realization of Jesus' second coming at stake in the Christian hope in v. 28b. Rather, the author utilizes this conjunction to point to the situation in which Jesus' eschatological appearance will happen in an unspecified timing in the future.[4] The lexeme παρρησία (4x) occurs for the first time regarding the believers' "confidence" when this eschatological event happens in the future in v. 28c (cf. 1 John 4:17). The remaining three occurrences of this

---

1. The lexeme νῦν occurs a total of four times in 1 John 2:18, 28; 3:2; 4:3.
2. Schnackenburg, *Johannine Epistles*, 152.
3. Culy, *1, 2, 3 John*, 62.
4. Louw and Nida, *Greek-English Lexicon of the New Testament*, 1:632 (semantic domain 67.32).

lexeme are concerned with the believers' confidence in the present (1 John 3:21; 5:14) or at the end of time (1 John 4:17) in this letter. The first-person plural subjunctive αἰσχυνθῶμεν (v. 28d) in the aorist tense can be in the passive or middle voice. If this subjunctive verb is really a passive verb,[5] the implicit agent of the indirect causation in regard to the believers' shame is either God or Jesus. Nevertheless, it deserves notice that the prepositional phrase ἀπ' αὐτοῦ is juxtaposed with this subjunctive verb above (i.e., αἰσχυνθῶμεν) to depict vividly someone feeling disgrace and thus shrinking back from Jesus at the time when he comes in v. 28d.[6] Regardless of the passive or middle voice of the first-person plural aorist subjunctive verb αἰσχυνθῶμεν, it is evident that the author urges his audience to remain in Jesus in light of his future coming.[7]

The author utilizes the third-class conditional sentence to introduce the new topic of born of God and further links this topic with the ethical notion of acting justly in 1 John 2:29. The protasis is made up of the two clauses in v. 29a–b. The apodosis is made up of the ensuing two clauses in v. 29c–d. In the protasis, the author employs the second-person plural perfect active subjunctive verb εἰδῆτε (v. 29a) to express that the believers are in the state of knowing the righteous nature of God (cf. 1 John 1:9) or possibly Jesus (cf. 1 John 2:1; 3:7). In the apodosis, the author shifts to use the present tense (i.e., the second-person plural present active indicative verb γινώσκετε) to move forward the main line of the discourse in v. 29c. Furthermore, the third-person singular perfect passive indicative verb γεγέννηται is utilized to give prominence to the idea of the divine begetting at the end of the apodosis in v. 29d. This is the first occurrence of the lexeme γεννάω (10x) in this epistle.[8] Since God is presumably the referent of the personal pronoun αὐτοῦ in the prepositional phrase ἐξ αὐτοῦ (v. 29d) that precedes this perfect passive indicative verb (i.e., γεγέννηται) above, he is the agent who brings about the spiritual birth. The author avails himself of the embedded participial clause πᾶς ὁ ποιῶν τὴν δικαιοσύνην to realize the generic subject to affirm that everyone who practices righteousness has been born of God in 1 John 2:29d. There are altogether three occurrences of

---

5. See Culy, *1, 2, 3 John*, 63–64; Schnackenburg, *Johannine Epistles*, 153. However, Brown thinks that the first-person plural aorist subjunctive verb αἰσχυνθῶμεν is in the middle voice in 1 John 2:28. See Brown, *Epistles of John*, 381.

6. Schnackenburg, *Johannine Epistles*, 153.

7. The prepositional phrase ἐν τῇ παρουσίᾳ αὐτοῦ is used temporally to express the unknown time of Jesus' future appearance in 1 John 1:28 (cf. 1 Cor 15:23; 1 Thess 2:19; 3:13; 4:15; 5:23; 2 Thess 2:1, 8; Jas 5:7, 8; 2 Pet 1:16; 3:4).

8. The lexeme γεννάω is found altogether ten times in 1 John 2:29; 3:9 (2x); 4:7; 5:1 (3x), 4, 18 (2x).

the lexeme δικαιοσύνη in this letter (1 John 2:29; 3:7, 10). In each case, this lexeme occurs in connection with the present active nominative masculine singular participle ποιῶν. The author's employment of the action verb ποιέω points to the emphasis on the experiential meaning with respect to just behaviors. Moreover, the occurrence of the lexeme δικαιοσύνη in the apodosis in v. 29d harks back to the cognate adjective δίκαιος in the protasis in v. 29b. As a corollary, the correlation between God's righteous nature and his children's righteous conduct is underscored.

b. The Hope of God's Children (3:1–3)

This section begins with the second-person plural aorist active imperative verb ἴδετε, which functions as the attention-getting device in 1 John 3:1a. The author develops the topic of the believers' status as God's children and particularly deals with the implication of their filial relationship to the deity in this section. Following the imperative verb ἴδετε above, the author puts forward the indirect question regarding that what kind of love the Father has given us in 1 John 3:1b. The complement ποταπὴν ἀγάπην, which is the object of the third-person singular perfect active indicative verb δέδωκεν, is fronted to emphasize the Father's marvelous love in v. 1b.[9] Furthermore, the perfect tense is used to give prominence to God's action of bestowing love on the believers. This is the only occurrence of the lexeme ποταπός (v. 1b) from semantic domain 58 ("nature, class, example") in the Johannine writings. The lexeme ἀγάπη has appeared twice pertaining to a person's love for God in 1 John 2:5 and 2:15. However, the believers are evidently the recipients of the Father's love in the present instance in 1 John 3:1 in view of the expressed actor (i.e., ὁ πατήρ as the subject) and the beneficiary (i.e., the inclusive first-person plural dative plural pronoun ἡμῖν as the indirect object) of the action of giving in v. 1b. The author expounds the content of the divine love by virtue of the subsequent ἵνα-clause in v. 1c, in which the believers are referred to as the "children of God" (cf. the fronted complement τέκνα θεοῦ in this ἵνα-clause). The phrase τέκνα θεοῦ is found a total of four times in the whole epistle (1 John 3:1, 2, 10; 5:2; cf. John 1:12; 11:52). This is the first time the lexeme τέκνον, which is the root word of the diminutive form τεκνίον,[10] appears with reference to the believers' status as God's children. The passive voice of the predicator κληθῶμεν (v. 1c) with the perfective aspect hints at

---

9. The lexeme δίδωμι occurs for the first time in 1 John 3:1 in this epistle (cf. 1 John 3:23, 24; 4:13; 5:11, 16, 20).

10. The diminutive form τεκνίον is detected altogether six times in 1 John 2:1, 12, 28; 3:18; 4:1; 5:21 (cf. John 13:33).

an indirect causality with God as the implicit agent of the verbal process. The author continues to affirm the believers' relationship to God in v. 1d. As indicated via the two subsequent negative clauses, the world does not know that the believers are God's children because it does not know God (cf. John 17:25) or Jesus (cf. John 1:10) in v. 1e–f.[11] The third-person singular present active indicative verb γινώσκει with the imperfective aspect is employed for conveying the message that the world does not know the believers in the primary clause in v. 1e. The third-person singular aorist active indicative verb ἔγνω with the perfective aspect is used to indicate that the world does not know God or Jesus in the secondary clause in v. 1f.

After addressing his audience affectionately as "beloved" (cf. the vocative plural ἀγαπητοί),[12] the author reiterates the assertion that the believers are God's children now in 1 John 3:2a (cf. v. 1). The placement of the complement τέκνα θεοῦ prior to the predicator ἐσμέν is emphatic in v. 2a. The author creates the subtle contrast between the believers' present and future situations through the use of the two temporal adjuncts νῦν (v. 2a) and οὔπω (v. 2b) and the first-person plural future verb ἐσόμεθα (v. 2b). The author avers that what the believers will be is not yet revealed in v. 2b. The embedded finite clause τί ἐσόμεθα is utilized to realize the indirect question (i.e., "what we will be") serving as the subject of the third-person singular aorist passive indicative verb ἐφανερώθη in v. 2b. Despite that what the believers will be has not yet been made known, they will be like Jesus when he appears in v. 2c–e. The implicit subject of the predicator φανερωθῇ (v. 2d) could be the foregoing embedded finite clause τί ἐσόμεθα (v. 2b) or Jesus. The strength of the former understanding is that the two predicators ἐφανερώθη (v. 2b) and φανερωθῇ (v. 2d) have in common the same subject, i.e., "what we will be."[13] That said, the latter understanding (i.e., Jesus is the implicit subject of the predicator φανερωθῇ in v. 2d) is preferred because he is probably the referent of the two personal pronouns αὐτῷ (v. 2e) and αὐτόν (v. 2f) in the immediate co-text.[14] At any rate, the author underlines the notion of a likeness to Jesus by placing the complement ὅμοιοι αὐτῷ in the thematic position at the forefront of the clause in v. 2e.[15] Moreover, the author uses the statements to supply the additional information that the

---

11. The prepositional phrase διὰ τοῦτο probably points forward to the ensuing ὅτι-clause in 1 John 3:1. See Brown, *Epistles of John*, 392.

12. The vocative plural ἀγαπητοί (6x) appears for the second time in 1 John 3:2 (cf. 1 John 2:7; 3:21; 4:1, 7, 11).

13. Brown, *Epistles of John*, 393–94.

14. Yarbrough, *1–3 John*, 178; Culy, *1, 2, 3 John*, 69.

15. The lexeme ὅμοιος is found only once in 1 John 3:2 in the whole letter.

firm grounds for the believers' future expectation of Christ-likeness is that they will see him just as he is in v. 2f–g.

It is the author's conviction that the Christian hope regarding the glorious state of God's children has a bearing on their daily conduct in the present.[16] There is a shift from the use of the inclusive "we" in the preceding co-text to the generic participant with respect to the class of individuals in 1 John 3:3a. The referent of the dative masculine singular pronoun αὐτῷ (v. 3a) is probably Jesus. It is said that everyone who has "this hope" on Jesus purifies himself or herself. This is the only occurrence of the lexeme ἐλπίς pertaining to the Christian hope in the Johannine writings. The antecedent of the reflexive pronoun ἑαυτόν, which is inclusive of both male and female genders, is the embedded participial clause πᾶς ὁ ἔχων τὴν ἐλπίδα ταύτην ἐπ' αὐτῷ that functions as the generic subject in v. 3a. The author makes use of the comparative clause beginning with the conjunction καθώς to correlate such a person with Jesus, who is pure in v. 3b (cf. Jesus' sinlessness in 1 John 3:5). The nominative masculine singular demonstrative pronoun ἐκεῖνος is employed to refer to Jesus altogether six times in this letter (1 John 2:6; 3:3, 5, 7, 16; 4:17). Notice that the demonstrative pronoun ἐκεῖνος (whose referent is Jesus) and the nominative masculine singular adjective ἁγνός are juxtaposed to heighten the connection of Jesus with the notion of moral purity in v. 3b. Both of the two lexemes ἁγνίζω (v. 3a) and ἁγνός (v. 3b) from semantic domain 88 ("moral and ethical qualities and related behavior) are found only once in 1 John 3:3 in the whole epistle. It is likely that the author does not simply use the statement to describe any person holding fast to the hope of Christ-likeness but rather subtly exhorts his audience to live a morally pure life in 1 John 3:3.

---

16. See Leung, "Ethics and *Imitatio Christi* in 1 John," 126–27.

1 JOHN 3:4–12

OUTLINE:

I. Body (1:5—5:12)

    A. Adhering to and Behaving in Conformity with the Christian Beliefs (1:5—2:27)

    B. Living as God's Children in View of Christ's Future Coming (2:28—4:6)

        1. The Hope for Jesus' Manifestation (2:28—3:3)

        2. The Disparity Between God's Children and the Devil's Children (3:4–12)

            a. God's Children Should Avoid Sin (3:4–6)

            b. God's Children versus the Devil's Children (3:7–12)

2. The Disparity Between God's Children and the Devil's Children (3:4–12)

The author has associated God's children with the ethical notions of righteous conduct and moral purity in 1 John 2:28—3:3. He continues to assert the necessity and importance of the believers' abstinence from sins in the present section in 1 John 3:4–12. There is a total of ten occurrences of the two cognate lexemes ἁμαρτία (6x; vv. 4 [2x], 5 [2x], 8, 9) and ἁμαρτάνω (4x; vv. 6 [2x], 8, 9) from semantic domain 88 ("moral and ethical qualities and related behavior") in this section. Both of these two lexemes carry the negative meaning related to sins and opposed to the positive notion of righteousness or moral purity. The present section is constitutive of two units,

1 John 3:4–6 and 3:7–12. The beginning of the second unit is signaled by the appearances of the vocative plural παιδία, the imperative πλανάτω, and the two cognate lexemes δικαιοσύνη and δίκαιός in v. 7. While it is common for commentators to consider a paragraph break at the end of v. 10 (more on this below), the nine clauses altogether constitute a clause complex in 1 John 3:10b–12e. Therefore, this commentary analyzes 1 John 3:7–12 as a self-contained unit in which the author explicates the hallmarks of God's children in contradistinction to the devil's children.

a. God's Children Should Avoid Sin (3:4–6)

The author intimates the topical shift to "sin" by employing the two semantically related lexemes ἁμαρτία and ἀνομία in 1 John 3:4a. Akin to the grammatical construction of the generic participant (i.e., πᾶς ὁ ποιῶν τὴν δικαιοσύνην) in 1 John 2:29 (cf. John 8:34; 1 John 3:7, 8), the embedded participial clause πᾶς ὁ ποιῶν τὴν ἁμαρτίαν is utilized to encode the generic subject as "everyone who practices sin" in v. 4a. In contrast to the person who does what is right (1 John 2:29d) or lives a morally pure life (1 John 3:3a), everyone who commits sin also commits lawlessness (1 John 3:4a). The author heightens the connection between the two notions of committing a sin and committing lawlessness by placing the two accusative phrases τὴν ἁμαρτίαν and τὴν ἀνομίαν adjacent to each other in v. 4a. Moreover, the author elaborates the notion of sin by identifying it with the feature of "lawlessness" in v. 4b. The lexeme ἀνομία is detected altogether twice in v. 4a and v. 4b in this letter and is absent from other Johannine writings.[1] The author has spoken of the future manifestation of the antichrist or Jesus in the preceding co-text (1 John 2:18, 28; 3:2). Moreover, the noun ἀνομία and its cognate adjective ἄνομος occur with respect to the appearance of God's eschatological adversary in 2 Thessalonians 2:3–8.[2] Thus, it is unlikely that the lexeme ἀνομία is employed to simply evoke the negative overtone of a rebellion against God or a contempt of his precepts in 1 John 3:4a–b. Rather, the author probably avails himself of the lexeme ἀνομία to associate those who practice sin with God's final opponent.[3]

---

1. The lexeme ἀνομία occurs altogether fifteen times in the NT (Matt 7:23; 13:41; 23:28; 24:12; Rom 4:7; 6:19 [2x]; 2 Cor 6:14; 2 Thess 2:3, 7; Titus 2:14; Heb 1:9; 10:17; 1 John 3:4 [2x]). The opposite lexeme νομός does not occur in 1–3 John but is found a total of fifteen times in the Fourth Gospel (John 1:17, 45; 7:19 [2x], 23, 49, 51; 8:5, 17; 10:34; 12:34; 15:25; 18:31; 19:7 [2x]).

2. Lieu, *I, II, & III John*, 128.

3. Lieu, *I, II, & III John*, 128–29.

The author reminds his audience concerning the purpose of Jesus' appearance in the past in 1 John 3:5. The nominative masculine singular demonstrative pronoun ἐκεῖνος (cf. 1 John 2:6; 3:3, 5, 7, 16; 4:17), whose referent is Jesus, functions as the subject of the predicator ἐφανερώθη in v. 5b. The author utilizes the purpose clause headed by the conjunction ἵνα to indicate that Jesus came to take away sins in v. 5c (cf. John 1:29; 1 John 3:8). The complement τὰς ἁμαρτίας is placed in the emphatic position to draw attention to the topic of sin in this ἵνα-clause. There is an additional genitive first-person plural pronoun ἡμῶν following the accusative feminine plural noun ἁμαρτίας in 1 John 3:5c in codices Sinaiticus (ℵ or 01), Ephraemi Syri Rescriptus (C or 04), and Athous Lavrensis (Ψ or 044), and other manuscripts. However, this pronoun (i.e., ἡμῶν) was probably added by the copyists into the text to make explicit that the goal of Jesus' first coming is relevant to "our" sins. Thus, the original wording does not contain the additional genitive first-person plural pronoun ἡμῶν in v. 5c. The author uses the negative statement to provide the information that in Jesus there is no sin in 1 John 3:5d. This is the fourth time the lexeme ἁμαρτία appears in 1 John 3:4–6 (vv. 4a, b, 5c, d). The thrust of this negative statement as to Jesus' sinlessness is in the same wavelength of the foregoing assertion regarding Jesus' pure nature in 1 John 3:3. The antecedent of the dative masculine singular pronoun αὐτῷ in the prepositional phrase ἐν αὐτῷ (v. 5d) is the preceding demonstrative pronoun ἐκεῖνος (v. 5b), which is employed to denote Jesus.

Building on the Christological affirmation of Jesus' sinlessness in v. 5d, the author depicts two contrastive kinds of people in v. 6a and v. 6b–c. The first kind of people is expressed by the generic subject, which is constitutive of the embedded participial clause πᾶς ὁ ἐν αὐτῷ μένων in v. 6a. The author places the prepositional phrase ἐν αὐτῷ between the article ὁ and the participle μένων to underline the idea of remaining "in him (i.e., Jesus)" in v. 6a (cf. 1 John 2:27–28). The second kind of people is "everyone who sins" in v. 6b, in which the embedded participial clause πᾶς ὁ ἁμαρτάνων functions as the generic participant. The author is fond of utilizing various embedded participial clauses in connection with the adjective πᾶς to encode the generic participants in different places in this epistle (e.g., 1 John 2:23, 29; 3:3, 4, 6, 9, 10, 15; 4:7; 5:1, 18; cf. 2 John 9). It is apparent that the two classes of individuals above are in contradistinction to each other in 1 John 3:6. At one pole, everyone who remains in Jesus does not sin in v. 6a. Moreover, the author probably hints at the implicit directive "Do not sin!" to his audience by means of the generic statement in v. 6a.[4] At the opposite pole, everyone who

---

4. See Longacre, "Exhortation and Mitigation in First John," 21; Marshall, *Epistles of John*, 181.

sins has neither seen nor known Jesus in v. 6b–c. Given the Son's perfect unity with the Father in Johannine thought, it follows that the latter individual has not seen or known the Father either (cf. John 14:7, 9). Moreover, the negative portrayal of those committing sins and not having a personal relationship to Jesus is prominent in view of the twofold employment of the perfect tense in v. 6c (cf. the two predicators ἑώρακεν and ἔγνωκεν).

b. God's Children Versus the Devil's Children (3:7–12)

For the third and last time, the author employs the vocative plural noun παιδία to address his audience directly and attract their attention at the outset of 1 John 3:7a (cf. 1 John 2:14, 18).[5] Following this direct address, he puts forward the explicit command "Let no one lead you astray!" to attempt influencing their action. The negative nominative masculine singular indefinite pronoun μηδείς is the subject of the third-person singular present active imperative verb πλανάτω in v. 7a. Aside from the preceding directive (i.e., "Let what you heard from the beginning remain in you!") in 1 John 2:24, this is the only other explicit command that is expressed by the third-person singular imperative in this epistle. Despite the third-person construction of this command, the author indicates that it is directed towards his audience by utilizing the accusative second-person plural pronoun ὑμᾶς as the object of the imperative verb πλανάτω above in v. 7a. Since the lexeme πλανάω has been employed with reference to those who attempt to lead the believers astray in 1 John 2:26, it is likely that the command "Let no one lead you astray!" is concerned with the danger from the false teachers in 1 John 3:7a.

The author uses the generic subjects to refer to two antithetical groups of people in 1 John 3:7b and 3:8a. These two groups of people are encoded grammatically by the embedded participial clauses ὁ ποιῶν τὴν δικαιοσύνην (v. 7b) and ὁ ποιῶν τὴν ἁμαρτίαν (v. 8a), respectively. On the positive side, the person who practices righteousness is righteous in v. 7b. The author further uses the dependent clause beginning with the comparative conjunction καθώς to connect such a person with Jesus, who is characterized as righteous in v. 7c (cf. 1 John 2:1, 29). Notice that the complement δίκαιος is placed between the subject (i.e., the embedded participial clause ὁ ποιῶν τὴν δικαιοσύνην or the demonstrative pronoun ἐκεῖνος) and the predicator ἐστίν in both of the two clauses in v. 7b and v. 7c.[6] The implication of this

---

5. The textual reading παιδία (1 John 3:7) adopted in NA28 is different from that in NA27, in which the more common term τεκνία is found.

6. The demonstrative pronoun ἐκεῖνος is used to denote Jesus in 1 John 3:7 (cf. 1 John 2:6; 3:3, 5, 16; 4:17).

parallel structure (i.e., the subject is followed by the complement δίκαιος and subsequently the verb ἐστίν) is that the connection between the person and Jesus is heightened in these two clauses above. On the negative side, the individual who commits sin is of the devil in 1 John 3:8a (cf. v. 4). There are altogether four occurrences of the lexeme διάβολος, which functions as the title of Satan, in 1 John 3:8 (3x) and 3:10a in this letter (cf. John 6:70; 8:44; 13:2). As indicated via the ὅτι-clause in v. 8b, the reason why the individual committing sins is of the devil is that the devil has been sinning from the beginning.[7] The use of the present active indicative verb ἁμαρτάνει (v. 8b) with the imperfective aspect suggests an internal viewpoint from which the action of the devil's sinning is looked at as an ongoing process. It is probable that the author seeks to evoke the creation story regarding the serpent's tempting Eve that led to the fall of humanity (Gen 3:1–24), as well as the murder of Abel by Cain (Gen 4:1–16).[8] In fact, the author will subsequently mention Cain killing his brother and associate Cain with the evil one in 1 John 3:12. At any rate, the author declares that the Son of God appeared so that he might put an end to the works of the devil in v. 8c–d (cf. 1 John 3:5; John 12:31). The prepositional phrase εἰς τοῦτο functions as a marker of purpose for orienting the audience in the clause-initial position in v. 8c. The genitive construction τὰ ἔργα τοῦ διαβόλου is probably the subjective genitive and implicates the meaning concerning that "the works done by the devil" in v. 8d.[9] In view of the use of the third-person singular aorist active subjective verb λύσῃ (v. 8d) with the perfective aspect, the destruction of the devil's works by Jesus is depicted as a complete event.

The author resumes the topic of born of God and links it with the notion of the believers' sinlessness in the four clauses in 1 John 3:9a–d (cf. 1 John 3:6; 5:18). In the first and fourth clauses of this verse, the perfect passive nominative masculine singular participle γεγεννημένος (v. 9a) or the third-person singular perfect passive indicative verb γεγέννηται (v. 9d) is connected with the prepositional phrase ἐκ τοῦ θεοῦ to indicate that God is the agent of the action regarding the believers' spiritual birth. Notably, these two references to the believers' divine begetting (v. 9a, d) form an *inclusio* to frame the author's assertion apropos their sinlessness at the beginning and end of 1 John 3:9. As said in v. 9a–b, everyone who is born of God does not commit sin (cf. 1 John 2:29) because his seed remains in this person. The placement of the prepositional phrase ἐν αὐτῷ prior to the predicator

---

7. Following the conjunction ὅτι, the preposition phrase ἀπ' ἀρχῆς is marked in 1 John 3:8b.

8. Kruse, *Letters of John*, 123; Brown, *Epistles of John*, 406.

9. Culy, *1, 2, 3 John*, 77; Sherman and Tuggy, *Semantic and Structural Analysis*, 61.

μένει is emphatic in the ὅτι-clause in v. 9b.[10] The lexeme σπέρμα is a *hapax legomenon* in 1 John 3:9b in this letter and absent from the other two Johannine epistles (cf. John 7:42; 8:33, 37; Rev 12:17). Since the author has mentioned the indwelling of the anointing (i.e., the Spirit) in the believers in 1 John 2:27, it is possible to construe God's "seed" as referring to the Spirit and particularly pertinent to the divine begetting (cf. John 3:5).[11] That said, the author probably employs the lexeme σπέρμα from semantic domain 58 ("nature, class, example") to connote the general sense that God's nature resides in his children because they are born of him in 1 John 3:9b.[12]

As asserted in v. 9c–d, the person in whom God's seed remains is not able to sin because he or she is born of God. The present active infinitive ἁμαρτάνειν is the complement of the third-person singular present active indicative verb δύναται in v. 9c.[13] The author places the prepositional phrase ἐκ τοῦ θεοῦ prior to the predicator γεγέννηται to stress the idea of born "of God" in v. 9d. There is a debate over the implication of the author's employment of the present tense (cf. ἁμαρτίαν οὐ ποιεῖ [v. 9a] and οὐ δύναται ἁμαρτάνειν [v. 9c]) regarding the believers' sinlessness (cf. 1 John 3:6, 9; 5:18). The matter is complicated when the relevant assertions about the believers' impeccability are read alongside the foregoing statements that presuppose the possibility of God's children to sin in 1 John 1:9 and 2:1. While it is common to explain the author's choice of the present tense with respect to the habitual sins (cf. NIV, NLT),[14] this understanding has two drawbacks. First, the present tense with the imperfective aspect does not necessarily implicate a continuous action but rather expresses an internal perspective of the event or action. Second, the present tense is employed to portray a particular sin rather than a habit of sinning in 1 John 5:16.[15] Another approach to interpreting the author's use of the present tense vis-à-vis the believers' sinlessness is that a

---

10. The referent of the personal pronoun αὐτῷ in the dative case is probably not God in 1 John 3:9b. However, Longacre thinks that God is the referent of both of the two personal pronouns (i.e., αὐτοῦ and αὐτῷ) in v. 9b. Thus, the author says that the descendant of God abides in him. See Longacre, "Exhortation and Mitigation in First John," 23.

11. Kruse, *Letters of John*, 124–25; Jobes, *1, 2, and 3 John*, 146–47; Brown, *Epistles of John*, 411.

12. Akin, *1, 2, 3 John*, 148–49; Sherman and Tuggy, *Semantic and Structural Analysis*, 62.

13. The lexeme δύναμαι is found only twice in 1 John 3:9 and 4:20 in this letter.

14. Contra Akin, *1, 2, 3 John*, 142–44; Burge, *Letters of John*, 150; Sherman and Tuggy, *Semantic and Structural Analysis*, 61–62.

15. Smalley, *1, 2, 3 John*, 151–52; Lieu, *I, II, & III John*, 131; Yarbrough, *1–3 John*, 183.

specific sin is in view in 1 John 3:6 and 3:9.[16] In other words, God's children do not and cannot commit specifically this sin, not any sin in general. While this interpretation is viable, there is no hint that the author seeks to limit the notion of "sin" to a particular sin in 1 John 3:4–12. The third view considers that the relevant statements about the sinlessness of God's children (vv. 6, 9) pertain to their ideal situation, which will be actualized at the eschaton.[17] Furthermore, the author speaks of the believers' eschatological reality in the future to encourage his audience to avoid sinning in the present. Therefore, the covert command "Do not sin!" is probably conveyed in the subtle way by the statements in 1 John 3:6 and 3:9.[18] While it is impossible to decide with certainty, the third view seems to pose the least difficulty and thus is tentatively adopted in this commentary.

The author elucidates the means by which God's children and the devil's children are manifest in 1 John 3:10. The word group τὰ τέκνα τοῦ θεοῦ καὶ τὰ τέκνα τοῦ διαβόλουis in the neuter plural functions as the subject of the third-person singular verb ἐστίν in v. 10a. It is not uncommon for the neuter plural noun to connect with a verb in the singular in Greek language.[19] This is the third time the articular or anarthrous construction (τὰ) τέκνα (τοῦ) θεοῦ is found with reference to the believers as God's children in this epistle (cf. 1 John 3:1, 2, 10; 5:2). The other articular construction τὰ τέκνα τοῦ διαβόλου with reference to the devil's children in the word group above is distinct in 1 John 3:10 in the NT. The author probably utilizes the prepositional phrase ἐν τούτῳ (v. 10a) to anticipate the following two negative clauses in v. 10b–c, in which the two distinguishing marks of the devil's children are pointed out. The author firstly indicates that everyone who does not do what is right is not of God in v. 10b (cf. 1 John 2:29; 3:7). The lexeme δικαιοσύνη occurs for the third and last time in v. 10b in this epistle. The author subsequently uses the elliptical clause (i.e., καὶ ὁ μὴ ἀγαπῶν τὸν ἀδελφὸν αὐτοῦ) to intimate that the person who does not love a Christian brother or sister is likewise not a child of God in v. 10c. The embedded participial clause ὁ μὴ ἀγαπῶν τὸν ἀδελφὸν αὐτοῦ functions as the generic subject in this elliptical clause above. Despite the lack of a finite verb, the implicit predicator ἐστίν with the negative polarity adjunct οὐκ and the prepositional phrase ἐκ τοῦ θεοῦ can be inferred from the prior clause (cf. οὐκ ἔστιν ἐκ τοῦ

---

16. Yarbrough, *1–3 John*, 183–84; Kruse, *Letters of John*, 126–32.

17. Thielman, *Theology of the New Testament*, 545–49; Marshall, *Epistles of John*, 182–83; Schnackenburg, *Johannine Epistles*, 258–60; Potterie, "Impeccability of the Christian," 186, 195–96.

18. Longacre, "Exhortation and Mitigation in First John," 21, 23; Leung, "Metaphorical Expressions of the Commands in 1 John" (forthcoming).

19. Mathewson and Emig, *Intermediate Greek Grammar*, 156–57.

θεοῦ in v. 10b) in v. 10c.[20] It is probable that the author does not repeat these clausal constituents to avoid redundancy and thereby focuses attention on those not loving their fellow Christians in v. 10c (cf. 1 John 2:9–11). In a nutshell, the devil's children are manifest by their lack of right conduct and communal love. Conversely speaking, the two hallmarks of God's children are practicing righteousness and loving other members in God's family.

The author employs the conjunction ὅτι to introduce the grounds for distinguishing the devil's children by their lack of love for the Christian brothers and sisters at the beginning of 1 John 3:11a. The author reminds his audience of the message which they have heard from the beginning. That is to say, they have heard this message since the time they received the gospel centered upon Jesus Christ (cf. 1 John 2:7). The lexeme ἀγγελία occurs for the second and last time in v. 11a in this letter (cf. 1 John 1:5). Aside from these two occurrences in 1 John 1:5 and 3:11, this lexeme (i.e., ἀγγελία) is not found in other NT documents. The more common word ἐπαγγελία attested in codices Sinaiticus (א or 01), Ephraemi Syri Rescriptus (C or 04), Porphyrianus (P^{apr} or 025), and Athous Lavrensis (Ψ or 044), and a number of minuscules (e.g., 1243, 1611, 1739, 1852, 1881, 2344) was probably originated with the copyists replacing the rare lexeme ἀγγελία by this word in 1 John 3:11a.[21] While the importance of loving the Christian brothers and sisters has been repeatedly affirmed in the preceding co-text (cf. 1 John 2:10; 3:10), the author utilizes the combination of the inclusive first-person plural present active subjective verb ἀγαπῶμεν and the accusative plural reciprocal pronoun ἀλλήλους for the first time to encode the love commandment in v. 11b. There are altogether 7 instances of the hortatory subjunctive verb ἀγαπῶμεν in the NT and all of them are present in the Johannine epistles (1 John 3:11, 18, 23; 4:7, 12; 5:2; 2 John 5). The wording of the covert directive (i.e., ἀγαπῶμεν ἀλλήλους) in v. 11b is akin to that of the new commandment of loving one another (i.e., ἀγαπᾶτε ἀλλήλους) that Jesus gave to his disciples in the Fourth Gospel (John 13:34; 15:12, 17). The shift from the second-person plural expression on Jesus' lips in this Gospel to the first-person plural construction is understandable given the different speaker and recipient in 1 John 3:11b (i.e., the author speaking to his audience in this epistle versus Jesus speaking to his disciples in the Fourth Gospel). Moreover, the author not only uses the device of the inclusive first-person plural (cf. ἀγαπῶμεν) to invite his audience to join in with him to

---

20. Culy, *1, 2, 3 John*, 79.

21. The variant ἐπαγγελία is also found in place of the word ἀγγελία in 1 John 1:5 in a number of manuscripts (e.g., C, P^{apr}, 1243, 1611, 1739, 1852, 1881, 2344). Yet this variant is in all likelihood not original. See Yarbrough, *1–3 John*, 51.

practice the mutual love in the Christian community, but also to express solidarity with them in v. 11b.

While there is no OT quotation in this epistle, the author alludes to the story of Cain killing his brother so as to set forth the negative example opposed to the brotherly love in 1 John 3:12a–e. The total four occurrences of the third-person singular indicative verbs are in either the imperfect tense (i.e., ἦν [v. 12a, d]) or aorist tense (i.e., ἔσφαξεν [v. 12b, c]) in the first four clauses in v. 12a–d, whereas the fifth clause is without a verb in v. 12e. Cain is depicted as the active participant because he is the subject of the total four occurrences of the two indicative verbs above in v. 12a–d. The author avails himself of the altogether five ranking clauses to provide the supplemental information to expound the "message" (v. 11) as regards loving the fellow Christians in God's family in 1 John 3:12. Since the author does not supply any background information concerning the murder committed by Cain, it can be presumed that the audience are familiar with the narrative as unfolded in Genesis 4:1–16. From the author's viewpoint, the fact that Cain killed his brother points to his connection with the evil one (cf. 1 John 2:13, 14; 5:18, 19).

The author gives a negative appraisal of the character and behavior of Cain, who is presented as the representative example of the devil's children in 1 John 3:12. The author avails himself of the combination of the negative polarity adjunct οὐ and the comparative conjunction καθώς (cf. John 6:58; 14:27) to convey the idea of a dissimilarity to Cain in v. 12a.[22] The lexeme σφάζω (1 John 3:12b, c; cf. Rev 5:6, 9, 12; 6:4, 9; 13:3, 8; 18:24) from semantic domain 20 ("violence, harm, destroy, kill") is a strong word bearing the connotation of slaughtering or violent killing. Rather than evincing straightly the cause of Cain murdering his brother, the author engages his audience by means of the rhetorical question containing the adjunctive phrase χάριν τίνος in v. 12c. Although the lexeme χάριν is generally a "marker of reason" and postposition following its object,[23] in the present instance this lexeme precedes the genitive neuter singular interrogative pronoun τίνος functioning as the object in v. 12c.[24] It is evident that the author does not merely use the rhetorical question to demand information from his audience about the reason of Cain murdering his brother (v. 12c), because the author subsequently spells out the answer of this question in v. 12d–e. While

---

22. Yarbrough, *1–3 John*, 179–80, 198; Smalley, *1, 2, 3 John*, 174.

23. Culy, *1, 2, 3 John*, 81. There are altogether nine occurrences of the lexeme χάριν in the NT (Luke 7:47; Gal 3:19; Eph 3:1, 14; 1 Tim 5:14; Titus 1:5, 11; 1 John 3:12; Jude 16). This lexeme often functions as the "marker of reason." See Louw and Nida, *Greek-English Lexicon of the New Testament*, 1:780.

24. Smalley, *1, 2, 3 John*, 175.

the elliptical clause τὰ δὲ τοῦ ἀδελφοῦ αὐτοῦ δίκαια does not have a verb in v. 12e, the implicit predicator ἦν can be presumed. Thus, Cain killed his brother because Cain's deeds were evil (v. 12d) but his brother's deeds were righteous (v. 12e).[25] There is an ellipsis in the subject in v. 12e, in which the implicit nominative neuter plural noun ἔργα is presumed. Granted that both of the two genitive constructions τὰ ἔργα αὐτοῦ (v. 12d) and τὰ . . . (ἔργα) τοῦ ἀδελφοῦ αὐτοῦ (v. 12e) are the subjective genitive, the author depicts Cain or his brother as the actor carrying out the wicked or just deeds, respectively. The lexeme δίκαιος appears for the sixth and last time in 1 John 3:12e in this letter (cf. 1 John 1:9; 2:1, 29; 3:7 [2x]). Both of the two lexically related adjective δίκαιος (cf. the last occurrence in v. 12e) and noun δικαιοσύνη (cf. the last occurrence in v. 10b) do not recur in the discourse subsequent to 1 John 3:12 in this epistle.

---

25. See Culy, *1, 2, 3 John*, 81.

1 JOHN 3:13–18

OUTLINE:

I. Body (1:5—5:12)

    A. Adhering to and Behaving in Conformity with the Christian Beliefs (1:5—2:27)

    B. Living as God's Children in View of Christ's Future Coming (2:28—4:6)

        1. The Hope for Jesus' Manifestation (2:28—3:3)

        2. The Disparity Between God's Children and the Devil's Children (3:4–12)

        3. Laying Down Our Lives for Others' Sake (3:13–18)

3. Laying Down Our Lives for Others' Sake (3:13–18)

Having given a negative appraisal of Cain as the representative example of the devil's children (cf. 1 John 3:12), the author seeks to promote the believers' mutual love within the Christian community in 1 John 3:13–18. The communal sense is intimated in view of the clustering of a total of five occurrences of the lexeme ἀδελφός in this passage (vv. 13a, 14c, 15a, 16c, 17b). The author utilizes the first-class conditional construction to realize the negative command to his audience not to be surprised if the world hates them in 1 John 3:13. The apodosis (v. 13a) is followed by the protasis beginning with the conditional conjunction εἰ (v. 13b). This negative command, which is encoded by the second-person plural present active imperative verb θαυμάζετε with the negative polarity adjunct μή, has the effect of grabbing the audience's attention in v. 13a at the outset of this section. While the author employs the vocative plural noun ἀδελφοί (v. 13a) to address the audience as his Christian brothers and sisters directly,[1] this does not imply an equality in regard to the tenor relation between the author and his audience. It is probable that the author uses this vocative plural noun to enhance the Christian solidarity with his audience and further evoke a contrast with Cain, who lacked a love for his brother and killed him (cf. 1 John 3:12). There is an intensification of the world's hostile relation to the believers, from the world not knowing them in 1 John 3:1d in the preceding co-text, to the world hating them in 1 John 3:13b. The lexeme μισέω, which is an antonym of the lexeme ἀγαπάω, appears for the third time in v. 13b in this letter (cf. 1 John 2:9, 11; 3:13, 15; 4:20). The author stresses that the audience are the object of the world's hatred by placing the complement (i.e., ὑμᾶς) prior to the subject (i.e., ὁ κόσμος) in v. 13b.

Despite the world's antagonism towards the believers, they know that they have passed from death to life because they love the Christian brothers and sisters in 1 John 3:14. The first-person plural nominative pronoun ἡμεῖς (v. 14a) is the subject of the ensuing three first-person plural perfect or present active indicative verbs in v. 14a–c. The author avails himself of the two first-person plural perfect active indicative verbs οἴδαμεν (v. 14a; cf. 1 John 3:2; 5:15 [2x], 18, 19, 20) and μεταβεβήκαμεν (v. 14b) to give prominence to the assertion regarding the Christian certitude of passing from death to life.[2] The two prepositional phrases ἐκ τοῦ θανάτου and εἰς τὴν ζωήν are utilized to portray the transferal of the believers' locality from the realm of death to the realm of life in v. 14b (cf. John 5:24).[3] The predicator ἀγαπῶμεν in the first-person plural and the present tense is in the indicative, not subjunctive, mood in the ὅτι-clause in v. 14c. The implication is that the believers' love for other members in God's family is the reason or grounds for the Christian surety of possessing the eternal life in the present. The author does not employ the accusative plural reciprocal pronoun ἀλλήλους to bring out the idea of mutuality in v. 14c (cf. 1 John 3:11). Rather, he utilizes the articular accusative plural noun ἀδελφούς to be the object of the predicator ἀγαπῶμεν so that the presumed contrast of the Christian love opposed to Cain killing his brother will be perceptible in v. 14c. The author shifts to use the generic participant to depict the kind of individuals lacking

---

1. There are altogether fifteen occurrences of the lexeme ἀδελφός in this letter (1 John 2:9, 10, 11; 3:10, 12 [2x], 13, 14, 15, 16, 17; 4:20 [2x], 21; 5:16). The author employs the vocative masculine plural form (i.e., ἀδελφοί) of this lexeme to refer to his audience only once in 1 John 3:13.

2. The lexeme μεταβαίνω occurs only once in 1 John 3:14 in this epistle. Kruse, *Letters of John*, 135.

3. The lexeme θάνατος is found a total of six times in 1 John 3:14 (2x); 5:16 (3x), 17.

love (presumably for the Christian brothers and sisters) and remaining in the realm of death in 1 John 3:14d. Without passing from death to life, it is obvious that such a person continues to be in the state of (spiritual) death.[4] The author uses the embedded participial clause ὁ μὴ ἀγαπῶν to encode the generic subject with reference to the person who does not love in v. 14d. Since the predicator ἀγαπῶν does not have a specified complement in this embedded participial clause, some scribes attempted to clarify the object of the person's love by adding the words τὸν ἀδελφόν or τὸν ἀδελφὸν αὐτοῦ in 1 John 3:14d (cf. 1 John 2:9, 10, 11; 3:10, 12, 14, 15, 16, 17; 4:20, 21).[5] Nevertheless, the shorter reading adopted in NA28 is preferable on account of transcriptional probability and the textual evidence from codices Sinaiticus (ℵ and 01), Alexandrinus (A or 02), and Vatincanus (B or 03), and other manuscripts.[6]

The author avers that anyone who hates the fellow believers is a murderer in 1 John 3:15a, in which the embedded participial clause πᾶς ὁ μισῶν τὸν ἀδελφὸν αὐτοῦ functions as the generic subject. The author further uses the linguistic device of mental projection (cf. the mental verb οἴδατε with the epexegetical conjunction ὅτι) to bring out the idea that every murderer does not have the eternal life remaining in him or her in v. 15b-c. The word group ζωὴν αἰώνιον in the feminine singular accusative is modified by the embedded participial clause ἐν αὐτῷ μένουσαν that follows in v. 15c. The lexeme αἰώνιος occurs a total of six times and always in connection with the lexeme ζωή with reference to the eternal life in this epistle (1 John 1:2; 2:25; 3:15; 5:11, 13, 20). The antecedent of the dative masculine singular pronoun αὐτῷ in the embedded participial clause above is the nominative masculine singular noun ἀνθρωποκτόνος that precedes in v. 15c. The lexeme ἀνθρωποκτόνος from semantic domain 20 ("violence, harm, destroy, kill") is detected only twice in 1 John 3:15 in the whole letter. Aside from these two occurrences in this letter, this lexeme is employed to denote the devil as a "murderer" from the beginning in John 8:44. It is worth noting that the lexeme ἀνθρωποκτόνος is semantically related to the lexeme σφάζω, which has been used for portraying Cain killing his brother in 1 John 3:12. The rhetorical implication is that the author tactfully associates any person hating his or her Christian brothers and sisters with Cain, who is a child of the devil.

---

4. Campbell, *1, 2, and 3 John*, 116.

5. The variant τὸν ἀδελφόν is found in C, Ψ, 5, 81, 307, etc. The other variant τὸν ἀδελφὸν αὐτοῦ is present in P^{apr}, 436, 442, 1448, etc. See Culy, *1, 2, 3 John*, 84; Metzger, *Textual Commentary on the Greek New Testament*, 643.

6. Metzger, *Textual Commentary on the Greek New Testament*, 643.

As asserted in 1 John 3:16, the act of Jesus laying down his life for the believers is the motivating basis and the model upon which they should follow suit in their dealings with other members in God's family. The prepositional phrase ἐν τούτῳ is cataphoric and used to point forward to the means by which the believers know love in v. 16a.[7] Notice that the relevant statement about knowing love above is prominent in view of the use of the perfect tense (cf. ἐγνώκαμεν).[8] The author underlines the notion that the believers are the beneficiary of Jesus' loving self-sacrifice by placing the prepositional phrase ὑπὲρ ἡμῶν adjacent to the demonstrative pronoun ἐκεῖνος, which is the subject with reference to Jesus in v. 16b (cf. 1 John 2:6, 3:3, 5, 7; 4:17). The believers are urged to follow in Jesus' footsteps and lay down their lives for the welfare of other members in God's family in v. 16c. The nominative first-person plural pronoun ἡμεῖς (v. 16c) is the subject of the first-person plural present active indicative verb ὀφείλομεν (cf. 1 John 3:6; 4:11), whose complement is the embedded infinitival clause τὰς ψυχὰς θεῖναι (cf. John 10:11, 15, 17, 18; 15:13). It is evident that the author draws on the linguistic resource to attempt establishing the correlation between Jesus laying down his life for our sake and the believers' obligation to lay down their lives for the sake of the fellow Christians in v. 16b–c.[9] The two lexemes ψυχή (2x) and τίθημι (2x) are present only in 1 John 3:16b–c in the whole epistle. In both of the two instances of the latter lexeme τίθημι, the aorist tense with the perfective aspect is employed to portray the complete action of Jesus' or the believers' self-sacrifice for others' sake in v. 16b or v. 16c.[10]

The author goes on to posit the situation in which anyone who has the world's material possessions (v. 17a) and sees his or her Christian brother or sister having a need (v. 17b), but shows no compassion to him or her (v. 17c). The masculine singular nominative relative pronoun ὅς, which is followed by the postpositive elided conjunction δ' and the possibility adjunct ἄν, does not have an antecedent at the beginning of v. 17a (cf. 1 John 2:5; 4:15). This headless relative pronoun (i.e., ὅς [v. 17a]) is the subject of the following two third-person singular present active subjunctive verbs ἔχῃ (v. 17a) and θεωρῇ (v. 17b) and the ensuing third-person singular aorist active subjunctive verb κλείσῃ (v. 17c). The author employs the lexeme βίος for the second and last time to depict the material goods that one possesses in the world in v. 17a (cf. 1 John 2:16). Rather than denoting only the rich people

---

7. Culy, *1, 2, 3 John*, 86.

8. The first-person plural perfect active indicative verb ἐγνώκαμεν is detected three times in 1 John 2:3; 3:16; 4:16.

9. Leung, "Ethics and *Imitatio Christi* in 1 John," 127–29; Bennema, *Mimesis in the Johannine Literature*, 115–16.

10. Leung, "Ethics and *Imitatio Christi* in 1 John," 127–29.

owning the luxurious goods, it is likely that the author speaks of generally any believer who has the livelihood and the world's possessions.[11] The entire word group τὸν ἀδελφὸν αὐτοῦ χρείαν ἔχοντα constitutes the complement of the predicator θεωρῇ in v. 17b. In the subsequent clause, the author uses another word group κλείσῃ τὰ σπλάγχνα αὐτοῦ as an idiomatic expression to convey the figurative sense of shutting off one's compassion to a Christian brother or sister having a need in v. 17c. The author further utilizes the interrogative adjunct πῶς to realize the rhetorical question (i.e., "How does the love of God abide in him?") to engage his audience and make a point in v. 17d. This is the only time this interrogative adjunct (i.e., πῶς) occurs to introduce a question in the Johannine epistles.[12] The genitive construction ἡ ἀγάπη τοῦ θεοῦ can be construed as either the objective genitive (i.e., our love for God) or subjective genitive (i.e., love that comes from God or God's love for us) in v. 17d.[13] In any case, the point of the rhetorical question is that the "love of God" does not find expression in the person having the material possessions and seeing a fellow believer lacking the necessities in life but having no pity on him or her.[14] As a corollary, the believers should willingly provide financial assistance to the needy members in the Christian community.

For the fourth time, the author employs the vocative plural τεκνία to attract his audience's attention and position himself over them at the outset of 1 John 3:18a (cf. 1 John 2:1, 12, 28; 4:4; 5:21). The author uses the first-person plural present active subjunctive verb ἀγαπῶμεν in connection with the negative polarity adjunct μή to realize the prohibition against loving merely with word or tongue. Despite the lack of a specified complement with this hortatory subjunctive (i.e., ἀγαπῶμεν), it can be presumed that the object of the believers' love is primarily the Christian brothers and sisters in v. 18a (cf. 1 John 3:11, 14; 4:7). Since both of the two lexemes λόγος and γλῶσσα in the adjunctive phrase λόγῳ μηδὲ τῇ γλώσσῃ (v. 18a) fall in semantic domain 33 ("communication"), it is apparent that the concern of loving merely with word or tongue lies in that our love to the fellow believers is

---

11. Yarbrough, *1–3 John*, 203; Smalley, *1, 2, 3 John*, 186.

12. The interrogative adjunct πῶς is employed to usher in a direct or indirect question a total of twenty times in the Fourth Gospel (John 3:4, 9, 12; 4:9; 5:44, 47; 6:42, 52; 7:15; 8:33; 9:10, 15, 16, 19, 21, 26; 11:36; 12:34; 14:5, 9).

13. Culy thinks that the genitive construction ἡ ἀγάπη τοῦ θεοῦ is the objective genitive in 1 John 2:17. In contrast, Campbell, Brown, and Stott believe that this genitive construction is the subjective genitive. See Culy, *1, 2, 3 John*, 89; Campbell, *1, 2, and 3 John*, 117; Brown, *Epistles of John*, 450; Stott, *Letters of John*, 415.

14. Kruse mentions the possibility of Deut 15:7–9 as the OT background of the communal love in 1 John 3:17. See Kruse, *Letters of John*, 138.

shown only through speech. It is probable that the articular dative noun γλώσσῃ is not merely synonymous to the preceding dative noun λόγῳ but rather signifies the source of the utterances (i.e., the "word" that comes from the "tongue").[15] The author uses the subsequent elliptical clause headed by the elided adversative conjunction ἀλλ' (v. 18b) to counter what has been said in the prior clause in v. 18a. While this elliptical clause (v. 18b) does not contain a verb, the first-person plural present active subjunctive verb ἀγαπῶμεν can be implied from the prior clause in v. 18a. As an upshot, an alternative voice is rhetorically evoked in such a way that the contesting position of loving merely with word or tongue is acknowledged but denied right away.[16] Contrary to simply talking about loving one another, it is mandatory for the believers to show love to others in deed and truth (cf. the prepositional phrase ἐν ἔργῳ καὶ ἀληθείᾳ) in v. 18b.[17] The anarthrous dative noun ἀληθείᾳ (cf. the sixth and only occurrence of the lexeme ἀλήθεια without an article) in the prepositional phrase above can be construed to express the idea of loving genuinely or with sincerity.[18] Alternatively, the author may seek to indicate that the "truth" is the source and basis of the believers' loving acts towards others in v. 18b.[19] The likelihood of the latter understanding increases if the "tongue" is considered as the source of the speeches in v. 18a.[20] Furthermore, the author will speak of the believers as belonging to the "truth" soon in 1 John 3:19.[21] At any rate, the author emphasizes that Christian love must be acted out, particularly in respect of providing financial aid to the needy in God's family.

---

15. Brown, *Epistles of John*, 451–52.

16. For the rhetorical effect of evoking alternative "voices" in the text, see Martin and Rose, *Working with Discourse*, 53–54.

17. The lexeme ἔργον occurs for the third and last time in 1 John 3:18 in this letter (cf. 1 John 3:8, 12). The preceding two occurrences of this lexeme are in the plural and concerning the "deeds" of the devil or Cain.

18. Stott, *Letters of John*, 146; Kruse, *Letters of John*, 138.

19. Jobes, *1, 2, and 3 John*, 159; Brown, *Epistles of John*, 452.

20. Brown, *Epistles of John*, 452.

21. Lieu, *I, II, & III John*, 152.

1 JOHN 3:19–24

OUTLINE:

II. Body (1:5—5:12)

    A. Adhering to and Behaving in Conformity with the Christian Beliefs (1:5—2:27)

    B. Living as God's Children in View of Christ's Future Coming (2:28—4:6)

        1. The Hope for Jesus' Manifestation (2:28—3:3)

        2. The Disparity Between God's Children and the Devil's Children (3:4-12)

        3. Laying Down Our Lives for Others' Sake (3:13-18)

        4. The Christian Confidence and God's Twofold Commandment (3:19-24)

4. The Christian Confidence and God's Twofold Commandment (3:19–24)

To begin the present section in 1 John 3:19-24, the author intimates that the believers will know that they are of the truth by loving the Christian brothers and sisters in deed and truth in v. 19a-b. The dative neuter singular demonstrative pronoun τούτῳ in the prepositional phrase ἐν τούτῳ (v. 19a) points backward to the exhortation in v. 18, in which the author asserts that the believers should not simply talk about loving other people but rather showing love to them in deed and truth.[1] Despite the connection with the

---

1. Jobes, *1, 2, and 3 John*, 165.

preceding co-text, this commentary will analyze the passage 1 John 3:19–24 as a self-contained unit on account of the following five observations. First, a number of new lexemes appear for the first time in this passage (e.g., πείθω [v. 19c], καρδία [vv. 19c, 20a, 20b, 21a], καταγινώσκω [vv. 20a, 21a], μέγας [v. 20c], αἰτέω [v. 22a], ἀρεστός [v. 22c], πιστεύω [v. 23b], and πνεῦμα [v. 24e]). Second, there is a topical shift to prayer in v. 22. Third, aside from the repeated occurrences of the two aforementioned lexemes καρδία (4x) and καταγινώσκω (2x), the author employs the lexemes ἐντολή four times (vv. 22b, 23a, 23d, 24a),[2] γινώσκω three times (vv. 19a, 20c, 24c), τηρέω twice (vv. 22b, 24a), δίδωμι twice (vv. 23d, 24e), and μένω twice (v. 24a, d) to enhance the literary coherence of this section. Fourth, the main participant is consistently the inclusive "we" throughout 1 John 3:19–24, in which there are altogether eleven finite verbs and seven personal pronouns in the first-person plural.[3] There is no second-person plural expression in 1 John 3:19–24. Fifth, while the demonstrative pronoun ἐκεῖνος has been employed with reference to Jesus a couple of times in the preceding co-text (1 John 2:6; 3:3, 5, 7, 16; cf. 1 John 4:17), this demonstrative pronoun is absent from 1 John 3:19–24. Instead of the demonstrative pronoun ἐκεῖνος, the author refers to Jesus Christ explicitly by name in 1 John 3:23. In short, it is proper to consider 1 John 3:19–24 as a self-contained unit.

Among the total twenty-five occurrences of the lexeme γινώσκω in this epistle,[4] this lexeme occurs only once in the middle voice in 1 John 3:19a. The author employs the first-person plural future middle verb γνωσόμεθα to draw attention to the presumed subject, namely the inclusive "we" whose referent includes the author and his audience in v. 19a. The author places the prepositional phrase ἐκ τῆς ἀληθείας prior to the predicator ἐσμέν to underline the believers' characteristic that they are "of the truth" in v. 19b. As affirmed in v. 19c, one of the implications of loving the fellow Christians in deed and truth is that we will convince our heart before God. That is to say, we will be confident in God's presence. The prepositional phrase ἔμπροσθεν αὐτοῦ pertaining to the circumstance of location (i.e., in front of God) is assigned the thematic place to orient the audience for what will be unfolded in the clause in v. 19c. The antecedent of the genitive masculine singular

---

2. The lexemes ἐντολή is absent from the foregoing units in 1 John 2:12—3:18.

3. The eleven finite verbs in the first-person plural are: γνωσόμεθα (v. 19a), ἐσμέν (v. 19b), πείσομεν (v. 19c), ἔχομεν (v. 21b), αἰτῶμεν (v. 22a), λαμβάνομεν (v. 22a), τηροῦμεν (v. 22b), ποιοῦμεν (v. 22c), πιστεύσωμεν (v. 23b), ἀγαπῶμεν (v. 23c), and γινώσκομεν (v. 24c). The seven personal pronouns in the first-person plural include the four instances of ἡμῶν (vv. 19c, 20a, b, 21a) and the three instances of ἡμῖν (vv. 23d, 24d, 24e).

4. The lexeme γινώσκω (25x) is present in 1 John 2:3 (2x), 4, 5, 13, 14 (2x), 18, 29; 3:1 (2x), 6, 16, 19, 20, 24; 4:2, 6 (2x), 7, 8, 13, 16; 5:2, 20.

pronoun αὐτοῦ in this prepositional phrase above (v. 19c) is the genitive masculine singular noun θεοῦ that precedes in v. 17d. The author utilizes the first-person plural future verb πείσομεν in connection with the complement τὴν καρδίαν ἡμῶν to portray the believers' future expectation of being confident in God's presence in v. 19c. Notably, all of the four occurrences of the lexeme καρδία are found in the present section in this letter (1 John 3:19, 20 [2x], 21). In each case, the inclusive first-person plural genitive pronoun ἡμῶν is employed in connection with the lexeme καρδία to indicate that the believers, including the author and his audience, are in view.

The three consecutive clauses are headed by the conjunctions ὅτι, ὅτι, and καί respectively in 1 John 3:20a–c. The meaning of the beginning word group ὅτι ἐάν is debatable in v. 20a. It is possible to render the initial word ὅτι as the reading ὅ τι, which is the accusative neuter singular form of the indefinite relative pronoun ὅστις.[5] Furthermore, the ensuing word ἐάν (v. 20a) in this word group above can be construed as functioning akin to the probability adjunct ἄν (cf. ἐάν in 1 John 3:22). The corollary is that the predicator πείσομεν in the prior clause in v. 19c takes a double accusative—namely, the object phrase τὴν καρδίαν ἡμῶν (v. 19c) and the reformulated indefinite relative clause ὅ τι ἐὰν καταγινώσκῃ ἡμῶν ἡ καρδία (v. 20a). If the above understanding of the word group ὅτι ἐάν is accepted, the author expresses that whatever (or in effect whenever) our heart condemns us in v. 20a.[6] The strength of this understanding is that it avoids the grammatical difficulty arising from the redundant repetition of the conjunction ὅτι in the two consecutive clauses in v. 20a and v. 20b (cf. v. 19b). Nevertheless, the above understanding requires that the word ἐάν to be construed alike a probability adjunct in v. 20a but the subsequent occurrence of this word is apparently a conditional conjunction rather than a probability adjunct in 1 John 3:21a.[7]

The alternative approach to the word group ὅτι ἐάν is to construe the initial word ὅτι as functioning to be a causal (or possibly epexegetical) conjunction at the outset of 1 John 3:20a.[8] Furthermore, the conditional conjunction ἐάν in this word group above is utilized to usher in the third-class protasis. Therefore, the author says that we will be confident before God because if our heart condemns us in v. 20a. The strength of this reading is that the usual and straightforward sense of the word group ὅτι ἐάν is retained. That said, the redundant repetition of the conjunction ὅτι in

---

5. See Marshall, *Epistles of John*, 197n4; Smalley, *1, 2, 3 John*, 191.
6. See Stott, *Letters of John*, 149; Smalley, *1, 2, 3 John*, 191.
7. Brown, *Epistles of John*, 456.
8. Brown thinks that both of the two occurrences of the conjunction ὅτι are epexegetical in 1 John 3:20. See Brown, *Epistles of John*, 456–58.

v. 20a and v. 20b remains difficult to comprehend. While certainty is not possible, the former understanding (i.e., ὅτι is rendered as ὅ τι) above is tentatively adopted in this commentary because it seems to pose the least difficulty and make a good sense in the flow of discourse.[9] Since God will purify the believers from all uncleanness if they confess their sins (cf. 1 John 1:9), the author avers that it is unnecessary for their conscience to be overburdened by guilt due to the condemnation of their own heart. In view of the foregoing exhortations in 1 John 3:17–18, the believers' inner accusation is probably concerned with personal guilt owing to their failure to live out the authentic love in the community. The author lays out the grounds of the ease of the believers' conscience before God in v. 20b-c. The entire word group μείζων . . . τῆς καρδίας ἡμῶν is the complement of the predicator ἐστίν in the ὅτι-clause in v. 20b. Following the initial conjunction ὅτι, the author separates the comparative adjective μείζων from other constituents of the complement above and places this comparative adjective alone in the emphatic position to accentuate the notion of the "greatness" of God in v. 20b. Since God is greater than our heart and he knows all things, the ultimate judge of the believers is not their own conscience but the omniscient God.[10] As an upshot, the believers will be confident in God's presence in whatever their hearts accuse them, and particularly that regarding the practice of loving others in deed and truth.

For the third time, the author employs the vocative plural ἀγαπητοί to enhance rapport with his audience and attract attention at the beginning of 1 John 3:21 (cf. 1 John 2:7; 3:2, 21; 4:1, 7, 11; 3 John 1, 2, 5, 11). He utilizes the third-class conditional statement to indicate that we have confidence in God's presence if our heart does not condemn us in v. 21a–b. The lexeme καταγινώσκω has previously occurred with reference to the inner accusation of our heart in v. 20a (cf. Gal 2:11). In line with this meaning, this lexeme is used to intimate the idea of "judg[ing] something to be bad" in the protasis in v. 21a.[11] The author places the complement παρρησίαν at the forefront to underline the notion of confidence in the apodosis in v. 21b. The lexeme παρρησία is detected a total of four times in this letter. This lexeme is employed twice with respect to the believers' confidence at Jesus' future coming or in the day of judgment (1 John 2:28; 4:17), and twice with respect to the believers' confidence when coming to God through prayer in the present (1 John 3:21; 5:14). The author elaborates the implication of

---

9. Stott, *Letters of John*, 149; Smalley, *1, 2, 3 John*, 191.

10. Wahlde, *Three Johannine Letters*, 134.

11. Louw and Nida, *Greek-English Lexicon of the New Testament*, 1:364 (semantic domain 30.118).

our approaching God with confidence in case we have a clear conscience in v. 22a. Following the initial conjunction καί, the embedded relative clause ὃ ἐὰν αἰτῶμεν as the complement is fronted to give emphasis to whatever the believers petition God in v. 22a. The author encourages his audience by telling them that the believers receive from God whatever they ask if they have a clear conscience before him. There is no hint that the believers can manipulate God to get anything they want because the author will subsequently point out the condition of answered prayers is that the petition is in accordance with God's will in 1 John 5:14. In fact, the author says that the grounds of God granting the believers' entreaty is that they keep his commandments and do the things that are pleasing in his sight in v. 22b–c. Notice that the complement τὰς ἐντολὰς αὐτοῦ or τὰ ἀρεστά is marked in the respective clause in v. 22b or v. 22c. In brief, the petitioner must conduct his or her life congruent with the precepts of God.

There is a cluster of four occurrences of the lexeme ἐντολή from semantic domain 33 ("communication") in 1 John 3:22–24. The accusative plural form (i.e., ἐντολάς) of this lexeme occurs twice pertaining to the notion of keeping God's commandments in general in v. 22b and v. 24a. The nominative or accusative singular form (i.e., ἐντολή or ἐντολήν) of this lexeme occurs altogether twice with respect to the single commandment of God in v. 23a and v. 23d respectively.[12] The nominative feminine singular demonstrative pronoun αὕτη (v. 23a) points forward to the ensuing ἵνα-clause, which is used to explicate the content of the commandment of God in v. 23b. The two aspects of the single commandment in v. 23b–c are framed by the altogether four occurrences of the lexeme ἐντολή in the surrounding co-text (vv. 22b, 23a, 23d, 24a). The first aspect of this commandment (v. 23b) is concerned with the doctrinal belief in the name of the Son of God, Jesus Christ. The word group τῷ ὀνόματι τοῦ υἱοῦ αὐτοῦ Ἰησοῦ Χριστοῦ as a whole is the complement of the first-person plural aorist active subjunctive verb πιστεύσωμεν in v. 23b.[13] The author utilizes the genitive construction τοῦ υἱοῦ αὐτοῦ Ἰησοῦ Χριστοῦ (v. 23b) to modify the dative noun ὀνόματι,

---

12. Campbell notes that the "switch from plural to singular indicates that all God's commands are essentially summed up in the single command" in 1 John 3:23 (Campbell, *1, 2, and 3 John*, 127).

13. The verb πιστεύω usually takes the object in the dative case. The textual reading πιστεύσωμεν adopted in NA28 is supported by B, 307, 642,1175, 1735, and some Byzantine manuscripts. The variant πιστεύωμεν, which is in the present tense, is attested in ℵ, A, C, Ψ, a number of minuscules, and the Byzantine witnesses. Despite the wide attestation of this latter variant, it was probably the outcome of the copyists' attempt to harmonize the verbal tense of the aorist active subjunctive verb πιστεύσωμεν with the following first-person plural present active subjunctive verb ἀγαπῶμεν in 1 John 3:23. Therefore, the textual reading πιστεύσωμεν is likely to be original. See Culy, *1, 2, 3 John*, 97.

which serves as the head in this word group above. The lexeme πιστεύω (9x) appears for the first time in 1 John 3:23 in this epistle (cf. 1 John 3:23; 4:1, 16; 5:1, 5, 10 [3x], 13). The second aspect of the commandment of God is concerned with the mutual love within the Christian community in v. 23c (cf. 1 John 5:1). The shift from the aorist tense with the perfective aspect (cf. πιστεύσωμεν) in v. 23b to the present tense with the imperfective aspect (cf. ἀγαπῶμεν) in v. 23c suggests that the emphasis of the two-part commandment lies in the ethical dimension of loving one another.[14] In addition, the Christological belief regarding Jesus' status as God's Son (v. 23b) is the presumed basis of the believers' practice of communal love (v. 23c).[15] It should be remarked that the author does not simply use the statements to inform his audience about the content of God's commandment but rather urges them to believe in the name of God's Son, Jesus Christ, and to love one another in 1 John 3:23. Yet, the way by which the author attempts affecting his audience's behavior is not through the use of the imperative to set forth the exhortation straightforwardly. Rather, the two implicit directives regarding the Christological belief and the communal love are expressed metaphorically (i.e., incongruent mood choices in grammar) through the statements and by using the construction containing the lexeme ἐντολή and the conjunction ἵνα in v. 23 (see "Tenor" in "Introduction").[16] The rhetorical effect is to soften the directives and make them sound less threatening. As a corollary, the audience will be inclined to act in accordance with the author's demand.

The author concludes the present section by portraying the positive kind of individuals who keep God's commandments in 1 John 3:24. As indicated in v. 24a-b, such an individual remains in God (or Jesus) and God (or Jesus) remains in him or her. While the elliptical clause καὶ αὐτὸς ἐν αὐτῷ does not have a verb in v. 24b, the third-person singular present active indicative verb μένει can be inferred from the prior clause in v. 24a. The author speaks of the means by which the believers know of the abiding presence of God (or Jesus) in v. 24c-e. The prepositional phrase ἐν τούτῳ (v. 24c) is instrumental and points forward to the elliptical clause in v. 24e, in which the prepositional phrase ἐκ τοῦ πνεύματος is employed to express the means and reason as regards the Christian assurance of God's abiding presence in the believers (cf. 1 John 4:13). In addition, the source of this assurance from the Spirit is also intimated through this prepositional phrase

14. Longacre, "Exhortation and Mitigation in First John," 21.
15. Culy, *1, 2, 3 John*, 97.
16. For the different degrees of the mitigated commands in 1 John, see Miehle, "Theme in Greek Hortatory Discourse," 156; Sherman and Tuggy, *Semantic and Structural Analysis*, 2.

above in v. 24e. The author further utilizes the embedded relative clause οὗ ἡμῖν ἔδωκεν to modify the preceding genitive singular noun πνεύματος and thereby indicates that God or Jesus gave the Spirit to the believers in v. 24e. The implicit subject of the third-person singular aorist active indicative verb ἔδωκεν could be God (cf. John 14:16, 26) or Jesus (cf. John 15:26; 16:7). Although the relative pronoun οὗ above is in the genitive case, it is the complement of the predicator ἔδωκεν. It is possible that the author chooses to employ the genitive instead of the accusative case to encode this complement in order to heighten the linkage between the embedded relative clause οὗ ἡμῖν ἔδωκεν and the genitive noun πνεύματος that precedes in v. 24e. The effect of this "case attraction" (i.e., the case of the relative pronoun οὗ is attracted to the case of its antecedent, namely πνεύματος) is that the notion of the indwelling of the Spirit is accentuated (cf. Rom 5:5; 8:14–16).[17] At any rate, it is worth noting that the author employs the lexeme πνεῦμα (12x) from semantic domain 12 ("supernatural beings and powers") to denote the Spirit for the first time in 1 John 3:24e in this letter.[18] By referring explicitly to the Spirit (v. 24e) at the end of the present section, the author paves the way for the subsequent discussion apropos the test of the spirits that will be unfolded in 1 John 4:1–6.

---

17. In contrast, Culy thinks that the grammatical feature of case attraction has "no pragmatic function" (*1, 2, 3 John*, 99).

18. There are altogether twelve occurrences of the lexeme πνεῦμα in 1 John 3:24; 4:1 (2x), 2 (2x), 3, 6 (2x), 13; 5:6 (2x), 8.

1 JOHN 4:1–6

OUTLINE:

II. Body (1:5—5:12)

    A. Adhering to and Behaving in Conformity with the Christian Beliefs (1:5—2:27)

    B. Living as God's Children in View of Christ's Future Coming (2:28—4:6)

        1. The Hope for Jesus' Manifestation (2:28—3:3)

        2. The Disparity Between God's Children and the Devil's Children (3:4-12)

        3. Laying Down Our Lives for Others' Sake (3:13-18)

        4. The Christian Confidence and God's Twofold Commandment (3:19-24)

        5. Test the Spirits (4:1-6)

5. Test the Spirits (4:1–6)

There is a change in tone from the assurance of the audience's knowledge about God's abiding presence at the end of the prior section in 1 John 3:19-24 to the warning about the threat posed by the false teachers in the present section in 1 John 4:1-6. The author deals with the matter of discerning the spirits so as to enable his audience to differentiate between the Spirit of truth and the spirit of deception. On the one hand, this section is lexically tied with the prior section through the recurrences of the lexeme πνεῦμα (cf. 1 John 3:24; 4:1 [2x], 2 [2x], 3, 6 [2x]). On the other hand, it is proper to consider the present section in 1 John 4:1–6 as a semantically and structurally unified unit on account of the following five observations. First, the author signals the beginning of a new section by employing the vocative plural ἀγαπητοί and the two second-person plural present active imperative verbs πιστεύετε and δοκιμάζετε to speak to his audience directly in 1 John 4:1.[1] Second, the semantic coherence of this section is enhanced in part through the altogether fifteen occurrences of the two lexemes πνεῦμα (7x; see above) and θεός (8x) from semantic domain 12 ("supernatural beings and powers") in 1 John 4:1–6.[2] In addition, the lexeme κόσμος is found a total of six times (vv. 1d, 3e, 4d, 5a, 5b, 5c). Third, the author increases the internal unity of this section by utilizing the literary device of the *inclusio*, which is made up of the two occurrences of the word group ἐν τούτῳ γινώσκετε in 1 John 4:2a and 4:6d.[3] Fourth, there is a parallelism in the structures of the three independent clauses in v. 4a (ὑμεῖς ἐκ τοῦ θεοῦ ἐστε), v. 5a (αὐτοὶ ἐκ τοῦ κόσμου εἰσίν), and v. 6a (ἡμεῖς ἐκ τοῦ θεοῦ ἐσμεν). In each of these three independent clauses above, the personal pronoun in the nominative plural functions as the subject and is succeeded by the prepositional phrase and subsequently the predicator. Fifth, the author avails himself of the two prepositional phrases ἐκ τοῦ θεοῦ (6x; cf. vv. 1c, 2b, 3a, 4a, 6a, 6c) and ἐκ τοῦ κόσμου (2x; cf. v. 5a, 5b) to establish the antithesis between the two notions of belonging to (or originating with) God and belonging to (or originating with) the world in this section.

As noted above, the author employs the affective lexeme ἀγαπητός (cf. 1 John 2:7; 3:2, 21; 4:1, 7, 11) from semantic domain 25 ("attitudes and emotions") for the fourth time to address his audience directly as his "beloved" in v. 1a. This affective address has the effect of softening the following two commands and making them sound less threatening in 1 John 4:1a–c. The author has used the lexeme πιστεύω to explicate that an aspect of God's twofold commandment is to believe in the name of his Son, Jesus Christ, in 1 John 3:23 in the preceding co-text. At the outset of the present section, the author employs the second-person plural present active imperative verb πιστεύετε in conjunction with the negative polarity adjunct μή to encode the prohibition "Do not believe every spirit!" in v. 1a. Notice that the complement παντὶ πνεύματι (v. 1a) is marked to stress the idea of "every spirit." In contrast to this prohibition above, the author sets forth the positive

---

1. Among the total six occurrences of the vocative plural ἀγαπητοί in this letter (1 John 2:7; 3:2, 21; 4:1, 7, 11), there are four instances in which this vocative plural is located at the beginning of a new section (cf. 1 John 2:7; 4:1, 7, 11).

2. The lexeme θεός is detected a total of eight times in the present section (1 John 4:1c, 2a, 2b, 3a, 4a, 6a, 6b, 6c).

3. Sherman and Tuggy, *Semantic and Structural Analysis*, 77.

command, "Test the spirits to see whether they are from God!" in v. 1b–c. The conjunction εἰ is utilized to introduce the indirect question regarding that whether a spirit is of God in v. 1c. The placement of the prepositional phrase ἐκ τοῦ θεοῦ (v. 1c) prior to the predicator ἐστίν suggests that the source of the spirit is in the author's interest. As an implication of issuing the two negative and positive directives above (v. 1a–c), the author orients his audience to expect that the messages that will be unfolded are primarily pertinent to discerning a spirit at the beginning of this section. The author further explains that it is necessary to put the spirits to test because many false prophets have gone out (cf. the third-person plural perfect active indicative verb ἐξεληλύθασιν) into the world in v. 1d. This is the first and only time the lexeme ψευδοπροφήτης from semantic domain 53 ("religious activities") is used to denote the false teachers in the three Johannine epistles. The author has spoken of the false teachers as "many antichrists" in 1 John 2:18 and will subsequently associate them with the spirit of the antichrist in 1 John 4:3. It is probable that the false teachers purport to possess the Spirit and thus speak with the authority of God.[4] Therefore, the author exhorts his audience to exercise spiritual discernment to test the spirits.

The author goes on to provide information concerning how the believers recognize the Spirit of God in 1 John 4:2. The construction τὸ πνεῦμα τοῦ θεοῦ is found only once in v. 2a in the Johannine writings.[5] While the predicator γινώσκετε (v. 2a) in the second-person plural and present tense could be in the indicative or imperative mood, it is more likely that this predicator is in the indicative mood because the author never sets forth a command subsequent to the prepositional phrase ἐν τούτῳ in other places in this epistle.[6] The dative neuter singular demonstrative pronoun τούτῳ in this prepositional phrase (v. 2a) points forward to the ensuing assertion that every spirit that confesses that Jesus Christ has come in the flesh is from God in v. 2b. The entire word group πᾶν πνεῦμα ὃ ὁμολογεῖ Ἰησοῦν Χριστὸν ἐν σαρκὶ ἐληλυθότα is the subject of the predicator ἐστίν in v. 2b. The prepositional phrase ἐν σαρκί preceding the accusative masculine singular perfect active participle ἐληλυθότα in this word group above is utilized to express the manner of the manifestation of Jesus Christ in a physical body (cf. 2 John 7; 1 Tim 3:16). As an antithesis of the Christological affirmation in v. 2b, every spirit that does not confess Jesus is not from God in 1 John 4:3a (cf. 1 John 2:22).[7] The notion of Christ's coming in the

---

4. Jobes, 1, 2, and 3 John, 176–77.
5. Brown, Epistles of John, 491.
6. Brown, Epistles of John, 491.
7. It is uncommon to use the negative polarity adjunct μή to negate an indicative

flesh is presupposed albeit the absence of the words ἐν σαρκὶ ἐληλυθότα in v. 3a. The author further identifies such a spirit (cf. v. 3a) as the spirit of the antichrist in v. 3b.[8] This is the fourth and last occurrence of the lexeme ἀντίχριστος in this epistle (1 John 2:18 [2x], 22; 4:3; cf. 2 John 7). The author reminds his audience that they have heard of the coming of the spirit of the antichrist in v. 3c–d (cf. 1 John 2:18). In fact, the spirit of the antichrist is already in the world in v. 3e. The word group ἐν τῷ κόσμῳ ἐστίν is framed by the two temporal adjuncts νῦν and ἤδη (v. 3e) to underscore the location of the present outworking of the spirit of the antichrist in the world. From the author's perspective, the spirit of the antichrist is currently operating actively through the false teachers' distorted Christology to attempt leading the believers astray.

The author places the nominative second-person plural pronoun ὑμεῖς in the thematic position to attract attention and signal the topical shift from the spirit(s) to his audience at the beginning of 1 John 4:4a (cf. 1 John 2:20a, 24a, 27a).[9] While there is a cluster of five occurrences of the lexeme πνεῦμα in the preceding co-text in vv. 1–3, this lexeme is not detected throughout vv. 4a–6c until its recurrence in the final clause in v. 6d in this section. Turning the focus to the audience as his "dear children," the author assures them that they belong to God and have overcome the false teachers in v. 4a–b. This is the fifth time the author employs the vocative neuter plural noun τεκνία (6x) to address the audience directly in v. 4a (1 John 2:1, 12, 28; 3:18; 4:4; 5:21; cf. John 13:33). The perfect active second-person plural indicative verb νενικήκατε has occurred twice pertaining to the young men's victory over the evil one in 1 John 2:13–14. For the third time, the author employs this perfect active second-person plural indicative verb above to portray and give prominence to the Christian conquest over the false prophets in 1 John 4:4b.[10] It is avowed that the believers have withstood against the false prophets' evil deception. The underlying causality of the believers' spiritual victory is spelt out in v. 4c–d, in which the author asserts that the one who is in his audience is greater than the one who is in the world (cf. John 16:33). The two nominal groups ὁ ἐν ὑμῖν (v. 4c) and ὁ ἐν τῷ κόσμῳ (v. 4d) are contrastive to each other. Some scholars believe that the first nominal group ὁ ἐν

---

verb in Koine Greek. For the possible explanations of the use of this negative polarity adjunct in connection with the third-person singular present active indicative verb ὁμολογεῖ in 1 John 4:3a, see Culy, *1, 2, 3 John*, 102.

8. The antecedent of the neuter nominative singular demonstrative pronoun τοῦτο (v. 3b) is the entire word group πᾶν πνεῦμα ὃ μὴ ὁμολογεῖ τὸν Ἰησοῦν that precedes in v. 3a.

9. Brown, *Epistles of John*, 497.

10. Stott, *Letters of John*, 157.

ὑμῖν refers to the Spirit of God in v. 4c.[11] The weakness of this reading is that there is a grammatical incongruence if the masculine singular article ὁ in this nominal group is treated as the specifier of the implicit neuter singular noun πνεῦμα. Alternatively, it is possible to construe the first nominal group ὁ ἐν ὑμῖν with reference to God or Jesus (cf. John 16:33).[12] On the whole, the understanding that this nominal group refers to God is more likely because the author speaks of God abiding in the believers through the indwelling of the Spirit a number of times in this letter (cf. 1 John 3:24; 4:12–13, 15).[13] Notice that the comparative adjective μείζων, which functions as the complement of the ensuing predicator ἐστίν, is marked in the clause to draw attention to the notion of greatness of God (or less likely Jesus) in v. 4c. The second nominal group ὁ ἐν τῷ κόσμῳ above is the subject of the implied predicator ἐστίν in the elliptical clause beginning with the conjunction ἤ in v. 4d. The referent of "the one who is in the world" is most probably the evil one (cf. 1 John 2:13–14), who is denoted as the prince of this world in the Fourth Gospel (John 12:31; 14:30; 16:11).[14] By indicating God's or Christ's unmatched superiority over the devil, the author endeavors to encourage his audience to continue standing firm against the deceptive teaching.

The nominative masculine plural pronoun αὐτοί functions as the expressed subject of the predicator εἰσίν at the outset of 1 John 4:5a. In view of this expressed subject, the author intimates the shift of topic from the audience to the people who are of the world in v. 5a.[15] The prepositional phrase διὰ τοῦτο is anaphoric in v. 5b and is utilized to suggest that the logical relationship between v. 5a and v. 5b–c is one of cause-and-effect. Given the people's connection with the world (v. 5a), they speak from the world and the world listens to them (v. 5b–c). The author does not simply use the word ἀκούει from semantic domain 31 ("hold a view, believe, trust") to mean hearing something but rather accepting something and believing it in v. 5c (cf. v. 6).[16] The implication is that those who belong to the world respond positively to the message of the false teachers, which is in alignment with the worldly viewpoint.

Akin to the thematic function of the two preceding nominative plural pronouns ὑμεῖς (v. 4a) and αὐτοί (v. 5a), the author uses the nominative

11. See, e.g., Campbell, *1, 2, and 3 John*, 136; Brown, *Epistles of John*, 497–98; Stott, *Letters of John*, 157.

12. Jobes thinks that "he who is in you" refers to Jesus Christ (*1, 2, and 3 John*, 182).

13. Marshall, *Epistles of John*, 208n16.

14. Kruse, *Letters of John*, 148–49; Campbell, *1, 2, and 3 John*, 136.

15. Campbell, *1, 2, and 3 John*, 137.

16. Louw and Nida, *Greek-English Lexicon of the New Testament*, 1:372 (semantic domain 31.56).

plural pronoun ἡμεῖς to encode the topical theme and thereby creates an expectation for what will follow at the outset of 1 John 4:6a. Furthermore, it is likely that the reference to "we" (v. 6a) is antithetical to the foregoing reference to "they" (v. 5a). If the first-person plural pronoun ἡμεῖς (v. 6a) above is exclusive, the referent is the author along with other true teachers.[17] Alternatively, it is probable that the author avails himself of the device of the inclusive "we" to enhance the Christian solidarity with his audience, who are included as part of the referent of the first-person plural pronoun ἡμεῖς in v. 6a.[18] Both of the exclusive and inclusive readings of this first-person plural pronoun in v. 6a are possible but the latter reading seems to be more fitting in the author's rhetorical strategy within the immediate co-text. Furthermore, the inclusive understanding of the "we" (v. 6a) is in line with the author's employment of the ensuing first-person plural present active indicative verb γινώσκομεν to refer to himself and the audience in v. 6d. At any rate, the author uses the generic statements to portray the two contrastive classes of people in regard to their different relationships to God and their varied responses to the apostolic teaching in 1 John 4:6b–c. On the positive side, the person who knows God listens to the author, other true teachers, and the audience in v. 6b (cf. v. 5c). On the negative side, any person who does not belong to God does not listen to the author, other true teachers, and the audience in v. 6c. The prepositional phrase ἐκ τοῦ θεοῦ occurs for the sixth time in v. 6c in the present section (cf. 1 John 4:1c, 2b, 3a, 4a, 6a, 6c). The author concludes his discourse apropos discerning the spirits in v. 6d, in which the prepositional phrase ἐκ τούτου is utilized to express agency or instrument. The genitive neuter singular demonstrative pronoun τούτου (v. 6d) in this prepositional phrase above is anaphoric and probably points backward to what has been said in vv. 5a–6c or the whole discourse in vv. 1a–6c.[19]

The lexeme πλάνη occurs only once in 1 John 4:6d in this epistle. However, the cognate verb πλανάω is employed with respect to those endeavoring to lead the believers astray in 1 John 2:26 and 3:7. Simply put, the author has spelt out two tests by which the believers can distinguish between the Spirit of truth (cf. 1 John 5:6; John 14:17; 15:16; 17:13) and the spirit of deception in this section in 1 John 4:1–6. The first test is whether the person upholds the belief of Jesus Christ coming in the flesh (cf. vv. 2–3). The second test is whether the person pays heed to the Christian message that is proclaimed

---

17. Lieu, *I, II, & III John*, 173; Stott, *Letters of John*, 158; Sherman and Tuggy, *Semantic and Structural Analysis*, 77; Marshall, *Epistles of John*, 209n19.

18. Kruse and Jobes think that the first-person plural pronoun ἡμεῖς is inclusive in 1 John 4:6a. Kruse, *Letters of John*, 150–51; Jobes, *1, 2, and 3 John*, 183.

19. See Brown, *Epistles of John*, 500.

by the author and other believers or true teachers (cf. vv. 5–6c). This latter test does not imply that the believers' status is elevated to be on a par with the apostles. The author's chief concern is to expose that the propaganda of the false teachers does not originate from God and is at variance with the Christian faith. Given this chief concern, the author avers that those who reject the Christian proclamation by him and other believers or true teachers actually do not possess the Spirit of truth.

1 JOHN 4:7—5:4

OUTLINE:

I. Body (1:5—5:12)

    A. Adhering to and Behaving in Conformity with the Christian Beliefs (1:5—2:27)

    B. Living as God's Children in View of Christ's Future Coming (2:28—4:6)

    C. Acting in Conformity with God's Loving Nature (4:7—5:12)

        1. Showing Love to the Christian Brothers and Sisters (4:7—5:4)

            a. The Reason to Love (4:7–10)

            b. Relying on God's Love (4:11–16b)

            c. Perfect Love Drives out Fear (4:16c–18)

            d. Loving God Involves Loving Fellow Believers (4:19–21)

            e. Love, Obedience, and Spiritual Victory (5:1–4)

C. Acting in Conformity with God's Loving Nature (4:7—5:12)

1. Showing Love to the Christian Brothers and Sisters (4:7—5:4)

Having exhorted his audience to exercise spiritual discernment in 1 John 4:1–6, the author seeks to influence them to practice the mutual love within the community in 1 John 4:7—5:4. The author creates coherence of this unit by employing the three cognate lexemes ἀγαπάω (19x), ἀγάπη (13x), and ἀγαπητοί (2x) from semantic domain 25 ("attitudes and emotions") altogether thirty-four times in 1 John 4:7—5:4.[1] In fact, the important topic of love predominates in the discourse until the transitional section in 1 John 5:1-4, in which both of the two lexemes ἀγαπάω and ἀγάπη occur for the last time in 1 John 5:2c and 1 John 5:3a, respectively, in this epistle. In this transitional section above, the author gradually shifts the focus from promoting the communal love to deal with the matter pertaining to the true faith that conquers the world. There is no consensus among the commentators on the structure of the discourse in 1 John 4:7—5:4.[2] On the basis of various linguistic features, including the occurrence of the vocative plural, the clustering of certain semantically related lexemes, and the change in topic, the discourse in 1 John 4:7—5:4 can be divided into five sections (i.e., 1 John 4:7-10, 4:11-16b, 4:16c-18, 4:19-21, 5:1-4). The commentary below will point out how the author uses different linguistic devices to signal the beginning of each section when necessary. The overall train of thoughts in these five sections is delineated as follows: (i) 1 John 4:7-10: The love of God is the reason and motivational basis of our obedience to the commandment to love one another. (ii) 1 John 4:11-16b: God has shown his love towards us through the sending of his Son to be the Savior of the world. (iii) 1 John 4:16c-18: The perfection of love in us causes us to have confidence in the judgment day. (iv) 1 John 4:19-21: We cannot truly love God without loving the Christian brothers and sisters. (v) 1 John 5:1-4: Loving God involves keeping his commandments and loving other members in his family. Furthermore, God's commandments are not burdensome because everyone who is born of God has conquered the world.

a. The Reason to Love (4:7–10)

The author hints at the topical shift from testing the spirits to the believers' mutual love by utilizing the vocative plural ἀγαπητοί (cf. 1 John 2:7; 3:2, 21; 4:1, 7, 11) to address his audience affectionately and repeating the covert

---

1. The three cognate lexemes ἀγαπάω (19x; cf. 1 John 4:7 [2x], 8, 10 [2x], 11 [2x], 12, 19 [2x], 20 [3x], 21 [2x]; 5:1 [2x], 2 [2x]), ἀγάπη (13x; cf. 1 John 4:7, 8, 9, 10, 12, 16 [3x], 17, 18 [3x]; 5:3), and ἀγαπητοί (2x; cf. 1 John 4:7, 11) occur frequently in the present unit in 1 John 4:7—5:4.

2. For example, Schnackenburg divides 1 John 4:7—5:4 into five sections (i.e., 4:7-10; 4:11-16; 4:17-18; 4:19—5:2; 5:3-4). Smalley observes the overall train of thought in 1 John 4:7—5:4 and divides this passage into four sections (i.e., 4:7-10; 4:11-16; 4:19-20; 4:21—5:4). Jobes discerns six small sections in 1 John 4:7—5:3 (i.e., 4:7-10; 4:11-14; 4:15-16; 4:17-18; 4:19-21; 5:1-3). See Schnackenburg, *Johannine Epistles*, 197–98; Smalley, *1, 2, 3 John*, 225; Jobes, *1, 2, and 3 John*, 186–201.

command to love one another in 1 John 4:7a. This covert command, which echoes the second aspect of God's twofold commandment in 1 John 3:23, is realized by the hortatory subjunctive ἀγαπῶμεν in connection with the reciprocal pronoun ἀλλήλους in v. 7a. In view of the use of the inclusive first-person plural ἀγαπῶμεν, the author invites his audience to join with him to practice the communal love. The author heightens the rhetorical force of the love commandment by virtue of the linguistic device of alliteration. Each of the first three words in the construction ἀγαπητοί ἀγαπῶμεν ἀλλήλους starts with the first letter alpha in Greek alphabet in v. 7a.[3] As indicated subsequently in v. 7b, the believers should love one another because the source of love is God. The articular nominative feminine singular noun ἀγάπη is placed adjacent to the prepositional phrase ἐκ τοῦ θεοῦ to underline the idea of love originating from God in v. 7b. The author uses the generic statements to associate God's children with the attribute of love in v. 7c–d. It is stated that everyone who loves has been born of God (v. 7c) and knows him (v. 7d). The lexeme γεννάω occurs in the perfect tense for the fourth time in 1 John 4:7c in this epistle (cf. 1 John 2:29; 3:9 [2x]). While the nominative masculine singular present active participle ἀγαπῶν does not have a complement in the embedded participial clause πᾶς ὁ ἀγαπῶν (v. 7c), it can be presumed that the object of the person's love is the Christian brothers and sisters. The implication is that loving other members in God's family is a distinguishing feature of his children. In accordance with the foregoing assertion that the believers can be sure of truly knowing God by obeying his commandments (cf. 1 John 2:3), the author affirms that the person who complies with the love commandment knows God and has a relationship to him in v. 7d.

As an antithesis of the positive depiction of the individual in 1 John 4:7, the author uses the negative generic statement to portray any person failing to love and not knowing God accordingly in 1 John 4:8a. The negative portrayal of the latter kind of people is in keeping with the author's sayings that everyone who does not love the Christian brothers and sisters does not belong to God and remains in death in the preceding co-text (cf. 1 John 3:10, 14).[4] The embedded participial clause ὁ μὴ ἀγαπῶν constitutes the subject of the third-person singular aorist active indicative verb ἔγνω, which is negated by the polarity adjunct οὐκ in v. 8a. The change from the present tense (cf. γινώσκει) in the mainline of the discourse in v. 7d to the aorist tense (cf. ἔγνω) in v. 8a may intimate that the author puts the emphasis

---

3. Brown, *Epistles of John*, 513; Sherman and Tuggy, *Semantic and Structural Analysis*, 79.

4. Jobes, *1, 2, and 3 John*, 190.

on the former positive example. The author explains that one cannot truly know God without love because God is love in v. 8b. There is a progression of ideas from the notion of love originating from God (v. 7b) to the notion of love being an attribute of God (v. 8b). It is worthy of mention that the clausal structure of the declaration "God is love" (i.e., ὁ θεὸς ἀγάπη ἐστίν) in 1 John 4:8b is akin to that of the foregoing assertion "God is light" (i.e., ὁ θεὸς φῶς ἐστίν) in 1 John 1:5b. In both of these two constructions above, the subject (i.e., ὁ θεός) is followed by the complement (i.e., ἀγάπη or φῶς) and subsequently the predicator ἐστίν. Moreover, the author points out God's nature to lay the grounds for the ethical mandate of loving one another in 1 John 4:8b or walking in the light in 1 John 1:5b.

The author elaborates the means by which the love of God is manifest among the believers in 1 John 4:9a–c. The prepositional phrase ἐν τούτῳ is cataphoric and used instrumentally at the outset of the main clause in v. 9a, which is followed by the two subordinate clauses that are headed by the conjunction ὅτι in v. 9b or ἵνα in v. 9c. The author utilizes the ὅτι-clause to convey the message that God's love is manifest through the sending of his own Son into the world in v. 9b. The complement (i.e., τὸν υἱὸν αὐτοῦ τὸν μονογενῆ) is placed in the thematic position to draw attention to God's one and only Son in this ὅτι-clause in v. 9b, in which the only occurrence of the lexeme μονογενής from semantic domain 58 ("nature, class, example") is present in this letter (cf. John 1:14, 18; 3:16, 18). While the aorist tense is used in v. 9a (cf. ἐφανερώθη) and v. 9c (cf. ζήσωμεν), the author employs the perfect tense (cf. ἀπέσταλκεν) to give prominence to the portrayal of God sending his one and only Son in v. 9b. This is the first time the lexeme ἀποστέλλω occurs with respect to God sending his Son for the benefit of the believers or the world (cf. 1 John 4:9, 10, 14). As expressed via the ἵνα-clause, the purpose of God sending his Son into the world is that we may live through the Son in v. 9c (cf. John 3:16). The lexeme ζάω is found only once in 1 John 4:9 in the whole letter. The cognate lexeme ζωή occurs altogether thirteen times in this letter (1 John 1:1, 2 [2x]; 2:25; 3:14, 15; 5:11 [2x], 12 [2x], 13, 16, 20), albeit its absence from the present section in 1 John 4:7—5:4. The antecedent of the genitive masculine singular pronoun (i.e., αὐτοῦ) in the prepositional phrase δι' αὐτοῦ (v. 9c) is the preceding masculine accusative singular noun υἱόν (v. 9b) with reference to the Son of God.

The author avails himself of the prepositional phrase ἐν τούτῳ again to orient his audience for what will follow at the beginning of 1 John 4:10 (cf. v. 9). The preceding occurrence of this prepositional phrase is concerned with the means of the manifestation of God's love in v. 9. In the present instance, the author utilizes the prepositional phrase ἐν τούτῳ (v. 10a) to anticipate the subsequent declaration regarding that what love consists of in v.

10b–d. He evinces that love is not defined by that we love God through the negative statement in v. 10b. The first-person plural perfect active indicative verb ἠγαπήκαμεν (v. 10b) is employed to heighten the idea that our love for God is not what love at bottom entails. As an antithesis to the negative statement above, the author uses the elided adversative conjunction ἀλλ' in connection with the epexegetical conjunction ὅτι to introduce the positive assertion that love consists of that God loved us in v. 10c. The antecedent of the nominative masculine singular pronoun αὐτός (v. 10c) is the accusative masculine singular noun θεόν that precedes in v. 10b. To expound the idea of God's love for the believers, the author affirms that God sent his own Son to be the atoning sacrifice for our sins in v. 10d. The adjunctive phrase ἱλασμὸν περὶ τῶν ἁμαρτιῶν ἡμῶν (v. 10d) is utilized to express that which causes God to send his Son to die for us. The lexeme ἱλασμόν from semantic domain 40 ("reconciliation, forgiveness") occurs for the second and last time in 1 John 4:10d in this epistle (cf. 1 John 2:2). The author has previously said that Jesus is the "atoning sacrifice" for our sins, and not only for ours but also for the sins of the whole world in 1 John 2:2. Furthermore, God cleanses the believers from all sins by means of Jesus' blood (1 John 1:7, 9). In line with these sayings in the preceding co-text, the author avers that God loved us and sent his Son to sacrifice his own life as the atonement for our sins so that God might forgive our sins in 1 John 4:10. Simply put, love is fundamentally defined by God's love for us and what he has done to bring salvation to the sinners.[5]

b. Relying on God's Love (4:11–16b)

For the sixth and last time, the author employs the vocative plural ἀγαπητοί to show affection and speak to his audience directly at the beginning of 1 John 4:11 (cf. 1 John 2:7; 3:2, 21; 4:1, 7). He uses the first-class conditional statement to promote the mutual love in the Christian community. The premise that God loves us is realized through the protasis containing the conditional conjunction εἰ in v. 11a. The adjunct οὕτως (v. 11a) subsequent to this conditional conjunction harks back to what was just said regarding God's sending his Son (v. 10). On account of the above premise concerning God's sacrificial love for us, the author infers that the believers are obliged to love one another through the apodosis in v. 11b. The first-person plural nominative pronoun ἡμεῖς functions as the subject of the first-person plural present active indicative verb ὀφείλομεν, which takes the embedded infinitival clause ἀλλήλους ἀγαπᾶν as the complement in this apodosis. It

---

5. Marshall, *Epistles of John*, 215.

is evident that the author underlines the correlation between God and the believers and thereby accentuates the Christian obligation to obey the love commandment. Worthy of notice is that the author places the accusative masculine plural reciprocal pronoun ἀλλήλους prior to the present active infinitive ἀγαπᾶν (v. 11b) to emphasize the object (i.e., one another in the Christian community) of our love. The lexeme ὀφείλω appears for the third and last time in 1 John 4:11b in this epistle (cf. 1 John 2:6; 3:16). In all of these three instances of this lexeme, the believers' ethical duty is based or modelled upon the act of Jesus or God.[6]

The author says that no one has ever seen God in 1 John 4:12a (cf. John 1:18; 5:37; 6:46). The accusative masculine singular noun θεόν is fronted to focus on "God" at the outset of v. 12a, in which the negative indefinite pronoun οὐδείς functions as the subject. The matter of the invisibility of God will be dealt with subsequently in 1 John 4:20. In the present co-text, the author attempts to promote the believers' communal love by means of the third-class conditional sentence in v. 12b-d. If the believers love one another (v. 12b), God remains in them (v. 12c) and his love reaches the state of perfection in them (v. 12d). The idea as to God's continual indwelling in or among the believers is present in a number of places in this letter (cf. 1 John 3:24; 4:12, 13, 15, 16).[7] The wording of the protasis (i.e., ἐὰν ἀγαπῶμεν ἀλλήλους) in v. 12b resonates with the foregoing implicit command (i.e., ἀγαπῶμεν ἀλλήλους), which is expressed by the hortatory subjunctive in 1 John 4:7a. The apodosis is made up of the two conjoined clauses linked by the coordinating conjunction καί in v. 12c-d. The author makes use of the perfect periphrastic construction τετελειωμένη ἐστίν to portray love reaching the state of perfection in v. 12d (cf. 1 John 1:4). Although the genitive construction ἡ ἀγάπη αὐτοῦ (v. 12d) can be construed as either the objective or subjective genitive, the latter understanding in the sense that God is the ultimate source of love is preferred because "God" is the subject in the prior clause in v. 12c. In short, the author seeks to encourage his audience to love the fellow believers by elucidating the desirable outcomes, which are enjoying God's abiding presence and bringing his love to full expression in 1 John 4:12.

The way by which the believers can have assurance of their mutually abiding relationship with God is elaborated in 1 John 4:13a-d. The prepositional phrase ἐν τούτῳ at the beginning of v. 13a anticipates the ὅτι-clause that follows in v. 13d. While the elliptical clause καὶ αὐτὸς ἐν ἡμῖν is without

---

6. Leung, "Ethics and *Imitatio Christi* in 1 John," 124–29.

7. The lexeme μένω is found altogether six times in 1 John 4:11–16 (vv. 12, 13, 15, 16 [3x]). In all of these six instances, this lexeme is connected with a prepositional phrase beginning with ἐν.

a predicator in v. 13c, the third-person singular present active indicative verb μένει can be implied and accordingly the author speaks of God remaining in us through this elliptical clause. The antecedents of the dative singular masculine pronoun αὐτῷ (v. 13b), the nominative singular masculine pronoun αὐτός (v. 13c), and the genitive singular masculine pronoun αὐτοῦ (v. 13d) are the same nominative singular masculine noun θεός that precedes in v. 12c. It has been declared that we can know God's indwelling in us by the Spirit whom he gave us in 1 John 3:24. Reminiscent of this foregoing declaration, the author avows that we can have the assurance of our mutually abiding relationship with God by virtue of the fact that he has given us of his Spirit in 1 John 4:13d. This latter avowal is prominent in light of the use of the perfect tense (i.e., δέδωκεν). It is probable that the prepositional phrase ἐκ τοῦ πνεύματος αὐτοῦ (v. 13d) expresses the partitive meaning in the sense that the believers are granted "a share in the Spirit," which is the evidence of their mutually abiding relationship with God.[8]

Following the initial conjunction καί, the first-person plural ἡμεῖς is probably exclusive with reference to the author and his co-workers in 1 John 4:14a.[9] Thus, the audience are not included as part of the referent of the exclusive "we." This first-person plural pronoun (i.e., ἡμεῖς) in the nominative case above is the subject of both of the subsequent first-person plural perfect active indicative verb τεθεάμεθα (v. 14a) and present active indicative verb μαρτυροῦμεν (v. 14b).[10] The author utilizes the linguistic device of the verbal projection to usher in the indirect locution vis-à-vis the Christian testimony, which pertains to that the Father has sent the Son to be the savior of the world in v. 14b–c. The predicator μαρτυροῦμεν (v. 14b) from semantic domain 33 ("communication") is used to project the indirect locution above, which is introduced by the subordinating conjunction ὅτι in v. 14c. The adjunctive phrase σωτῆρα τοῦ κόσμου, which is appositional to the accusative masculine singular noun υἱόν that precedes, is employed to point out the cause or purpose of the Father sending his Son in v. 14c. The only occurrence of the lexeme σωτήρ is present in this adjunctive phrase above in the three Johannine letters (cf. John 4:42). In both of 1 John 4:14c and John 4:42, the genitive construction σωτῆρα τοῦ κόσμου is the objective

---

8. Marshall, *Epistles of John*, 219; cf. Culy, *1, 2, 3 John*, 112; Brown, *Epistles of John*, 522.

9. Schnackenburg, *Johannine Epistles*, 219; Stott, *Letters of John*, 166–67; Jobes, *1, 2, and 3 John*, 196. For the alternative view that the author employs the device of the inclusive "we" in 1 John 4:14, see Marshall, *Epistles of John*, 220.

10. The combination of the two predicators τεθεάμεθα and μαρτυροῦμεν in 1 John 4:14 echoes with the relevant expressions concerning the eyewitness testimony in 1 John 1:1–2 in the prologue to this epistle.

genitive and in regard to the fact that Jesus came to bring salvation to the people of the world. The third-person singular perfect active indicative verb ἀπέσταλκεν appears for the third and last time in v. 14a in this letter (cf. 1 John 4:9, 10). In view of the twofold employment of the perfect tense (i.e., τεθεάμεθα [v. 14a] and ἀπέσταλκεν [v. 14c]), the author attaches importance to the notion of the eyewitness testimony regarding the Son's salvific mission in the world.

Instead of using the device of the first-person plural in v. 14, the author uses the generic subject to portray the whole class of people who acknowledge that Jesus is the Son of God in 1 John 4:15 (cf. 1 John 5:5). This generic subject is realized by the embedded relative clause ὃς ἐὰν ὁμολογήσῃ ὅτι Ἰησοῦς ἐστιν ὁ υἱὸς τοῦ θεοῦ in v. 15a. The Christological confession apropos Jesus' divine sonship above is in tune with the preceding assertion in 1 John 4:2, in which it is affirmed that every spirit that confesses that Jesus Christ has come in the flesh is from God. The author depicts that the person who acknowledges Jesus as the Son of God enjoys the mutually abiding relationship with God in 1 John 4:15b-c (cf. 1 John 3:24; 4:13, 16). The antecedents of both of the dative masculine singular pronoun αὐτῷ (v. 15b) and the nominative masculine singular pronoun αὐτός (v. 15c) are the entire embedded relative clause above in v. 15a. The author avails himself of the personal pronoun ἡμεῖς to hint at the topical shift from any person acknowledging Jesus as God's Son (v. 15) to the inclusive "we" with respect to the believers at the outset of v. 16. It is said that we have known and believed the love that God has in us. The lexeme ἀγάπη recurs in v. 16b since its prior occurrence as regards the perfection of God's love in the believers in 1 John 4:12d. The present saying is prominent in view of the combination of the two first-person plural perfect active indicative verbs ἐγνώκαμεν (v. 16a) and πεπιστεύκαμεν (v. 16b), which altogether have the effect of heightening the sense of a "complete trust and reliance."[11] Among the total nine occurrences of the lexeme πιστεύω in this epistle, this lexeme occurs in the perfect tense only once in 1 John 4:16b. The believers can be sure of their relationship to God given that they know and have put their trust on the love that God has in them. The author probably employs the prepositional phrase ἐν ἡμῖν to point out that the divine love is with respect to the believers or this love is manifest in the individual believers or Christian community at the end of v. 16b.[12]

---

11. Louw and Nida, *Greek-English Lexicon of the New Testament*, 1:375 (semantic domain 31.85).

12. Culy, *1, 2, 3 John*, 114; Smalley, *1, 2, 3 John*, 243; Brown, *Epistles of John*, 525-56; Marshall, *Epistles of John*, 221.

c. Perfect Love Drives Out Fear (4:16c–18)

For the second time, the author characterizes God as bearing the attribute of love through the use of the relational process clause (cf. the relational verb ἐστίν) in 1 John 4:16c (cf. v. 8). The wording of the construction ὁ θεὸς ἀγάπη ἐστίν (v. 16c) is reminiscent of the preceding affirmation of God's loving nature in 1 John 4:8b. In both of these two instances, the author places the complement (i.e., ἀγάπη) immediately after the subject (i.e., ὁ θεός) to enhance the connection between God and the notion of love. Since God is love, the person who remains in love remains in God and God remains in such a person in v. 16d–e (cf. 1 John 4:13, 15; John 15:9–10). There is a total of twenty-four occurrences of the lexeme μένω in this epistle.[13] The last three occurrences of this lexeme are present in the two clauses in 1 John 4:16d (2x) and 4:16e. In view of the foregoing exhortations regarding the communal love (cf. 1 John 4:7, 11–12), it is likely that the depiction of "abiding in love" (v. 16d) is not simply concerned with the reciprocal love between God and the believers but also the Christian obligation to love one another. It merits mention that the two clauses have a parallel structure in v. 16d and v. 16e. In both of these two clauses, the coordinating conjunction καί is followed in sequence by the subject (i.e., ὁ μένων ἐν τῇ ἀγάπῃ or ὁ θεός), the prepositional phrase (i.e., ἐν τῷ θεῷ or ἐν αὐτῷ), and the predicator μένει. Unlike the use of the ellipsis in the verbless clause in v. 13c or v. 15c, the author utilizes the third-person singular present active indicative verb μένει to be the predicator in v. 16e. As an outcome, the mutually abiding relationship between God and the person who abides in love is stressed in 1 John 4:16d–e.

The author uses the prepositional phrase ἐν τούτῳ to indicate the means by which love reaches perfection with the believers at the beginning of 1 John 4:17a. It is possible to construe the dative neuter singular demonstrative pronoun τούτῳ in this prepositional phrase above to anticipate the ensuing clause headed by the conjunction ὅτι in v. 17c.[14] That said, it is more likely that this prepositional phrase (v. 17a) is utilized to hark back to what the author has just said in v. 16d–e. The reason why the anaphoric reading of the prepositional phrase ἐν τούτῳ (v. 17a) is preferred is that the main clause in v. 17a and the ὅτι-clause in v. 17c are not in straight succession but rather separated by the ἵνα-clause in v. 17b (i.e., ἵνα παρρησίαν ἔχωμεν ἐν

---

13. The altogether twenty-four occurrences of the lexeme μένω are found in 1 John 2:6, 10, 14, 17, 19, 24 (3x), 27 (2x), 28; 3:6, 9, 14, 15, 17, 24 (2x); 4:12, 13, 15, 16 (3x).

14. Sherman and Tuggy, *Semantic and Structural Analysis*, 86–87; Longacre, "Exhortation and Mitigation in First John," 33.

τῇ ἡμέρᾳ τῆς κρίσεως).[15] Thus the author propounds that love "has reached perfection" (the perfect middle or passive indicative verb τετελείωται, cf. 1 John 2:5; 4:12, 18) with the believers by means of their mutually abiding relationship with God (cf. v. 16d-e). The meaning of the prepositional phrase μεθ' ἡμῶν is not evident in 1 John 4:17a. Nevertheless, it is probable that the author employs this preposition phrase to evoke the sense of an association with the believers as regards the perfection of love. Since the believers must show their love for God through loving other members in his family, the believers play a part in bringing about the full realization of love in the Christian community.

As said in v. 17b, the upshot of the perfection of love is that the believers may have confidence in the day of judgment. The idea of the judgment day pertains to the Jewish concept concerning the day of the Lord in the OT (cf. Isa 2:12-22; Joel 2:1-11, 32; Amos 5:18-20; Zeph 1:14-18) and Second Temple Judaism (cf. *Jub.* 5.10; 24.30; *Pss. Sol.* 15.13; *4 Ezra* 7.113).[16] The author gives emphasis to the positive notion of "confidence" by placing the accusative singular feminine noun παρρησίαν in the emphatic position prior to the predicator ἔχωμεν in 1 John 4:17b. This is the third time the lexeme παρρησία appears in this letter (cf. 1 John 2:28; 3:21; 4:17; 5:14). The eschatological overtone as to being confident in the judgment day in v. 17b echoes with the author's preceding directive given to his audience in 1 John 2:28, in which they are urged to abide in God or Jesus so that they may have "confidence" at the time when Jesus returns. The author further points out that the reason of the believers' confidence in the day of judgment is their present conformity to Jesus in this world in 1 John 4:17c-d.[17] It is apparent that there is a linkage between eschatology and ethics within the conceptual framework of this epistle (cf. 1 John 3:3; 4:17). The author heightens the corresponding relation between Jesus and the believers by employing the comparative conjunction καθώς (v. 17c) and the two pronouns ἐκεῖνος (v. 17c; cf. 1 John 2:6; 3:3, 5, 7, 16) and ἡμεῖς (v. 17d), which denote Jesus and the believers respectively.[18] Aside from the comparative clause in 1 John 4:17c, the following construction καθὼς ἐκεῖνος . . . ἐστιν is also found in 1 John 3:3b and 3:7c. In both of these two latter instances, Jesus' pure or righteous nature is expressed by the respective complement in the relevant

---

15. The following scholars think that the prepositional phrase ἐν τούτῳ is anaphoric in 1 John 4:17a. See Lieu, *I, II, & III John*, 193; Brown, *Epistles of John*, 526-27; Marshall, *Epistles of John*, 223; Yarbrough, *1-3 John*, 257; Jobes, *1, 2, and 3 John*, 204.

16. See Schnackenburg, *The Johannine Epistles*, 222-23n79; Brown, *Epistles of John*, 528.

17. Leung, "Ethics and *Imitatio Christi* in 1 John," 129-30.

18. Bennema, *Mimesis in the Johannine Literature*, 61, 132-34.

clauses (1 John 3:3b, 7c). However, there is no complement to specify what is compared between Jesus and the believers in 1 John 4:17c–d.[19] Nevertheless, the believers' likeness to Jesus is probably pertinent to the continually loving relationship with God (cf. v. 16), which is inseparable from the Christian commitment to practice the communal love.

Although the final judgment can be a cause for fear, the believers need not be afraid to be condemned because they follow in Jesus' footsteps in this world. The nominative masculine singular noun φόβος is placed at the forefront of the clause to emphasize the idea of the absence of fear in love in 1 John 4:18a.[20] All of the three occurrences of the lexeme φόβος from semantic domain 25 ("attitudes and emotions") are clustered in 1 John 4:18 (v. 18a, b, c) in this letter. In addition, the cognate lexeme φοβέομαι is present in v. 18d. Following the elided adversative conjunction ἀλλ᾿, the author employs the action verb βάλλει in connection with the locative adjunct ἔξω to portray vividly that perfect love "casts out" fear in v. 18b. It is explained that perfect love eliminates fear because fear has to do with the final punishment by God in v. 18c. The lexeme κόλασις occurs only once in 1 John 4:18 in the Johannine writings (cf. Matt 25:46). Earlier the author has affirmed that the believers have confidence in the day of judgment because of the perfection of love, which is achieved by virtue of their mutually abiding relationship with the loving God in 1 John 4:16–17. On the contrary, the person who is afraid of God's punishment on the day of judgment has not yet reached perfection in regard to love in v. 18d. The lexeme τελειόω appears for the fourth and last time in 1 John 4:18d in this epistle (cf. 1 John 2:5; 4:12, 17). In all of these four instances, a perfect form of the lexeme τελειόω is employed with an emphasis on the state of the perfection or full realization of love.

d. Loving God Involves Loving Fellow Believers (4:19–21)

Akin to the use of the inclusive first-person plural nominative pronoun ἡμεῖς in 1 John 4:14a and 4:16a, the author avails himself of this personal pronoun to be the emphatic subject of the predicator ἀγαπῶμεν and thereby points out that the believers are the topic of the message at the outset of

---

19. The first-person plural future verb ἐσόμεθα is found in lieu of the reading ἐσμεν in 1 John 4:17 in Codex Sinaiticus (ℵ or 01) and minuscules 876, 1832, and 2138. Yet this former variant (i.e., ἐσόμεθα) was probably the outcome of the scribal assimilation to the predicator ἐσόμεθα in 1 John 3:2 and thus is not original. See Yarbrough, *1–3 John*, 266; Smalley, *1, 2, 3 John*, 223n1.

20. Sherman and Tuggy, *Semantic and Structural Analysis*, 87.

1 John 4:19a. It is likely that this predicator (i.e., ἀγαπῶμεν [v. 19a]) in the first-person plural and present tense is not a hortatory subjunctive but rather is in the indicative mood.[21] Since the predicator ἀγαπῶμεν above does not have a complement, some scribes probably attempted to clarify that God is the object of the believers' love by supplying the unspecified complement in v. 19a (e.g., τὸν θεόν in codices Sinaiticus [ℵ or 01] and Vaticanus Graecus [048] and the Syriac and Bohairic versions, or αὐτόν in codex Athous Lavrensis [Ψ or 044] and the Byzantine witnesses). Nevertheless, the textual reading (i.e., ἡμεῖς ἀγαπῶμεν) without the complement and adopted in NA28 is likely to be authentic.[22] It is uncertain whether the author thinks of the believers' love for God or others in v. 19a.[23] Alternatively, it is possible that the author speaks of love as being the believers' distinguishing characteristic in general and without a specific object of the Christian love in mind.[24] In any case, the reason or basis of our love is that God first loved us in v. 19b. The nominative masculine singular pronoun αὐτός, which is the subject of the third-person singular aorist active indicative verb ἠγάπησεν, refers to God in v. 19b. Subsequent to this pronoun (i.e., αὐτός), the adjunct πρῶτος (v. 19b) is used to provide the additional information that God takes the initiative to show love towards the believers (presumably by sending his one and only Son, cf. 1 John 4:10, 14). While the present tense with the imperfective aspect (cf. ἀγαπῶμεν) is employed in the primary clause in v. 19a, the author shifts to use the aorist tense with the perfective aspect (cf. ἠγάπησεν) to suggest that God's love for us is conceived of as a whole in the secondary clause in v. 19b.

The author utilizes the third-class conditional statement to depict any person who professes to love God but hates his or her Christian brothers and sisters in 1 John 4:20a–c. Following the conditional conjunction ἐάν, the indefinite pronoun τις is the generic subject of the third-person singular aorist active subjunctive verb εἴπῃ in v. 20a and the subsequent third-person singular present active subjunctive verb μισῇ in v. 20c. The author avails himself of the word group ἀγαπῶ τὸν θεόν to realize the direct speech uttered by the generic participant in v. 20b. As lofty as this profession, "I love God," seems to be, it is proven to be false by the person's hatred against fellow believers. The author indicates his negative appraisal of this person

---

21. Kruse, *Letters of John*, 169n192; Stott, *Letters of John*, 170; cf. Schnackenburg, *Johannine Epistles*, 225.

22. Metzger, *Textual Commentary on the Greek New Testament*, 645.

23. Kruse believes that the implicit object of the believers' love is God in 1 John 4:19a. See Kruse, *Letters of John*, 169n192; cf. *NLT* ("we love each other"); Schnackenburg, *Johannine Epistles*, 225.

24. Smalley, *1, 2, 3 John*, 250; Brown, *Epistles of John*, 532.

by denoting him or her as a liar in the apodosis in v. 20d (cf. 1 John 1:6; 2:4). Notice that the complement ψεύστης is marked for emphasizing the person's identification as a liar in this apodosis. The author has expressed his unfavorable judgment of any individual hating his or her fellow believers a number of times in the preceding co-text (cf. 1 John 2:9, 11; 3:15). It is evident that the person who hates the Christian brothers and sisters neither has a true relationship to God nor loves him genuinely. The author further explains that any person not loving fellow Christians, whom he or she has seen, cannot love God, whom he or she has not seen in v. 20e. This explanatory statement is prominent in view of the twofold employment of the third-person singular perfect active indicative verb ἑώρακεν. It is worthy of notice that the ranking clause in v. 20e is the longest within the surrounding co-text in 1 John 4:7–21. The relatively long length of this ranking clause is partly due to the nesting of the altogether four embedded clauses, which are (1) the participial clause ὁ . . . μὴ ἀγαπῶν τὸν ἀδελφὸν αὐτοῦ, (2) the relative clause ὃν ἑώρακεν, (3) the relative clause ὃν οὐχ ἑώρακεν, and (4) the infinitival clause ἀγαπᾶν in v. 20e. As a rhetorical effect, the author builds suspense in such a way that the shocking idea regarding one's inability to love God (i.e., οὐ δύναται ἀγαπᾶν) is mentioned at the end of this ranking clause. Simply put, the author attempts to underscore the incompatibility between lacking love for the Christian brothers and sisters within our range of vision and loving the invisible God in v. 20e.

The author places the complement (i.e., ταύτην τὴν ἐντολήν) in the thematic position to orient the audience for what will be said concerning the commandment that the believers receive from God in 1 John 4:21. It is likely that God is the referent of the genitive masculine singular pronoun αὐτοῦ and thus the author speaks of the commandment from God in v. 21a. The accusative singular feminine demonstrative pronoun ταύτην (v. 21a) in this complement above points forward to the ensuing ἵνα-clause in v. 21b, in which the author avers that the person who loves God must also love his or her Christian brothers and sisters. The recurrence of the lexeme ἐντολή (v. 21a) resonates with the foregoing mention of God's twofold commandment to believe in the name of his Son and love one another in 1 John 3:23. In fact, the employment of this lexeme in connection with the epexegetical ἵνα-clause is suggestive of the implicit command to love the fellow Christians in 1 John 4:21. In a nutshell, the author indicates that a person's lack of love for other members in God's family invalidates his or her claim to love God and shows it to be an empty profession.

e. Love, Obedience, and Spiritual Victory (5:1–4)

The present section is transitional to the succeeding unit in 1 John 5:5-12. The author's dealing with the believers' mutual love draws to a close in 1 John 5:1-4, in which the last occurrences of the lexemes ἀγάπη (vv. 1b, 3a), ἀγαπάω (vv. 1b, 2b, c), and ἐντολή (vv. 2d, 3b, c) are present in this letter. Aside from the relevant word group τὰ τέκνα τοῦ θεοῦ (v. 2b), the author utilizes the construction γεννάω ἐκ τοῦ θεοῦ thrice to express the idea of born of God in this unit (vv. 1a, b, 4a; cf. 1 John 2:29; 3:9; 4:7; 5:18). The author also picks up the topic of faith in Jesus Christ by employing the lexeme πιστεύω in 1 John 5:1a. This lexeme has appeared for the first time with respect to God's commandment to believe in the name of his Son, Jesus Christ, in 1 John 3:23 and will recur a total of five times in 1 John 5:5-13 (vv. 5, 10 [3x], 13; cf. 1 John 4:1, 16) in the remainder of this epistle. The author says that everyone who believes that Jesus is the Christ has been born of God in v. 1a, in which the entire construction πᾶς ὁ πιστεύων ὅτι Ἰησοῦς ἐστιν ὁ Χριστός constitutes the generic subject. Furthermore, the prepositional phrase ἐκ τοῦ θεοῦ is used for intimating that God is the agent causing the spiritual birth in v. 1a. The author has affirmed that God's children must do what is right (1 John 2:29), avoid sin (1 John 3:9), and love fellow believers (1 John 4:7) in the preceding co-text. In line with these foregoing affirmations above, the author puts forward the general principle that everyone who loves the father loves the person born of him too in 1 John 5:1b.[25] On the one hand, it is possible that the two embedded participial clauses τὸν γεννήσαντα and τὸν γεγεννημένον ἐξ αὐτοῦ refer specifically to God and the believer as his child, respectively, in v. 1b.[26] On the other hand, these two embedded participial clauses above can be construed as evincing the general principle pertaining to any individual's loving relationships with his parent and siblings.[27] At any rate, the author evidently uses the generic statement to lend support to the exhortation that the believers' love for God must find expression in their love for his children in 1 John 5:1b.

---

25. Among the total ten occurrences of the lexeme γεννάω in this letter, there are only two instances in which this lexeme occurs in the aorist tense in 1 John 5:1b (cf. γεννήσαντα) and 5:18c (cf. γεννηθείς). All of the remaining eight occurrences of this lexeme are in the perfect tense (1 John 2:29d; 3:9a, 9d; 4:7c; 5:1a, 1b, 4, 18b).

26. Kruse, *Letters of John*, 171; Akin, *1, 2, 3 John*, 188; Jobes, *1, 2, and 3 John*, 208. Contra Augustine's understanding that the embedded participial clause τὸν γεγεννημένον ἐξ αὐτοῦ refers to Jesus Christ as the Son of God. See Augustine, *Homilies on the First Epistle of John*, 147.

27. Stott, *Letters of John*, 172; Marshall, *Epistles of John*, 227.

The author employs the combination of the prepositional phrase ἐν τούτῳ and the lexeme γινώσκω for the eighth and last time to elucidate how we can be sure that we love the children of God in 1 John 5:2 (cf. 1 John 2:3, 5; 3:16, 19, 24; 4:2, 13).[28] If the prepositional phrase ἐν τούτῳ above (v. 2a) is anaphoric, the believers can know that they love God's children whenever they love God by virtue of the general principle as set forth in v. 1b (i.e., everyone who loves the parent loves his child too).[29] If this prepositional phrase above (v. 2a) is cataphoric, the believers can be sure of their love towards the fellow Christians by loving God (cf. the complement τὸν θεόν is marked in v. 2c) and carrying out his commandments (cf. the complement τὰς ἐντολὰς αὐτοῦ is marked in v. 2d) in v. 2c-d. In this latter reading, the dative neuter singular demonstrative pronoun τούτῳ (v. 2a) is considered to point forward to the subsequent clause beginning with the subordinating conjunction ὅταν in v. 2c.[30] Given that the prepositional phrase ἐν τούτῳ with the lexeme γινώσκω is often used to refer to what will be said in the ensuing co-text (cf. 1 John 2:3, 5; 3:16, 24; 4:2, 13), the cataphoric reading of this prepositional phrase in 1 John 5:2a above is preferable. While the author's contention has been that our love for God is evidenced by our love for his children in the preceding co-text (e.g., 1 John 3:14–18; 4:7–12, 20; 5:1), it is probable that the author brings in the flip side of this contention in the reverse direction by pointing out that our love for God's children is evidenced by our love for him in 1 John 5:2.[31] In fact, the two notions of love for God and love for his children are intertwined in Johannine thinking. On the one hand, the believers cannot truly love God without loving the fellow Christians. On the other hand, genuine love for God's children takes root in love for him. The variant τηρῶμεν at the end of 1 John 5:2 that is found in a number of manuscripts (e.g., ℵ, A, P^pr, most of the minuscules and the Byzantine witnesses) probably arose as the outcome of the scribal attempt to harmonize with the common wording regarding "keeping God's commandments" in this letter (cf. 1 John 2:3, 4, 5; 3:22, 24; 5:3). The peculiar combination of the first-person plural present active subjunctive verb ποιῶμεν and the complement τὰς ἐντολὰς αὐτοῦ is the more difficult reading and thus likely to be authentic in v. 2d.[32]

---

28. Brown, *Epistles of John*, 535. The predicator ἀγαπῶμεν in the present tense is likely to be in the indicative, not subjunctive, mood in 1 John 5:2.
29. Marshall, *Epistles of John*, 227–28; Schnackenburg, *Johannine Epistles*, 125.
30. Brown, *Epistles of John*, 536–37; Culy, *1, 2, 3 John*, 121.
31. Brown, *Epistles of John*, 537–38.
32. Metzger, *Textual Commentary on the Greek New Testament*, 646.

The author provides the reason in support of the conceptual linkage between loving God and obeying his commandments in 1 John 5:3. The nominative feminine singular demonstrative pronoun αὕτη (v. 3a) points forward to the subsequent ἵνα-clause in v. 3b, in which the author expounds that doing what God commands is the defining feature of the believers' love for God. It is likely that the genitive construction ἡ ἀγάπη τοῦ θεοῦ is the objective genitive in v. 3b. This is the last time the lexeme ἀγάπη (18x) is detected in the whole letter (1 John 2:5, 15; 3:1, 16, 17; 4:7, 8, 9, 10, 12, 16 [3x], 17, 18 [3x]; 5:3). Notice that the complement τὰς ἐντολὰς αὐτοῦ is placed prior to the first-person plural present active subjunctive verb τηρῶμεν to focus attention on the notion of "God's commandments" in v. 3b (cf. 1 John 2:3; 3:22; 5:2). Upon pointing out that obedience is an essential feature of the Christian love for God, the author uses the negative statement to elaborate that God's commandments are not burdensome and difficult to obey in v. 3c.[33] As noted in 1 John 5:4a, the reason why the commandments of God are not burdensome for his children is that everyone who is born of God overcomes the world (cf. 1 John 2:14; 4:4). In fact, the believers' spiritual victory over the world and their power to withstand its temptations are grounded in the accomplished conquest of the world by Jesus Christ (cf. John 16:33). The fifth and last occurrence of the lexeme νικάω from semantic domain 39 ("hostility, strife") is present in the embedded participial clause ἡ νίκη ἡ νικήσασα τὸν κόσμον, which as a whole constitutes the subject in v. 4b (cf. 1 John 2:13, 14; 4:4; 5:4a). Notably, the author juxtaposes the lexically related noun νίκη and aorist active participle νικήσασα in this embedded participial clause above to accentuate the idea of victory over the world. This is the only time the lexeme νίκη is found in the Johannine epistles. The employment of the aorist tense with the perfective aspect (cf. the participle νικήσασα above) suggests that the overcoming of the world is conceived of as a complete event in v. 4b. It is the author's conviction that the believers' faith empowers them to conquer the world. The feminine singular nominative demonstrative pronoun αὕτη, which is the complement of the predicator ἐστίν,[34] points forward to the ensuing word group ἡ πίστις ἡμῶν in 1 John 5:4. This verse contains the only occurrence of the lexeme πίστις in the Johannine epistles and the Fourth Gospel. In the subsequent co-text, the author will expound that the correct belief about Jesus is necessary for the believers' spiritual victory over the temptations of the world in 1 John 5:5–12.

33. The lexeme ἐντολή is detected altogether fourteen times in 1 John 2:3, 4, 7 (3x), 8; 3:22, 23 (2x), 24; 4:21; 5:2, 3 (2x).

34. Cf. the word group καὶ αὕτη ἐστίν in 1 John 1:5; 2:25; 3:23; 5:4, 11, 12; 2 John 6. See Brown, *Epistles of John*, 192.

1 JOHN 5:5–12

OUTLINE:

II. Body (1:5—5:12)

    A. Adhering to and Behaving in Conformity with the Christian Beliefs (1:5—2:27)

    B. Living as God's Children in View of Christ's Future Coming (2:28—4:6)

    C. Acting in Conformity with God's Loving Nature (4:7—5:12)

        1. Showing Love to the Christian Brothers and Sisters (4:7—5:4)

        2. The True Faith in Christ as the Basis of Spiritual Victory (5:5-12)

            a. The three Witnesses of Christ (5:5-8)

            b. The Testimony of God (5:9-12)

2. The True Faith in Christ as the Basis of Spiritual Victory (5:5–12)

The present section in 1 John 5:5–12 is located in the final part of the letter body. The linkage of this section with the preceding discourse is established by reiterating the idea concerning the believers' victory over the world in v. 5a, in which the lexeme νικάω from semantic domain 39 ("hostility, strife") occurs for the sixth and last time in this letter (cf. 1 John 2:13, 14; 4:4; 5:4 [2x], 5). Having affirmed the conquering power of the true faith in 1 John 5:4, the author endeavors to expound the Christological content of this faith that is grounded in the person of Jesus Christ the Son of God. Furthermore, the author corroborates his Christological assertion by pointing out the witnesses to the Son. The predominance of the topic of testimony is evident in the concentration of the altogether ten occurrences of the two cognate lexemes μαρτυρέω (4x; cf. vv. 6, 7, 9, 10) and μαρτυρία (6x; cf. vv. 9 [3x], 10 [2x], 11) in this section in 1 John 5:5-12. The present section can be divided into two units, i.e., 1 John 5:5-8 and 5:9-12. In the first unit (1 John 5:5-8), the author underlines that the Spirit, the water, and the blood in concert bear witness to Jesus Christ, who has come to bring salvation to those who believe in him. The coherence of this unit is created in part through the repeated occurrences of the following three lexemes ὕδωρ (vv. 6 [3x], 8), αἷμα (vv. 6 [2x], 8), and πνεῦμα (vv. 6 [2x], 8) in 1 John 5:5-8. The second unit focuses on the testimony that God has testified about his Son in 1 John 5:9-12. God's gift of the eternal life is granted only to those who accept this testimony. Aside from the altogether six occurrences of the lexeme μαρτυρία (vv. 9 [3x], 10 [2x], 11), the author employs the two lexemes ζωή and ἔχω four times (vv. 11 [2x], 12 [2x]) and five times (vv. 10, 12 [4x]) respectively to enhance the internal coherence in this unit (i.e., 1 John 5:9-12). Both of these two latter lexemes are absent from the prior unit in 1 John 5:5-8.

a. THE THREE WITNESSES OF CHRIST (5:5-8)

The author makes use of the rhetorical question to engage his audience and accentuate the affirmation vis-à-vis Jesus' divine sonship in 1 John 5:5a-b at the beginning of this section. The clausal structure of this rhetorical question (i.e., τίς δέ ἐστιν . . . εἰ μὴ . . . ὅτι Ἰησοῦς ἐστιν ὁ υἱὸς τοῦ θεοῦ;) in v. 5a-b is reminiscent of that in 1 John 2:22a-b (i.e., τίς ἐστιν . . . εἰ μὴ . . . ὅτι Ἰησοῦς οὐκ ἔστιν ὁ Χριστός;). In the present instance, the interrogative pronoun τίς and the embedded participial clause ὁ νικῶν τὸν κόσμον are the complement and the subject respectively in the primary clause in v. 5a. The secondary clause starts with the word group εἰ μή, which functions as "a marker of contrast by designating an exception" in v. 5b.[1] As a corollary, the author tactually utilizes the rhetorical question to affirm that only the person who believes that Jesus is God's Son conquers the world in v. 5b (cf. 1 John 4:15). This affirmation is in tune with the foregoing saying, which is that everyone who believes that Jesus is the Christ has been born of God in 1 John 5:1a. Given these pertinent statements regarding Jesus' divine sonship or messianic status, it is evident that the faith that empowers the believers to

---

1. Louw and Nida, *Greek-English Lexicon of the New Testament*, 1:794 (semantic domain 89.131).

overcome the world's temptations and hostile forces takes root in correct Christology.

The means by which Jesus Christ came to accomplish his salvific mission is elucidated via the statements in 1 John 5:6a–c. The author provides the information that Jesus Christ came by water and blood—not by water only, but by water and blood. The antecedent of the nominative masculine singular demonstrative pronoun οὗτος (v. 6a) is the noun Ἰησοῦς that precedes in v. 5b.[2] Yet, the author makes explicit the referent of this demonstrative pronoun by the word group Ἰησοῦς Χριστός at the end of v. 6a in such a way that the audience's attention will be focused on God's Son.[3] This is the fifth time the compound name "Jesus Christ" is detected in this epistle (cf. 1 John 1:3; 2:1; 3:23; 4:2; 5:6, 20). The nominative masculine singular aorist active participle ἐλθών with the perfective aspect is employed to portray the "coming" of Jesus Christ by water and blood as a complete event in v. 6a. In the Fourth Gospel, "the coming one" is a predominant Christological designation (which is expressed by various forms of the participial construction ὁ ἐρχόμενος) regarding Jesus' messianic status (e.g., John 1:15, 27, 30; 4:25; 6:14; 11:27; 12:13; cf. John 1:9; 3:31; 7:27, 31, 41, 42).[4] The textual reading δι' ὕδατος καὶ αἵματος (1 John 5:6a) adopted in NA28 is supported by codices Vaticanus (B or 03) and Athous Lavrensis (Ψ or 044), the Vulgate, and the Byzantine witnesses. The anarthrous construction ὕδατος καὶ αἵματος is the object of the elided preposition δι' above in v. 6a. In addition to the two genitive nouns ὕδατος and αἵματος in this anarthrous construction above, the third genitive noun πνεύματος is found in the variant readings in a number of manuscripts including codices Sinaiticus (ℵ or 01), Alexandrinus (A or 02), and Porphyrianus (P^apr or 025).[5] Depending on the order of the two genitive nouns αἵματος and πνεύματος in the variant readings, Jesus Christ is depicted as coming "by water and blood and spirit" or "by water and spirit and blood," accordingly. In either case, the extra word πνεύματος was probably due to the influence by John 3:5 and is thus inauthentic in 1 John 5:6a.[6]

The two elliptical clauses (i.e., οὐκ ἐν τῷ ὕδατι μόνον and ἀλλ' ἐν τῷ ὕδατι καὶ ἐν τῷ αἵματι) are contrastive to each other in 1 John 5:6b–c, in which the notion of Jesus Christ coming by blood is emphasized. The author increases audience engagement by creating an expectation regarding

---

2. Culy, *1, 2, 3 John*, 124.
3. Culy, *1, 2, 3 John*, 124.
4. Köstenberger, *Theology of John's Gospel and Letters*, 319.
5. For the variants and manuscripts, see *Novum Testamentum Graecum*, 6.1:348.
6. Metzger, *Textual Commentary on the Greek New Testament*, 646.

the idea that Jesus Christ did not come only by water via the first negative elliptical clause above in v. 6b. To counter this expectation rhetorically (v. 6b), the author utilizes the subsequently elliptical clause beginning with the elided adversative conjunction ἀλλ' to aver that Jesus Christ came by water and by blood in v. 6c.[7] Notice that the preposition ἐν with the dative, instead of the preposition διά with the genitive (cf. v. 6a), is employed in both of the two elliptical clauses in v. 6b–c.[8] Despite the prior mention of Jesus coming in the flesh in 1 John 4:2 (cf. 2 John 7), there is no sufficient evidence to establish the case that the "water" is the symbol of Jesus' incarnation. The "blood" of Jesus has been referred to with respect to his sacrificial death in 1 John 1:7 (cf. 1 John 5:8; John 19:34). Most scholars construe that the two imageries of "water" and "blood" point to Jesus' baptism (or his baptizing work) and his death, respectively, in v. 6b–c.[9] The baptism of Jesus by John the Baptist was widely regarded as the starting point of Jesus' ministry in early Christianity and is explicitly mentioned in John 1:33, in which the prepositional phrase ἐν ὕδατι is present (cf. John 1:26, 31). Alternatively, it is possible to interpret the author's portrayal of Jesus Christ coming by water and blood in 1 John 5:6a as alluding to the flowing out of "blood and water" from Jesus' side at his crucifixion in John 19:34.[10] In other words, both of the two imageries "water" and "blood" point to Jesus' death in this epistle. Nevertheless, the likelihood of this allusion decreases when it is observed that the two words "water" and "blood" are in reverse order in 1 John 5:6a, as compared with the sequence of these two words in John 19:34. While it is difficult to determine with certainty, the former understanding that the "water" and the "blood" point to Jesus' baptism (or his baptizing work) and his death, respectively, is preferred in this commentary. At any rate, it is probable that the author's opponents undermine the salvific significance of Jesus' death albeit their acknowledgement of his baptism or baptizing ministry.

---

7. Contra Schnackenburg, *Johannine Epistles*, 233–34. It is unlikely that the "water" and the "blood" symbolize the two sacraments of baptism and eucharist respectively in 1 John 5:6.

8. The variant ἐν τῷ ὕδατι καὶ τῷ αἵματι (cf. the single preposition ἐν) is found in 1 John 5:6 in ℵ, 436, 442, 642, 1448, 2492, the Byzantine witnesses, and other manuscripts. This variant is considered as equal to the textual reading (i.e., ἐν τῷ ὕδατι καὶ ἐν τῷ αἵματι) in the critical apparatus in NA28.

9. Jobes, Campbell, and Marshall consider that the "water" is a symbol of Jesus' baptism. See Jobes, *1, 2, and 3 John*, 222; Campbell, *1, 2, and 3 John*, 156–58; Marshall, *Epistles of John*, 231–35. For Kruse and Yarbrough, the "water" points to Jesus' baptizing work. See Kruse, *Letters of John*, 174–78; Yarbrough, *1–3 John*, 282. All of the scholars above believe that the "blood" refers to Jesus' death.

10. Brown, *Epistles of John*, 566–67.

The author speaks of the Spirit as the one who testifies in 1 John 5:6d, in which the embedded participial clause τὸ μαρτυροῦν constitutes the complement of the predicator ἐστίν. As stated subsequently in v. 6e, the reason or basis of the Spirit's testifying work is that the Spirit is the truth (cf. John 15:26; 16:13). The witness given by the Spirit is presumably pertinent to Jesus' baptism (or his baptizing work) and especially his death in view of what was just said in v. 6a–c. The author puts forward another reason or basis as regards the Spirit's witnessing work in vv. 7–8a. There are three that testify, namely the Spirit, the water, and the blood. Following the subordinating conjunction ὅτι, the cardinal number τρεῖς is marked to underline "three" witnesses in 1 John 5:7. There is a scholarly consensus that the so-called Johannine Comma regarding the textual interpolation between 1 John 5:7 and 5:8 in several late Greek manuscripts (e.g., 61, 918, 2318, 2473, the margins of 88, 221, 429, 636) is not original.[11] The insertion of the Johannine Comma in effect adds the extra information that the Father, the Word, and the Holy Spirit are the three witnesses in heaven; and the Spirit, the water, and the blood are the three witnesses on earth. However, the author in all likelihood mentions only the latter three witnesses (i.e., the Spirit, the water, and the blood) of Jesus and without noting their earthly location in 1 John 5:7–8.[12] Since the Spirit is spoken of prior to the water and the blood, the Spirit's testimony is attached importance in v. 8a. The author's recourse to the three Christological witnesses above is in accord with the Jewish law that at least two or three testimonies are necessary to establish the conclusive evidence of any fact (cf. Deut 17:6; 19:15). Although all of the three nouns πνεῦμα, ὕδωρ, and αἷμα are neuter in v. 8a, the author employs the masculine plural nominative present active participle μαρτυροῦντες (v. 7) to depict vividly that the Spirit, the water, and the blood give testimonies. On the one hand, the use of this participle in the masculine is in tune with the author's understanding of the Spirit as a person. On the other hand, the author probably avails himself of the incongruence between the grammatical genders (i.e., the three neuter nouns in connection with the masculine participle above) to heighten the rhetorical effect of the assertions about the Christological witnesses in 1 John 5:7–8a.[13] As averred in v. 8b, the three witnesses (i.e., the Spirit, the water, and the blood) are in agreement (cf. the prepositional phrase εἰς τὸ ἕν). On the assumption that the "water" symbolizes Jesus' baptism or baptizing ministry and the "blood" symbolizes his

---

11. Metzger, *Textual Commentary on the Greek New Testament*, 647–49; Culy, *1, 2, 3 John*, 127; Yarbrough, *1–3 John*, 293. For a list of the manuscripts containing the so-called Johannine Comma, see *Novum Testamentum Graecum*, 4.1:350.

12. Culy, *1, 2, 3 John*, 127.

13. Marshall, *Epistles of John*, 237n20.

death, it is unbecoming to accept the reality of Jesus' baptism or baptizing ministry while repudiating the factuality of his crucifixion or subverting its salvific significance.

b. The Testimony of God (5:9–12)

After underlining the certitude and unity of the three witnesses of Jesus Christ the Son of God, the author uses the first-class conditional sentence to bring up the topic of the testimony of God in 1 John 5:9 (cf. v. 11). There is one occurrence of the lexeme μαρτυρία in each of the three clauses in v. 9a, v. 9b, and v. 9c. In addition, the first-person plural perfect active indicative verb μεμαρτύρηκεν is related to this lexeme (i.e., μαρτυρία) in the succeeding clause in v. 9d. Following the conditional conjunction εἰ, the author places the complement (i.e., the word group τὴν μαρτυρίαν τῶν ἀνθρώπων) prior to the predicator λαμβάνομεν to underline the human testimony in the protasis in v. 9a. The witness that John the Baptist bore to Jesus is referred to as a human testimony, which is less weighty than the Father's testimony to his Son in the Fourth Gospel (cf. John 5:33–36). That said, it is unlikely that the human testimony pertains to specifically the Baptist's witness in 1 John 5:9a because he is never mentioned explicitly in this epistle.[14] Rather, the author probably speaks of the general phenomenon that we accept human testimony in v. 9a.[15] The author continues to set forth the statement of fact that God's testimony is greater in v. 9b (cf. John 5:36–37). This is the third and last time the nominative masculine singular comparative adjective μείζων is employed with reference to the superiority of God in this letter (cf. 1 John 3:20; 4:4; 5:9). Granted the true premise that we generally accept human testimony, it can be readily inferred from this premise that we should accept God's greater testimony for his Son. However, the author does not spell out this consequent explicitly through an apodosis, which is missing in 1 John 5:9. Rather than speaking of our obligation to accept God's testimony, the author expounds that God's testimony is superior because it is the testimony that which he has testified about his Son in v. 9c–d. Each of the two clauses starts with the subordinating conjunction ὅτι in v. 9c and v. 9d. The function of this subordinating conjunction is causal in v. 9c, in which the nominative feminine singular demonstrative pronoun αὕτη points forward to the epexegetical ὅτι-clause in v. 9d. It is noteworthy that the author gives prominence to the affirmation that God has testified regarding his Son by employing the third-person singular perfect active indicative verb μεμαρτύρηκεν in v. 9d.

---

14. Contra Brown, *Epistles of John*, 586.
15. Jobes, *1, 2, and 3 John*, 223; Schnackenburg, *Johannine Epistles*, 238n123.

Among the total six occurrences of the lexeme μαρτυρέω in this letter, only the last two occurrences of this lexeme regarding the testimony of God are in the perfect tense in 1 John 5:9–10 (see below; cf. 1 John 1:2; 4:14; 5:6, 7). In view of this, the author seeks to accentuate God's testimony concerning his Son. It is unspecified whether the testimony of God is considered as completely distinct to the concerted witnesses of the Spirit, the water, and the blood in 1 John 5:9d (cf. 1 John 5:6–8). Yet, it is reasonable to presume that God's testimony about his Son is concerned with the unified testimony of these three witnesses.

There is a total of three occurrences of the lexeme πιστεύω in 1 John 5:10a–c. The author uses the two embedded participial clauses (i.e., ὁ πιστεύων εἰς τὸν υἱὸν τοῦ θεοῦ and ὁ μὴ πιστεύων τῷ θεῷ) to realize the two generic participants, which are antithetical to each other in v. 10a–b. As indicated in v. 10a, the person who believes in the Son of God has the testimony in himself or herself. The predicator ἔχει is employed in connection with the complement (i.e., τὴν μαρτυρίαν) to express the idea of accepting and holding fast to God's testimony about his Son in v. 10a.[16] It is likely that the prepositional phrase ἐν αὐτῷ (v. 10a) carries a reflexive sense and thus implicating the locative meaning of being in the person above.[17] In contrast to the person who believes in God's Son and possesses God's testimony (v. 10a), the individual who does not believe God has made him a liar (cf. 1 John 1:10) because this individual has not believed in the testimony which God has testified concerning his Son in v. 10b–c. The dative phrase τῷ θεῷ is the complement of the nominative masculine singular present active participle πιστεύων in v. 10b, in which the lexeme ψεύστης appears for the fifth and last time in this epistle (cf. 1 John 1:10; 2:4; 2:22; 4:20; 5:10). Both of the accusative masculine singular noun ψεύστην and pronoun αὐτόν (whose referent is God) are the complements of the predicator πεποίηκεν in 1 John 5:10b (cf. the similar structure in 1 John 1:10b). The implication is that the individual who does not believe God causes him to bear the feature of a liar and in effect God's truthful character is disclaimed. Notice that the author employs the perfect tense thrice to give prominence to the negative depiction of this individual in v. 10b–c (cf. πεποίηκεν [v. 10b], πεπίστευκεν [v. 10c], μεμαρτύρηκεν [v. 10c]). By underscoring the negative example in

---

16. The feminine accusative singular article τήν (v. 10a) harks back to the testimony of God in v. 9c. Note the variant τὴν μαρτυρίαν τοῦ θεοῦ in 𝔓[74], codex Alexandrinus (A or 02), and the Latin and Bohairic translations. See Marshall, *Epistles of John*, 241.

17. Yarbrough, *1–3 John*, 293; Brown, *Epistles of John*, 589. The variant ἐν ἑαυτῷ has been adopted in NA27. This variant is attested in codices Sinaiticus (א or 01) and Athous Lavrensis (Ψ or 044) and several minuscules (e.g., 5, 1243, 1611, 1739).

v. 10b–c, the author has rhetorically put weight on the preceding positive example of the person who believes in God's Son in v. 10a.[18]

The sixth and last occurrence of the lexeme μαρτυρία is concerned with God's testimony and the gift of the eternal life in 1 John 5:11 (cf. vv. 9 [3x], 10 [2x]). The nominative feminine singular demonstrative pronoun αὕτη (v. 11a), which is the complement of the predicator ἐστίν, points forward to the ensuing clause headed by the subordinating conjunction ὅτι in v. 11b. It merits mention that the clausal structure in v. 11a–b (i.e., αὕτη ἐστὶν ἡ μαρτυρία, ὅτι . . .) is parallel to that in v. 9c–d (i.e., αὕτη ἐστὶν ἡ μαρτυρία τοῦ θεοῦ, ὅτι . . .). In both of these two instances, the author avails himself of the identifying relational process clause (cf. the relational verb ἐστίν) and the subsequent ὅτι-clause to indicate the defining characteristic of God's testimony. In the present instance, the testimony of God is linked with the notion of the eternal life in 1 John 5:11. It is said that God has given eternal life to the believers (cf. the inclusive first-person plural pronoun ἡμῖν), who accept and hold fast to his testimony regarding his Son). Following the conjunction ὅτι, the complement ζωὴν αἰώνιον is marked and placed in the thematic position to orient the audience in v. 11b. The author further elaborates the notion of eternal life by indicating that this life is in the Son in v. 11c. The nominative feminine singular demonstrative pronoun αὕτη (v. 11c) is anaphoric and harks back to the "eternal life" mentioned in v. 11b. The author goes on to characterize the eternal life as being in the Son of God in 1 John 5:11c. It follows that the person who has the Son possesses this life, too, in 1 John 5:12a. In contrast, the person who does not have the Son of God does not possess the eternal life in v. 12b. It is apparent that the two generic participants, who are expressed by the two embedded participial clauses ὁ ἔχων τὸν υἱὸν and ὁ μὴ ἔχων τὸν υἱὸν τοῦ θεοῦ, respectively, are antithetical to each other in v. 12a–b. Furthermore, the placement of the complement τὴν ζωὴν prior to the predicator ἔχει is emphatic in v. 12b. Simply put, the author affirms the admirable upshot of the person having God's Son in 1 John 5:12a by presenting its opposite with the use of the negative statement in v. 12b. As a result, the positive outcome (i.e., the possession of the eternal life) of having the Son is rhetorically underscored.[19]

---

18. Sherman and Tuggy, *Semantic and Structural Analysis*, 96.
19. Sherman and Tuggy, *Semantic and Structural Analysis*, 97.

1 JOHN 5:13–21

OUTLINE:

I. Prologue (1:1–4)

II. Body (1:5—5:12)

III. Conclusion (5:13–21)

    A. Confidence in Prayer (5:13–17)

    B. Concluding Assurance and Exhortation (5:18–21)

III. CONCLUSION (5:13–21)

The author signals that he has reached the closing of his letter by indicating his main purpose of corresponding with his audience in 1 John 5:13. There is a change in participant from the generic subjects, the testimony or eternal life in the prior section in 1 John 5:5–12, to the author and his audience in 1 John 5:13a. In the closings of the other two Johannine epistles, the Elder expresses his desire to visit the addressee and sends a final greeting in 2 John 12–13 or 3 John 13–15. In addition, there is a peace benediction near the end of 3 John. Yet, these epistolary features above are missing in the conclusion in 1 John.[1] Rather than enhancing rapport with his audience, the author endeavors to reassure his audience that they possess the eternal life and belong to God in the concluding section of this letter. There are certain lexico-grammatical features that suggest the broad division of 1 John 5:13–21 into the two units in vv. 13–17 and vv. 18–21. For example, there is a cluster of altogether eight occurrences of various lexemes from

---

1. For the main features and function of the closing in ancient Hellenistic letters, see White, "Greek Documentary Letter Tradition," 91–95.

semantic domain 33 ("communication") in the first unit in vv. 13–17, as compared to the absence of any lexeme from this semantic domain in the second unit in vv. 18–21. These various lexemes from this semantic domain include γράφω (v. 13), αἰτέω (vv. 14, 15 [2x], 16), αἴτημα (v. 15), λέγω (v. 16), and ἐρωτάω (v. 16). Furthermore, the lexeme θάνατος appears a total of four times in 1 John 5:16–17 within the first unit but is not detected in the second unit. In contrast to the concentration of the two cognate lexemes ἁμαρτάνω (2x) and ἁμαρτία (4x) in vv. 16–17 in the first unit, the former lexeme ἁμαρτάνω appears once (cf. v. 18) and the latter lexeme is wanting in vv. 18–21. It is worth noting that the author creates the structural coherence of the second unit by starting each of the three clause complexes with the predicator οἴδαμεν at the outset of v. 18, v. 19, and v. 20. The commentary below will analyze the conclusion of this letter according to the two-part division in 1 John 5:13–21 as mentioned above.

A. Confidence in Prayer (5:13–17)

To begin to conclude his letter, the author affirms that his audience believe in the name of the Son of God and consequently possess the eternal life in 1 John 5:13 (cf. vv. 10–11; John 20:31). The neuter plural accusative demonstrative pronoun ταῦτα, which is the complement of the predicator ἔγραψα, is fronted to emphasize and intimate the topical theme at the outset of v. 13a. This is the last time the lexeme γράφω occurs in this letter. Among the total thirteen occurrences of this lexeme in this letter, only its first occurrence is in the first-person plural in 1 John 1:4 in the prologue to this letter. All of the remaining twelve occurrences of this lexeme are in the first-person singular (1 John 2:1, 7, 8, 12, 13 [2x], 14 [3x], 21, 26; 5:13). While the demonstrative pronoun ταῦτα (v. 13a) above could refer to just that which was said in the foregoing section in vv. 5–12, it probably refers to the whole letter.[2] The author has utilized the word group ταῦτα γράφομεν in connection with the ἵνα-clause to explain why he writes to his audience in 1 John 1:4 at the end of the prologue.[3] In a similar fashion, he uses the combination of the word group ταῦτα ἔγραψα ὑμῖν (cf. 1 John 2:1, 26) and the following ἵνα-clause to express the goal of his writing in 1 John 5:13. Thus the two purpose statements altogether form an *inclusio* to frame the letter body (i.e., 1 John 1:5—5:12) in 1 John 1:4 and 5:13. In the present instance, the author writes to his audience so that they may know that they have eternal life. The entire embedded participial clause τοῖς πιστεύουσιν εἰς τὸ ὄνομα τοῦ υἱοῦ τοῦ

---

2. Kruse, *Letters of John*, 188; Jobes, *1, 2, and 3 John*, 225.
3. Jobes, *1, 2, and 3 John*, 225.

θεοῦ serves as the definer of the dative second-person plural pronoun ὑμῖν that precedes in v. 13. The author makes use of this embedded participial clause to provide the additional information concerning the audience, who are portrayed as those believing in the name of the Son of God (cf. John 1:12; 3:18; 20:31). Notably, the two dependent clauses ἵνα εἰδῆτε and ὅτι ζωὴν ἔχετε αἰώνιον are placed between the demonstrative pronoun ὑμῖν and this embedded participial clause (i.e., τοῖς πιστεύουσιν εἰς τὸ ὄνομα τοῦ υἱοῦ τοῦ θεοῦ) above to stress the purpose (cf. the telic conjunction ἵνα) of this epistle in v. 13. Although the accusative feminine singular noun ζωήν is modified by the accusative feminine singular adjective αἰώνιον, the author draws attention to the notion of "life" by assigning this noun (i.e., ζωήν) the thematic position in the ὅτι-clause in v. 13. In short, it is of the author's interest that his audience are sure of their possession of the eternal life in the conclusion of this letter.

The author deals with the believers' confidence before God in relation to the matter of prayer in 1 John 5:14. While a total of three second-person plural expressions (i.e., ὑμῖν, εἰδῆτε, and ἔχετε) are employed with reference to the audience in v. 13, the author shifts to use the inclusive first-person plural expressions (i.e., ἔχομεν, αἰτώμεθα, and ἡμῶν) to show commonness with his audience in v. 14. The second-person plural will not be employed to denote the audience again until 1 John 5:21 at the end of this epistle (see below). The clausal structure (i.e., καὶ αὕτη ἐστὶν . . . ὅτι . . .) in v. 14a–b is reminiscent of that respecting the preceding clauses in v. 9c–d (i.e., ὅτι αὕτη ἐστὶν . . . ὅτι . . .) or v. 11a–b (i.e., καὶ αὕτη ἐστὶν . . . ὅτι . . .). The nominative feminine singular demonstrative pronoun αὕτη (v. 14a) anticipates the ensuing ὅτι-clause (v. 14b), which is appositional to this demonstrative pronoun (i.e., αὕτη) that precedes. The lexeme παρρησία (v. 14a) is employed for the fourth and last time to depict the believers' confidence in God (cf. 1 John 2:28; 3:21; 4:17; 5:14), who hears them if they ask him anything according to his will in v. 14b (cf. 1 John 3:21–22).[4] The lexeme θέλημα is found only twice in 1 John 2:17 and 5:14 in the whole epistle. In both of these two instances, the author speaks of the "will" of God. The placement of the accusative neuter singular indefinite pronoun τι, which functions as the complement of the first-person plural present middle subjunctive verb αἰτώμεθα, is emphatic in the third-class protasis in v. 14b. The implication is that the author seeks to emphasize "whatever" the believers ask God in accordance with his will. There is an occurrence of the lexeme αἰτέω pertaining to the believers' petition to God in v. 14b. This lexeme will subsequently be employed three times regarding the matter of prayer in v. 15c, v. 15e, and

---

4. Akin, *1, 2, 3 John*, 205.

v. 16b (cf. 1 John 3:22). It is probable that the author utilizes the first-person plural present middle subjunctive verb αἰτώμεθα to draw attention to the subject, which is encoded by the inclusive "we" with reference to the believers as the beneficiary of the answered prayers in v. 14b (cf. v. 15c).[5] Moreover, the notion of God hearing our petitions is affirmed twice through the two statements in v. 14c and v. 15b.

The third-class conditional sentence is made up of a total of five clauses in 1 John 5:15a–e. The first three clauses constitute the protasis in v. 15a–c and the succeeding two clauses constitute the apodosis in v. 15d–e. Since the premise is pertinent to the believers' certitude of their answered prayers, the protasis is actually used to express a statement of fact in v. 15a–c. Thus, since we are certain that God hears us as to whatever we ask (v. 15a–c), we know that we have the requests which we have asked from him (v. 15d–e). It can be presumed that the believers' petitions are in accordance with God's will on account of what was just said in 1 John 5:14. Notably, the author attaches importance to this positive consequent regarding the believers' certitude of answered prayers by employing the perfect tense (cf. ᾐτήκαμεν) in v. 15e. Furthermore, the rhetorical impact of this positive upshot vis-à-vis answered prayers is heightened through the use of the accusative neuter plural noun αἰτήματα (v. 15e), which is lexically related to this indicative verb above.

The author uses the third-class conditional statements to give information to his audience again in 1 John 5:16a–c. He tells them that if any person sees his Christian brother or sister committing a sin not resulting in (spiritual) death, this person should pray and God will give life to the sinner. The juxtaposition of the accusative masculine singular present active participle ἁμαρτάνοντα and the lexically related accusative feminine singular noun ἁμαρτίαν accentuates the rhetorical effect in v. 16a. In lieu of the second-person plural expressions with reference to the audience or the inclusive "we" (cf. vv. 13–15), the author shifts to use the generic subject without a specific referent and thereby softens the generic statements with respect to the sinner in v. 16a–c. It is probable that the author does not simply use the third-person singular future verb αἰτήσει to depict what the person will do for the sinner in v. 16b. Rather, the author utilizes this future verb above to intimate the covert directive in the third-person that the person has to pray for the Christian brother or sister who commits a sin not leading to death.[6] The outcome of this intercessory prayer is elaborated in v.

---

5. Culy, *1, 2, 3 John*, 133.

6. Jobes, *1, 2, and 3 John*, 234; Kruse, *Letters of John*, 190; Brown, *Epistles of John*, 611–12. Yet, Stott thinks that the author employs the future active form αἰτήσει to simply describe "the Christian's inevitable and spontaneous reaction" (*Letters of John*, 185).

16c, in which the third-person singular future active verb form δώσει does not have a specified subject. Since the indefinite pronoun τις is the generic subject of the two predicators ἴδῃ and αἰτήσει that precede in v. 16a–b, it is possible to construe that this indefinite pronoun is the unspecified subject of the predicator δώσει in v. 16c. Thus the person gives life to the sinful Christian in the sense that God, upon hearing this person's intercession for him or her, bestows life on this Christian who has not committed a mortal sin.[7] Nevertheless, the implicit subject of this predicator (i.e., δώσει) in v. 16c is probably God because he alone can give life to an individual, albeit the believer's petition can be the instrument via which the gift of life is granted to the sinner.[8] It deserves mention that there is a grammatical mismatch in number in regard to the dative plural masculine present active participle ἁμαρτάνουσιν and the dative singular pronoun αὐτῷ, whose referent is the sinner in v. 16c. Rather than focusing on an individual, it is possible that the author utilizes this grammatical mismatch in number to attract attention rhetorically and make reference to the whole class of people who have not committed a mortal sin.

As an antithesis to the sin not resulting in death, there is a sin that leads to death in 1 John 5:16d. The negative polarity adjunct οὐ is fronted to accentuate the negated idea in v. 16e, in which the author utilizes the first-person singular present active indicative verb λέγω to speak to his audience directly. Aside from the lexeme γράφω, this is the only instance in which the author employs the first-person singular form of a verb for self-reference in this epistle.[9] Following this negative polarity adjunct οὐ above, the feminine singular genitive demonstrative pronoun ἐκείνης in the prepositional phrase περὶ ἐκείνης (v. 16e) is used to point backward to the sin resulting in death (cf. v. 16a). In lieu of the lexeme αἰτέω (cf. 1 John 3:22; 5:14, 15 [2x], 16), the author employs another lexeme ἐρωτάω to express the idea of petitioning God in 1 John 5:16f (cf. 2 John 5).[10] The change of terminology does not suggest a significant difference in meaning pertaining to making request to God.[11] It is likely that the author does not simply use the third-person singular aorist active subjunctive verb ἐρωτήσῃ (v. 16f) to portray that the believer would pray, but rather implicates the covert command "he should

---

7. Stott, *Letters of John*, 185–86.
8. Marshall, *Epistles of John*, 236n17.
9. The prior occurrence of the first-person singular (cf. ἔγραψα) is present in 1 John 5:13 at the beginning of the letter closing. Regarding the saying verb λέγω in 1 John 5:16, Brown observes that "only here in 1 John does the author use of himself the first-person singular form of a verb other than 'write'" (*Epistles of John*, 612).
10. The lexeme ἐρωτάω occurs only once in 1 John 5:16 in this letter.
11. Marshall, *Epistles of John*, 246n19.

pray." Therefore, the author explicates that the exhortation to pray for the sinner is not given with respect to the sin that leads to death in v. 16e–f. Yet, it should be remarked that the author does not forbid the believers to intercede for the people who commit the mortal sin. It is rather the case that his treatment of the Christian intercession focuses on the sin that does not lead to death in 1 John 5:16.[12]

The author reminds his audience that all unrighteousness is sin but there is sin not leading to death in 1 John 5:17a–b. The coordinating conjunction καί serves as "a marker of emphasis" at the beginning of v. 17b.[13] The first occurrence of the lexeme ἀδικία is present in 1 John 1:9, in which the author asserts that God will forgive us our sins and cleanse us from all "unrighteousness" if we confess our sins to him. The corollary of this assertion in 1 John 1:9 is that there are times when Christians may commit a sin. Furthermore, the question arises of why a Christian can possess eternal life in spite of his or her wrongdoing. The author explicates that not all sin has the consequence of death, albeit all "unrighteousness" is considered as sin in 1 John 5:17. Thus, the believer who commits a sinful act can possess eternal life because this is not a mortal sin. There are different approaches to construe the distinction between the sin not resulting in death and the sin resulting in death in 1 John 5:16–17.[14] For example, the mortal sin in 1 John 5:16 can be linked with the unforgivable sin of blasphemy against the Holy Spirit in Jesus' saying in the Synoptic Gospels (Matt 12:31–32; Mark 3:28–30; Luke 12:10). Alternatively, it has been observed that the dealings of certain sins are distinguished into two types according to whether the sinner has acted unintentionally or intentionally in the Jewish laws in the OT (cf. Lev 4:2, 13, 22, 27; 5:15–18; Num 15:30–31; Deut 17:12). Moreover, the sins of idolatry, murder, and adultery are so abhorrent that they have the capacity of producing moral impurity, which degrades the status of the people, the temple, and the land of Israel in Jewish thinking.[15] In particular, the sin of idolatry or murder is mentioned in 1 John 3:15 and 5:21 in this letter. Nevertheless, it should be stressed that the distinction between

12. The author's saying in 1 John 5:16 resonates with Jesus' prayer to the Father in John 17:9 (cf. the two occurrences of the lexeme ἐρωτάω), in which Jesus does not pray for the world but for those the Father has given him. See Jobes, *1, 2, and 3 John*, 237; Brown, *Epistles of John*, 618.

13. Louw and Nida, *Greek-English Lexicon of the New Testament*, 1:811 (semantic domain 91.12); Sherman and Tuggy, *Semantic and Structural Analysis*, 99.

14. See the discussion in Jobes, *1, 2, and 3 John*, 234–37; Kruse, *Letters of John*, 190–94; Akin, *1, 2, 3 John*, 208–10.

15. The ultimate punishment of committing the heinous sins is expulsion from the land. See the discussion about the notion of moral impurity in Klawans, *Impurity and Sin in Ancient Judaism*, 21–42; Klawans, "Moral and Ritual Purity," 266–84.

the sin leading to death and the sin not leading to death must take into consideration the author's depiction of the two different kinds of people in 1 John 5:12.[16] There it is stated that the person who has the Son has eternal life but the person who does not have God's Son does not have life. The corollary is that the mortal sin is likely concerned with the refusal to believe in Jesus Christ the Son of God in 1 John 5:16 (cf. 1 John 3:23; 5:10, 12). Viewed against the background of the historical situation of this letter, the sin that leads to death can also be related to the secessionists who have left the church.[17] They neither acknowledge Jesus as the Christ and God's Son nor uphold the belief that he has come in the flesh. In any event, there is no hint that the children of God are associated with the sin that leads to death in this epistle.[18]

B. Concluding Assurance and Exhortation (5:18–21)

The matter of sin continues to be the topic of discussion in v. 18a–b, in which the last occurrence of the lexeme ἁμαρτάνω (v. 18b) is present. There are three clause complexes in v. 18a–d, v. 19a–c, and v. 20a–e. Each of these three clause complexes starts with the first-person plural perfect active indicative verb οἴδαμεν (vv. 18a, 19a, 20a; cf. v. 15), which is followed by the subordinating conjunction ὅτι (vv. 18b, 19b, 20b) to usher in the author's saying to his audience. The author has indicated that everyone who has been born of God does not commit sin because God's seed remains in the person in 1 John 3:9 (cf. 1 John 3:6). Now the author reassures his audience that everyone who has been born of God does not sin in 1 John 5:18b. In both of these two generic statements above, the subject is made up of the embedded participial clause πᾶς ὁ γεγεννημένος ἐκ τοῦ θεοῦ with reference to God's children in 1 John 3:9 or 5:18b.[19] While the full realization of the believers' sinlessness awaits the arrival of the eschaton, they are presently under the spiritual protection of God or his Son as they resist against the temptations of sin in this hostile world. Since the one who was born of God protects the believer, the evil one (i.e., the devil; cf. 1 John 3:8, 10) is not able

---

16. Jobes, *1, 2, and 3 John*, 235–36; Kruse, *Letters of John*, 194; Brown, *Epistles of John*, 617–18.

17. Wahlde, *Three Johannine Letters*, 204; Painter, *1, 2, and 3 John*, 317.

18. Akin, *1, 2, 3 John*, 210; Thompson, *1–3 John*, 143; Culpepper, *Gospel and Letters of John*, 274.

19. The combination of the lexeme γεννάω and the prepositional phrase ἐκ τοῦ θεοῦ or ἐξ αὐτοῦ is found in 1 John 2:29; 3:9; 4:7; 5:1, 4, 18.

to harm him or her in v. 18c–d.[20] The referent of the embedded participial clause ὁ γεννηθεὶς ἐκ τοῦ θεοῦ can be either the believer or God's Son in v. 18c. The author has employed a perfect form of the lexeme γεννάω to affirm the believers' status as God's children a number of times in the preceding co-text (cf. 1 John 2:29; 3:9 [2x]; 4:7; 5:1 [2x], 4, 18). Yet, he utilizes the aorist passive participle γεννηθείς to depict "the one who was born of God" in 1 John 5:18c.[21] It is noteworthy that the accusative masculine singular personal pronoun αὐτόν adopted previously in v. 18c in NA27 has been altered to the accusative masculine singular reflexive pronoun ἑαυτόν in NA28.[22] It follows that the one who was born of God in all likelihood refers to the believer in v. 18c. Thus the author portrays the believer guarding himself or herself, though God is presumably the ultimate agent who causes the believer's secure protection.[23] Alternatively, if the variant αὐτόν above (cf. NA27) is favored over the textual reading ἑαυτόν that was adopted in NA28, it is possible to construe that the author speaks of Jesus Christ the Son of God safeguarding the believers and so the devil is not able to destroy their faith in v. 18c–d.[24] This latter understanding is in consonance with Jesus' saying regarding his protection of the disciples in John 17:12, in which the lexeme τηρέω is found (cf. John 17:15). Whether "the one born of God" (v. 18c) denotes the believer or Jesus Christ, it is certain that God's children are protected spiritually from the harm of the devil and will not succumb to the secessionists' erroneous teaching accordingly.

The author deals with the Christian assurance of having a relationship to God in 1 John 5:19a–b. Following the subordinating conjunction ὅτι, the prepositional phrase ἐκ τοῦ θεοῦ is placed prior to the predicator ἐσμεν to underline the notion of belonging to God in v. 19b. In contrast to the believers' spiritual standing, the whole world exists in close association with the evil one in v. 19c (cf. John 12:31; 14:30; 16:11). This is the fifth and last time the devil is referred to as "the evil one" in this epistle (1 John 2:13, 14; 3:12;

20. The lexeme ἅπτω from semantic domain 20 ("violence, harm, destroy, kill") is a *hapax legomenon* in 1 John 5:18 in this letter.

21. Note that the accusative masculine singular aorist active participle γεννήσαντα is present in 1 John 5:1.

22. The reading αὐτόν adopted in NA27 is attested in codices Alexandrinus and Vatincanus and the Latin tradition. The textual reading ἑαυτόν, which is adopted in NA28, is attested in codices Sinaiticus and Athous Lavrensis and a number of the minuscules including 33, 81, and 322. See the discussion in Yarbrough, *1–3 John*, 321; Metzger, *Textual Commentary on the Greek New Testament*, 650.

23. Sherman and Tuggy, *Semantic and Structural Analysis*, 101; Culy, *1, 2, 3 John*, 137; Thompson, *1–3 John*, 146–67.

24. Kruse, *Letters of John*, 195; Smalley, *1, 2, 3 John*, 289–90; Marshall, *Epistles of John*, 252.

5:18, 19). The author has said that Jesus Christ is the atoning sacrifice not only for our sins but also for the sins of the whole world in 1 John 2:2. Yet, the individuals who repudiate this atoning sacrifice do not belong to God and thus continue to exist as part of the world, which lies under the power of the evil one in 1 John 5:19.

The first-person plural perfect active indicative verb οἴδαμεν recurs and is linked with the postpositive conjunction δέ, which serves as "a marker of additive relation" in 1 John 5:20a.[25] The author reminds his audience of the Christian certitude regarding the coming of God's Son to give understanding to the believers in v. 20b–c.[26] The lexeme ἥκω occurs only once in 1 John 5:20b in this epistle and is not detected in 2 or 3 John. This lexeme is present in Jesus' saying that he has come from God in John 8:42. The author foregrounds the depiction of the Son giving understanding to the believers by employing the third-person singular perfect active indicative verb δέδωκεν in v. 20c. As a result of what the Son has done for the believers, they may know the One who is true in v. 20d. Although the "true light" probably denotes Jesus in 1 John 2:8, it is likely that God is the referent of the "true one" (i.e., τὸν ἀληθινόν) in 1 John 5:20d (cf. John 17:3). In fact, the accusative masculine singular noun θεόν was inserted to specify God as the One who is true in this verse in codices Alexandrinus (A or 02) and Athous Lavrensis (Ψ or 044), minuscules 5, 33, and 436, and the Vulgate. Nevertheless, the reading without the additional θεόν in NA28 is the more difficult reading and supported by codices Sinaiticus (ℵ or 01), Vaticanus (B or 03), and Porphyrianus (P^{apr} or 025), as well as the Syriac and Byzantine witnesses.[27] As elaborated in v. 20e, the believers are in union with the One who is true because they are in union with his Son, Jesus Christ. The compound name "Jesus Christ" occurs in connection with the epithet "Son" a total of three times in this letter (1 John 1:3; 3:23; 5:20). The author indicates that the believers can be certain of their mutual indwelling with God by the Spirit whom God has given them (cf. 1 John 3:24; 4:13).[28] Simply put, the author attempts to assure his audience positively apropos their connection with the Father, the Son, and the Spirit.

The author continues to aver that "this one" (cf. the nominative masculine singular demonstrative pronoun οὗτος) is the true God and eternal life through the statement in 1 John 5:20f. The lexeme ἀληθινός from

---

25. Louw and Nida, *Greek-English Lexicon of the New Testament*, 1:789 (semantic domain 89.94).

26. The lexeme διάνοια is found only once in 1 John 5:20 in the Johannine writings.

27. Metzger, *Textual Commentary on the Greek New Testament*, 650–51.

28. Kruse, *Letters of John*, 197.

semantic domain 72 ("true, false") recurs in v. 20f (cf. v. 20d, e). It is debatable whether the referent of the demonstrative pronoun οὗτος (v. 20f) above is the Father or the Son. Some scholars think that this demonstrative pronoun refers to the Father because he is consistently denoted as "God" in the preceding co-text.[29] Nevertheless, it is likely that the referent of the demonstrative pronoun οὗτος (v. 20f) is Jesus Christ on account of the following four observations. First, the nearest noun to this demonstrative pronoun is Ἰησοῦ in the genitive case that precedes in v. 20e. Second, the author has employed the demonstrative pronoun οὗτος with reference to Jesus previously in 1 John 5:6a. Third, Jesus is spoken of as the eternal life in 1 John 1:2. Moreover, the author says that eternal life is bestowed on those who have the Son in 1 John 5:12. Fourth, Jesus Christ is explicitly portrayed as "God" in the Fourth Gospel (cf. John 1:1, 18; 20:28). In a nutshell, the author probably affirms Jesus' divinity by identifying him as the true God and the source of eternal life in 1 John 5:20f.[30]

The author draws his letter to a close by utilizing the vocative plural noun τεκνία to address his audience directly for the sixth and last time in 1 John 5:21 (cf. 1 John 2:12, 28; 3:7, 18; 4:4; 5:21). Following this direct address to his audience, the author issues the command to them to guard themselves from the idols in v. 21. This command is realized by the second-person plural aorist active imperative verb φυλάξατε in connection with the accusative neuter plural reflexive pronoun ἑαυτά and the subsequent prepositional phrase ἀπὸ τῶν εἰδώλων. It is of the author's concern that the believers should beware being attracted to or associated with the "idols," which are evidently antithetical to the "true God" just mentioned in v. 20f.[31] It should be noted that the combination of the second-person plural aorist active imperative verb φυλάξατε and the reflexive pronoun ἑαυτά is telling that the believers bear the responsibility of guarding their spiritual health despite that they are protected from the harm of the evil one (cf. v. 18). In addition, the employment of the aorist tense with the perfective aspect suggests that the action of keeping watch against the influence of the idols is viewed as complete. The lexeme φυλάσσω appears only once in 1 John 5:21 in this letter. This lexeme is employed to express the positive meaning of "guarding" one's life (John 12:25), "obeying" Jesus' words (John 12:47), or Jesus "guarding" the disciples (John 17:12) in the Fourth Gospel. Moreover, the combination of the lexeme φυλάσσω and the preposition ἀπό is used

---

29. Smalley, *1, 2, 3 John*, 294.

30. For the aforesaid arguments, see Yarbrough, *1–3 John*, 320; Akin, *1, 2, 3 John*, 214–15.

31. Campbell, *1, 2, and 3 John*, 170.

with respect to Jesus' command to guard from every kind of greed in Luke 12:15 and Paul's saying about the Lord guarding the believers from the evil one in 2 Thessalonians 3:3.[32] It is worthy of mention that the exhortation to the audience to keep themselves from the idols probably resonates with the polemics against idolatry in the Jewish tradition (e.g., Deut 4:28; Pss 115:3–8; 135:15–18; Isa 44:9–20; Jer 10:5; Zech 13:2).[33] The author does not spell out what the "idols" refer to in 1 John 5:21. Broadly speaking, there are four different understandings of the referent of these "idols."[34] Firstly, it is possible to consider the "idols" literally with reference to the physical statutes or images of the Greco-Roman deities. However, the author does not deal with any Greco-Roman deity or pagan cult explicitly in this epistle. Secondly, the "idols" can be understood metaphorically to represent the false beliefs concerning God or Christ and in particular the secessionists' incorrect Christology as regards Jesus' messiahship or filial relationship to God.[35] The third understanding of the "idols" is that they are a synonym for sin in view of the linkage between the notions of idolatry and sin in several Dead Sea scrolls (e.g., 1QS II, 11–12, 17; IV, 5; CD XX, 9).[36] According to this understanding, the author urges his audience to abstain from sins in 1 John 5:21.[37] Fourthly, it has been proposed that the "idols" do not have any specific referent but rather denote generally the evil world system of the ideas and practices against God.[38] It is difficult to determine with certainty the meaning of the "idols" in 1 John 5:21. That said, the second interpretation above is preferred in this commentary because it takes into account the historical situation as to the purpose of the author in writing this epistle. Therefore, the believers should guard themselves from the false beliefs opposed to the Christian convictions regarding God or his Son Jesus Christ, who alone is the way, the truth, and the life (cf. John 14:6).

---

32. For the biblical references, see Marshall, *Epistles of John*, 255n50.

33. Jobes, *1, 2, and 3 John*, 243.

34. Brown lists ten different understandings of the "idols" in 1 John 5:21. See Brown, *Epistles of John*, 626–29.

35. Jobes, *1, 2, and 3 John*, 243; Kruse, *Letters of John*, 202; Brown, *Epistles of John*, 628–29; Marshall, *Epistles of John*, 255–56; Campbell, *1, 2, and 3 John*, 170–71.

36. For the references in the Dead Sea Scrolls, see Marshall, *Epistles of John*, 255n53.

37. Marshall, *Epistles of John*, 255.

38. Lieu, *I, II, & III John*, 237.

COMMENTARY ON
2 JOHN

THE SECOND LETTER OF JOHN is the only NT epistle in which the author uses the figurative language of a woman with her children to identify the recipient (i.e., a Christian congregation with her members) in cryptic terms in the opening prescript (v. 1a; cf. v. 13). This brief letter is the second shortest book in the NT, consisting of a total of 245 words in altogether thirty-three ranking clauses.[1] Most of these ranking clauses are declarative clauses that are utilized to realize various assertive statements in the service of the persuasive goals in this epistle. While 2 John contains a greater number of words than 3 John, there are fewer ranking clauses in 2 John than 3 John. The latter epistle contains a total of 218 words in altogether thirty-eight ranking clauses (see "Commentary on 3 John"). Broadly speaking, the ranking clauses in 2 John are relatively packed with information partly due to the nesting of plenty of embedded participial or infinitival clauses in them. The relatively high lexical density of the ranking clauses in 2 John suggests that this letter has a more written "mode" than 3 John (see "Mode" in "Introduction").[2]

The two main participants are the Elder and the chosen lady in 2 John. If the nine first-person plural expressions (vv. 2 [2x], 3, 4, 5 [2x], 6, 8, 12) and one occurrence of the reciprocal pronoun ἀλλήλους (v. 5) are counted, there is a total of twenty-four direct or indirect participant references to

---

1. The altogether thirty-three ranking clauses are present in 2 John 1a, 1b, 1c, 1d–2, 3, 4a, 4b, 4c, 5a, 5b, 6a, 6b, 6c, 6d, 6e, 7a, 7b, 7c, 8a, 8b, 8c, 9a, 9b, 9c, 10a, 10b, 10c, 10d, 11, 12a, 12b, 12c, 13. The participial clause οἱ μὴ ὁμολογοῦντες Ἰησοῦν Χριστὸν ἐρχόμενον ἐν σαρκί is considered as an elliptical clause in v. 7b. The participial clause ὁ μένων ἐν τῇ διδαχῇ is considered as a minor clause in v. 9b. These two elliptical or minor clauses above are counted as two ranking clauses in 2 John in this commentary.

2. For the topic related to the lexical density, see Eggins, *Introduction to Systemic Functional Linguistics*, 92–93.

the Elder in this letter.³ There are altogether thirty (or twenty-nine) direct or indirect participant references to the chosen lady in 2 John, including the nine occurrences (or eight occurrences if the subject of the predicator εἰργασάμεθα [v. 8] is the exclusive "we") of the inclusive first-person plural expressions (vv. 2 [2x], 3, 4, 5 [2x], 6, 8 [?], 12), one occurrence of the relative pronoun οὕς (v. 1), and one occurrence of the reciprocal pronoun ἀλλήλους (v. 5).⁴ Aside from the Elder and the chosen lady, the false teachers are another participant that are referred to quite frequently in 2 John. There is a total of fifteen explicit or implicit references to the false teachers including the relevantly generic references in vv. 9–11.⁵ In view of this, it is apparent that the problem caused by the false teachers is of the Elder's concern.

As for the aim of 2 John, the Elder wrote this letter to attempt affecting the audience's behavior so that they would not welcome the false teachers or be succumbed to the negative influences of their erroneous Christology. In close connection with this aim, the Elder sought to promote the Christian way of life in the truth that entails mutual love and an obedience to God's commandments. It deserves mention that the three lexemes (i.e., ἀλήθεια [vv. 1, 2, 3, 4], ἀγάπη [vv. 1, 3, 6], ἐντολή [vv. 4, 5, 6]), which are loaded with positive connotations regarding the Christian living, occur in connection with each other in the prescript and the first half of the body in 2 John. As will be pointed out in the commentary below, the Elder endeavors to lay the theological and ethical basis of his subsequent warning to his addressee against the deceivers in the early sections of this letter.

3. The reference chain of the Elder is as follows: Ὁ πρεσβύτερος (v. 1); ἐγὼ (v. 1) ἀγαπῶ (v. 1); ἐγώ (v. 1); ἐν ἡμῖν (v. 2); μεθ' ἡμῶν (v. 2); μεθ' ἡμῶν (v. 3); Ἐχάρην (v. 4); εὕρηκα (v. 4); ἐλάβομεν (v. 4); ἐρωτῶ (v. 5); γράφων (v. 5); εἴχομεν (v. 5); ἀγαπῶμεν (v. 5) ἀλλήλους (v. 5); περιπατῶμεν (v. 6); εἰργασάμεθα (v. 8); ἔχων (v. 12); γράφειν (v. 12); ἐβουλήθην (v. 12); ἐλπίζω (v. 12) γενέσθαι (v. 12); λαλῆσαι (v. 12); ἡμῶν (v. 12). For the notion of participant references or reference chain, see Eggins, *Introduction to Systemic Functional Linguistics*, 37–40.

4. Below are all the explicit or implicit participant references to the chosen lady: ἐκλεκτῇ κυρίᾳ (v. 1); αὐτῆς (v. 1); οὕς (v. 1); ἐν ἡμῖν (v. 2); μεθ' ἡμῶν (v. 2); μεθ' ἡμῶν (v. 3); σου (v. 4); ἐλάβομεν (v. 4); σε (v. 5); κυρία (v. 5); σοι (v. 5); εἴχομεν (v. 5); ἀγαπῶμεν (v. 5) ἀλλήλους (v. 5); περιπατῶμεν (v. 6); ἠκούσατε (v. 6); περιπατῆτε (v. 6); βλέπετε (v. 8) ἑαυτούς (v. 8); ἀπολέσητε (v. 8); εἰργασάμεθα (v. 8 [?]); ἀπολάβητε (v. 8); ὑμᾶς (v. 10); λαμβάνετε (v. 10); λέγετε (v. 10); ὑμῖν (v. 12); ὑμᾶς (v. 12); ἡμῶν (v. 12); σε (v. 13); σου (v. 13).

5. The following reference chain illustrates the altogether fifteen explicit or implicit references to the false teachers: πολλοὶ πλάνοι (v. 7) ἐξῆλθον (v. 7); οἱ μὴ ὁμολογοῦντες (v. 7); οὗτός (v. 7); ὁ πλάνος (v. 7); ὁ ἀντίχριστος (v. 7); Πᾶς ὁ προάγων (v. 9); μὴ μένων (v. 9); τις (v. 10) ἔρχεται (v. 10); φέρει (v. 10); αὐτὸν (v. 10); αὐτῷ (v. 10); αὐτῷ (v. 11); αὐτοῦ (v. 11).

2 JOHN 1–4

OUTLINE:

I. Opening (vv. 1–4)
    A. The Prescript (vv. 1–3)
        1. The Sender and the Recipient (vv. 1–2)
        2. The Greeting (v. 3)
    B. An Expression of Rejoicing (v. 4)
II. Body (vv. 5–11)
III. Closing (vv. 12–13)

I. OPENING (VV. 1–4)

The opening of 2 John is constitutive of the prescript (vv. 1–3) and a transition (v. 4), in which the Elder expresses the cause of his joy.

A. The Prescript (vv. 1–3)

The three main components (i.e., superscription, adscription, salutation) of the opening of a Hellenistic letter are all found in the prescript in 2 John 1–3. This prescript contains fifty-nine words in altogether five ranking clauses (vv. 1a, 1b, 1c, 1d–2, 3). Compared to the Elder's brief self-introduction (word count: two) and the greeting (word count: twenty-one), much ink is spilled on the depiction of the recipient of this letter (word count: thirty-six). The corollary is that the Elder seeks to establish the relationship with his audience through the adscription so that they will be disposed to listen to what he has to say. Aside from the typical conventions in the opening of a Hellenistic letter, the coherence of the prescript of 2 John is enhanced semantically by the recurrences of the various lexemes from semantic domain 25 ("attitudes, emotions"; cf. ἀγαπῶ [v. 1b], ἀγάπη [v. 3]), semantic domain 72 ("true, false"; cf. ἀλήθεια [vv. 1b, 1d, 2, 3]), or semantic domain 12 ("supernatural beings and powers"; cf. θεός [v. 4], πατήρ [v. 4], υἱός [v. 4]). In addition, the two notions of "love" and "truth" are connected in v. 1b and v. 3 and consequently forming an *inclusio* at the beginning and end of the prescript.[1]

1. The Sender and the Recipient (vv. 1–2)

The customary formula of the prescript in the Hellenistic letters was, "From the sender (in the nominative case) to the recipient (in the dative case), Greetings (the present active infinitive χαίρειν)," though the recipient's name may sometimes appear prior to the sender's name in certain kinds of correspondences and particularly the official letters of petition sent by an inferior to a superior.[2] The author of 2 John simply uses the articular nominative masculine singular adjective ὁ πρεσβύτερος as substantive to introduce himself and without indicating his personal name (v. 1a; cf. 3 John 1). It is presumably the case that "the Elder" was a well-known figure and so his name was not necessary for identification. While the lexeme πρεσβύτερος is the comparative form of the adjective πρέσβυς, the thrust of the sender's self-designation is not that he was older than the recipient. Rather, "the Elder" is likely a title denoting the author as holding a position of authority in the churches (cf. Acts 14:23; 20:17; 1 Pet 5:1).[3] Nevertheless, the Elder should be advanced in years at the time 2 John was written because the recognized leader of a community was usually a senior male in antiquity.

The Elder uses the word group ἐκλεκτῇ κυρίᾳ καὶ τοῖς τέκνοις αὐτῆς in the dative case to identify the recipient of his letter in v. 1a. The lexeme κυρία is literally a title of respect for addressing a woman of a high social status or rank. That said, it is probable that the "chosen lady" refers to a Christian congregation figuratively in feminine terms rather than designating a respectable lady on account of the frequent references to God's people as a woman in the biblical traditions (e.g., Isa 61:10; 62:5; Jer 31:21, 32; Ezek 16:7–14; Hos 2:2, 16–20; 2 Cor 11:2; Eph 5:25–27; Rev 19:6–8; 22:17). It should be noted that apart from the use of the various second-person singular pronouns (vv. 4b, 5a, 5b, 13 [2x]), the Elder employs a second-person plural pronoun to denote the recipient a total of three times in the body of

---

1. Klauck, *Ancient Letters and the New Testament*, 30.
2. White, "Greek Documentary Letter Tradition," 87.
3. Jobes, *1, 2, and 3 John*, 255.

the letter (cf. ὑμᾶς in v. 10a, ὑμῖν in v. 12a, and ὑμᾶς in v. 12b). In fact, all of the seven finite verbs that are in the second person are various plural forms (i.e., ἠκούσατε [v. 6d], περιπατῆτε [v. 6e], βλέπετε [v. 8a], ἀπολέσητε [v. 8b], ἀπολάβητε [v. 8c], λαμβάνετε [v. 10c], λέγετε [v. 10d]).[4] This suggests that the recipient of 2 John is probably a congregation instead of a woman. While the lexeme ἐκλεκτός is not found in the other two Johannine epistles or the Fourth Gospel, the related verb ἐκλέγω is often employed to portray the disciples as chosen by Jesus in this Gospel (e.g., John 6:70; 13:18; 15:16 [2x], 19). Furthermore, the lexeme ἐκλεκτός or συνεκλεκτός occurs with reference to a Christian congregation in 1 Peter 1:1 and 5:13.[5] If the understanding that the "chosen lady" refers to a congregation is accepted, the co-recipient "her children" likewise is a metaphor of the believers belonging to this congregation.

The Elder expands the adscription by elaborating the description of the audience through three statements, which are realized by the three subordinate clauses in v. 1b, v. 1c, and vv. 1d–2, respectively. While the first subclause starts with the masculine plural accusative relative pronoun οὕς (v. 1b), the antecedent of this relative pronoun is constitutive of the feminine singular dative noun κυρίᾳ and the neuter plural dative noun τέκνοις that precede in v. 1a. This relative pronoun (i.e., οὕς) in the accusative case is the object of the first-person singular present active indicative verb ἀγαπῶ (v. 1b), whose meaning falls into semantic domain 25 ("attitudes and emotions"). In addition to this indicative verb above, there are altogether six words regarding emotion (i.e., ἀγάπη [v. 3], ἐχάρην [v. 4a], ἀγαπῶμεν [v. 5b], ἀγάπη [v. 6a], χαρά [v. 12c]) or desideration (i.e., ἐβουλήθην [v. 12a]) that fall into this semantic domain in the remainder of this letter. Since all of the emotive words above bear the overtone of either love or happiness, there is a high degree of positive affect in regard to the Elder's interpersonal relationship with his audience. It merits mention that the Elder adds the first-person singular pronoun ἐγώ to make explicit the subject of the first-person singular present active indicative verb ἀγαπῶ and thereby accentuates his own love towards them in v. 1b. Following this indicative verb, the prepositional phrase ἐν ἀληθείᾳ (v. 1b) can be construed to simply express the idea of sincerity or authenticity concerning the Elder's loving affection towards his audience (cf. 2 John 3, 4; 3 John 1, 3, 4).[6] However, the Elder probably utilizes this prepositional phrase (i.e., ἐν ἀληθείᾳ [v. 1b]) to intimate that his

---

4. Stott notes the use of the second-person singular or plural expressions in 2 John. See Stott, *Letters of John*, 203.

5. Yarbrough, *1–3 John*, 334.

6. Sherman and Tuggy, *Semantic and Structural Analysis*, 106.

love is grounded in the Christian faith shared by him and his audience in view of the subsequent emphasis on the truth's abiding presence with them (cf. v. 2). Notably, the two notions of "love" and "truth" are tied together in their first occurrences in v. 1b in this epistle.

The elliptical clause (i.e., καὶ οὐκ ἐγὼ μόνος) is verbless in v. 1c. Despite the lack of a predicator, the Elder presumably expresses that he is not the only person who loves the audience. The Elder utilizes the polarity adjunct οὐκ in connection with the adjective μόνος to negate the idea of aloneness and puts forward the negative understatement, "and not I alone," accordingly in v. 1c. This negative understatement paves the way for the subsequently contrastive assertion that the audience are loved by all who know the truth in vv. 1d–2. Compared with the brevity of the foregoing two clauses (i.e., v. 1b and v. 1c), the length of the clause beginning with the adversative conjunction ἀλλά is relatively long (word count: twenty-one) owing to the presence of the three embedded participial or finite clauses in vv. 1d–2. The first embedded participial clause (i.e., πάντες οἱ ἐγνωκότες τὴν ἀλήθειαν) as a whole constitutes the subject of the implicit third-person plural present active indicative verb ἀγαπῶσιν in v. 1d.[7] Among the total five occurrences of the lexeme ἀλήθεια in this letter (vv. 1b, 1d, 2, 3, 4b), this lexeme occurs in connection with an article only twice in v. 1d and v. 2. Given that the notion of "truth" is attached a theological importance in Johannine thought (cf. John 8:32; 14:6),[8] it is likely that "all who know the truth" (cf. the embedded participial clause above) refer broadly to the believers who are in relationship with God through his Son, Jesus Christ.[9] Furthermore, there is little doubt that the members of the Christian congregation which the Elder was belonged to are included as those knowing the truth (cf. v. 13).

The Elder provides the reason to explicate that all who know the truth love the audience because of the truth (cf. διά with the accusative) which abides in us and will be with us forever in v. 2. There is an embedded participial clause (i.e., τὴν μένουσαν ἐν ἡμῖν) and an embedded finite clause (i.e., καὶ μεθ' ἡμῶν ἔσται εἰς τὸν αἰῶνα) in this verse. It can be presumed that both of the two first-person plural dative or genitive pronouns ἡμῖν and ἡμῶν are with reference to the inclusive "we" in the two embedded participial or finite clauses above. The implication is that the Elder seeks to enhance solidarity with his audience by banding himself and his audience in the same group in which the truth resides now and forever.

---

7. Culy, *1, 2, 3 John*, 142.
8. Köstenberger, *Theology of John's Gospel and Letters*, 288–89.
9. Jobes, *1, 2, and 3 John*, 256.

2. The Greeting (v. 3)

In the opening of most Greek letters, the simple salutation is a single word using the present active infinitival form χαίρειν.[10] Yet this greeting formula is rarely found in the opening of the NT epistles except the epistolary opening in James 1:1 (cf. Acts 15:23; 23:26). The customary salutation found in the Pauline epistles is various forms of the expression χάρις ὑμῖν καὶ εἰρήνη (or χάρις ἔλεος εἰρήνη),[11] which is accompanied by the prepositional phrase headed by ἀπό to indicate the divine source of grace and peace.[12] In contrast to the verbless construction in the Pauline greetings, the Elder begins his salutation with the third-person singular future verb ἔσται followed by the prepositional phrase μεθ' ἡμῶν in 2 John 3. This future verb and this prepositional phrase above have appeared in connection with each other in v. 2. Their recurrence in reverse order serves to create emphasis in vv. 2–3, though what will be with us is not the truth but rather grace, mercy, and peace in v. 3.[13] It is worth noting that the Elder places the third-person singular future verb ἔσται in the clause-initial position to stress the surety of God's bestowal of grace, mercy, and peace upon the believers.[14] The subject (i.e., χάρις ἔλεος εἰρήνη) is made up of three nominative singular nouns in an asyndetic construction in v. 3. The first noun χάρις is cognate with the common verb of greeting χαίρειν in the Hellenistic letter.[15] This noun is also lexically related to the ensuing predicator ἐχάρην in the transitional unit to the letter body in v. 4. The second noun ἔλεος in this subject phrase above is a *hapax legomenon* in the Johannine writings. Both of these two lexemes (i.e., χάρις and ἔλεος) fall in semantic domain 88 ("moral and ethical qualities and related behavior") and thus have semantic associations. The third noun εἰρήνη is the only occurrence of a word from semantic domain 22 ("trouble, hardship, relief, favorable circumstances") in 2 John. It is likely that the inclusion of "peace" in the Elder's opening salutation takes root in

---

10. White, "Greek Documentary Letter Tradition," 87.

11. See, e.g., 1 Tim 1:2; 2 Tim 1:2.

12. See, e.g., ἀπὸ θεοῦ πατρὸς ἡμῶν καὶ κυρίου Ἰησοῦ Χριστοῦ in Rom 1:7. See also similar constructions in 1 Cor 1:3; 2 Cor 1:2; Gal 1:3; Eph 1:2; Phil 1:2; Col 1:2; 1 Thess 1:1; 2 Thess 1:2; 1 Tim 1:2; 2 Tim 1:2; Titus 1:4; Phlm 3. See Adams, "Paul's Letter Opening and Greek Epistolography," 46–48.

13. Klauck, *Ancient Letters and the New Testament*, 30.

14. Yarbrough, *1–3 John*, 336; Sherman and Tuggy, *Semantic and Structural Analysis*, 107.

15. Adams, "Paul's Letter Opening and Greek Epistolography," 47.

the Jewish notion of "shalom,"[16] which is one of God's eschatological blessings to his people (cf. the peace benediction in 3 John 15).

The Elder avails himself of the two conjoined prepositional phrases (i.e., παρὰ θεοῦ πατρὸς καὶ παρὰ Ἰησοῦ Χριστοῦ τοῦ υἱοῦ τοῦ πατρὸς) to add the information regarding the source of grace, mercy, and peace from God the Father and from Jesus Christ, the Son of the Father in v. 3.[17] The Elder indicates that these blessings originate from the deity through the employment of several words (i.e., θεός, πατήρ, υἱός) from semantic domain 12 ("supernatural beings and powers"). Compared to the absence of a mention of Jesus by name in 3 John, he is explicitly referred to in the opening (v. 3) and the body (vv. 7a, 9a, 9b) of 2 John. Aside from the opening greeting, the four lexemes θεός, πατήρ, Χριστός, and υἱός are found in close proximity to each other elsewhere in regard to the Elder's criticism of any person going beyond and not holding fast to the teaching of Christ in v. 9. In addition, the lexeme πατήρ occurs in v. 4 and the word group Ἰησοῦς Χριστός is present in v. 7. The two notions of "love" and "truth" have appeared in connection with each other in v. 1b. These two notions are linked again in reverse order in the prepositional phrase ἐν ἀληθείᾳ καὶ ἀγάπῃ, which constitutes the closing bookend of the *inclusio* at the end of the prescript in 2 John 3 (cf. v. 1b).[18] This is the fourth time the lexeme ἀλήθεια is detected in the opening of this letter (vv. 1b, 1d, 2, 3; cf. v. 4b). Since the Elder employs the preposition ἐν to govern both of the two anarthrous dative singular feminine nouns ἀληθείᾳ and ἀγάπῃ (v. 3), equal force is given to the two notions of "love" and "truth" in this prepositional phrase above.[19] As will be seen below, the intimate tie established between these two notions in the opening will prove crucial for the Elder's subsequent exhortations to his audience in the body of the letter. While a wish or prayer for the recipient's health often follows the prescript in ancient Greek letters (cf. 3 John 2), this epistolary feature is missing from the opening in 2 John.

---

16. Cf. the Jewish greetings in Ezra 4:17; 5:7. See Adams, "Paul's Letter Opening and Greek Epistolography," 47.

17. Instead of simply παρὰ Ἰησοῦ Χριστοῦ, the longer reading παρὰ κυρίου Ἰησοῦ Χριστοῦ is found in codices Sinaiticus and Porphyrianus, minuscules 5, 33, 307, 1175, 1448, 2344, and 2492, the Byzantine manuscripts, and the Syrian versions. However, it is unlikely that the longer reading above is authentic. The reason is that the scribes would not have deleted the title "Lord" had it been originally in the text. Furthermore, the reading (i.e., παρὰ Ἰησοῦ Χριστοῦ) adopted in NA28 is attested in codices Alexandrinus and Vaticanus. See Metzger, *Textual Commentary on the Greek New Testament*, 652.

18. Klauck, *Ancient Letters and the New Testament*, 30.

19. Brown, *Epistles of John*, 660.

B. An Expression of Rejoicing (v. 4)

There is no formal conjunction to connect the transitional unit in v. 4 with the foregoing prescript in vv. 1–3. However, the author creates the lexical link with this prescript by employing the lexeme ἀλήθεια the fifth and last time in the dependent clause headed by the conjunction ὅτι in v. 4b (cf. vv. 1b, 1d, 2, 3). Furthermore, the wording of the prepositional phrase παρὰ τοῦ πατρός (v. 4c) is reminiscent of that as regards the source of the divine favors in v. 3. Yet there is a change in participant from "all who know the truth" (v. 1d) to the Elder, who is the implicit subject of the two indicative verbs ἐχάρην and εὕρηκα in the first-person singular in v. 4a. In addition, there is a shift in finite verbs from the present (e.g., μένουσαν [v. 2]) or future form (e.g., ἔσται [vv. 2, 3]) to the aorist (e.g., ἐχάρην [v. 4a], ἐλάβομεν [v. 4c]) or perfect tense (e.g., εὕρηκα [v. 4b]) in 2 John 4. It is also noteworthy that several lexemes including περιπατέω (v. 4b; cf. v. 6b, 6e) and ἐντολή (v. 4c; cf. vv. 5a, 6b, 6c) appear for the first time in this verse. Therefore, verse 4 is considered as the transitional unit or the introduction to the body (i.e., vv. 5–11) of 2 John in this commentary.[20]

The Elder uses the main clause (v. 4a) to succinctly express his rejoicing and subsequently utilizes the two subclauses beginning with the conjunction ὅτι or καθώς to spell out the cause of his gladness in v. 4b–c. This main clause (i.e., Ἐχάρην λίαν) is brief, containing only two words in v. 4a. The two subordinate clauses comprise nine and six words, respectively, in v. 4b and v. 4c. The employment of the aorist tense with the perfective aspect (cf. the predicator ἐχάρην above) suggests that this transitional unit contains the supporting materials in v. 4 to set the stage of the Elder's messages in the epistolary body and particularly his request to his audience in v. 5.[21] Moreover, the Elder enhances rapport with the audience through the use of the emotive lexeme χαίρω in connection with the adverbial modifier λίαν, which serves to augment the positive affect of his happiness (cf. 3 John 3). The reason of the Elder's exceeding joy is ushered in by the causal conjunction ὅτι in v. 4b (cf. 3 John 3–4). While the aorist tense is employed in v. 4a and v. 4c, the Elder utilizes the first-person singular perfect active indicative verb εὕρηκα to give prominence to the explanatory statement concerning the cause of his gladness in v. 4b. It is said that he has found some of the lady's children walking in the truth. The prepositional phrase ἐκ τῶν τέκνων σου (v. 4b) is a partitive construction, which functions substantivally with the

---

20. Sherman and Tuggy, *Semantic and Structural Analysis*, 108–11.

21. According to Funk, it was not uncommon that the word group ἐχάρην λίαν is used to introduce the "background statement" of the petition (cf. 2 John 5) in the Hellenistic letter ("Form and Structure," 427).

implicit accusative plural pronoun τινάς to serve as the object of this indicative verb (i.e., εὕρηκα) above.[22] The lexeme περιπατέω literally means "walk" but the accusative masculine plural present active participle περιπατοῦντας (v. 4b) is used in a figurative way to convey the sense of a way of life in the truth in v. 4b (cf. 1 John 1:6, 7; 2:6, 11; 2 John 4, 6; 3 John 3). Thus the Elder affirms that his audience' daily living corresponds to their identity as the followers of Jesus Christ, who is the truth according to John 14:6.

The idea of walking in the truth is elaborated by means of the dependent clause beginning with the comparative conjunction καθώς in v. 4c. Given the use of the inclusive first-person plural aorist active indicative verb ἐλάβομεν (v. 4c), the Elder includes himself with the audience as the co-recipients of a commandment from the Father. The divine origin of this commandment is spelt out by virtue of the prepositional phrase παρὰ τοῦ πατρός. It is worthy of mention that the Elder does not employ a verb (e.g., ἐντέλλομαι) to encode the experiential meaning regarding that "we were commanded by the Father" or "the Father commanded us."[23] Rather, the Elder avails himself of the linguistic device of the "ideational grammatical metaphor" (e.g., nominalization) in such a way that the verbal process of commanding is reconstrued as a thing, that is, a "commandment" in v. 4c.[24] As a corollary, the Elder is enabled to place the accusative feminine singular noun ἐντολήν prior to the predicator ἐλάβομεν above in the thematic position of the καθώς-clause to orient the audience and underline the notion of "commandment" in v. 4c. In addition, the transitional unit in v. 4 can be readily linked with the ensuing co-text through the repeated occurrences of the lexeme ἐντολήν in vv. 5–6. In a nutshell, the Elder rejoiced greatly to find that some of the audience exemplifying a commendable way of living in accordance with the Father's commandment.

---

22. Culy, *1, 2, 3 John*, 144.

23. Brown, *Epistles of John*, 662.

24. According to the Hallidayan theory of language, the "ideational grammatical metaphor" is a kind of the "grammatical metaphor" that is concerned with the different ways of expressing the same experiential meaning. One of the common ways to encode the ideational grammatical metaphor is "nominalization." See Halliday and Matthiessen, *Halliday's Introduction to Functional Grammar*, 707–15; Martin and Rose, *Working with Discourse*, 106–12; Martin, *English Text*, 406–12.

2 JOHN 5–11

OUTLINE:

I. Opening (vv. 1–4)

II. Body (vv. 5–11)

    A. Exhortations to Love and Beware (vv. 5–8)

    B. Prohibitions Against Welcoming the Deceivers (vv. 9–11)

III. Closing (vv. 12–13)

II. BODY (VV. 5–11)

Having indicated his happiness caused by knowing the audience' way of life in the truth in the opening of the letter (v. 4), the Elder communicates the key messages to them in the letter body in 2 John 5–11. There are several discourse markers that point to the beginning of a new section and the body proper in v. 5a. These discourse markers include the occurrences of the transitional word group καὶ νῦν, the first-person singular present active indicative verb ἐρωτῶ with respect to petitioning, and the vocative singular noun κυρία used as a direct address to the audience. Furthermore, there is a change in tense from using the aorist tense in v. 4 (cf. the two predicators ἐχάρην and ἐλάβομεν) to the present tense (cf. the predicator ἐρωτῶ) in v. 5a. There is no consensus on the overall structure of the body in vv. 5–11. It is also debatable whether a new paragraph starts in v. 7. On the one hand, the deceivers come on scene as a new participant in v. 7a, in which the lexeme πλάνος appears for the first time in v. 7a (cf. the recurrence of this lexeme in v. 7c). On the other hand, the dependent clause begins with the causal subordinating conjunction ὅτι in v. 7a and thus is hypotactically related to the prior clause in v. 6e.¹ While certainty is not possible, v. 7 is linked to the preceding co-text in this commentary on account of the aforementioned clausal relation between v. 7a and v. 6e. Therefore, the first section of the body is present in vv. 5–8, in which the Elder deals with the believers' correct way of living. His first explicit command to the audience to watch out marks the sub-peak in v. 8. In the body's second section (vv. 9–11), the Elder mostly utilizes the generic statements to inform his audience concerning the danger from the false teachers. While the three lexemes ἀλήθεια (vv. 1 [2x], 2, 3, 4), ἀγάπη (vv. 1, 3, 6), and ἐντολή (vv. 4, 5, 6 [2x]) are predominant in the preceding co-text in vv. 1–8, they are absent from this latter section in vv. 9–11. In contrast, there is a concentration of three occurrences of the lexeme διδαχή with respect to the teaching of Christ in this section (vv. 9 [2x], 10). Notably, the two related prohibitions against receiving the false teachers are suggestive of the presence of a discourse peak in v. 10 near the end of the body.

A. Exhortations to Love and Beware (vv. 5–8)

The body opens with the Elder's request (cf. the predicator ἐρωτῶ) to his audience to love one another in v. 5.² The lexeme ἐντολή is found altogether three times (vv. 5a, 6b, 6c) and the prepositional phrase ἀπ' ἀρχῆς occurs altogether twice (vv. 5a, 6d) in this section in 2 John 5–8. The clustering of several words (e.g., ἐρωτῶ, ἐντολήν, γράφων) from semantic domain 33 ("communication") signals a change of topic in the initial independent clause in v. 5a, which is of the considerable length of sixteen words. Following the accusative second-person singular pronoun σε, the Elder uses the vocative singular κυρία (v. 5a) to speak to his audience to attract attraction and identify the receiver of his request. However, the content of the Elder's appeal is not readily perceptible within the surrounding co-text. It could be expressed through one of the three clauses that begin with the subordinating conjunction ἵνα in v. 5b, v. 6b, or v. 6e. Since the first ἵνα-clause is the closest to the saying verb ἐρωτῶ (v. 5a), it is likely that what the Elder calls on the lady to perform is presented through the statement (i.e., ἀγαπῶμεν ἀλλήλους) in v. 5b (cf. John 13:34; 15:32; 1 John 3:11, 18, 23; 4:7).³ While the second-person singular (e.g., σε [v. 5a], σοι [v. 5a]) or plural expressions

---

1. Culy, *1, 2, 3 John*, 147.
2. Funk notes that ἐρωτάω is one of the common verbs of petition in the Hellenistic letter. See Funk, "Form and Structure," 426.
3. Contra Lieu, who thinks that the content of the request is spelt out in v. 6e (i.e., ἵνα ἐν αὐτῇ περιπατῆτε). Lieu, *I, II, & III John*, 249–51.

(e.g., ἠκούσατε [v. 6d], περιπατῆτε [v. 6e]) abound in the immediate co-text, the Elder employs the first-person plural present active subjunctive verb ἀγαπῶμεν in connection with the reciprocal pronoun ἀλλήλους to invite his audience to join with him to practice mutual love in the community in v. 5b.[4]

It should be noted that the Elder utilizes the entire adjunctive construction (i.e., οὐχ ὡς ἐντολὴν γράφων σοι καινὴν ἀλλ᾽ ἣν εἴχομεν ἀπ᾽ ἀρχῆς) to provide supplementary information in v. 5a before spelling out the content of his request in v. 5b. This adjunctive construction above can be divided into two parts corresponding to two contrastive ideas. The first part of this construction contains the negative polarity adjunct οὐχ and the embedded participial clause ὡς ἐντολὴν γράφων σοι καινὴν. The Elder brings up the idea that a novel commandment is imposed on the audience, so as to refute this idea by way of negation. The textual reading (i.e., ἐντολὴν γράφων σοι καινὴν) adopted in NA28 differs from that (i.e., ἐντολὴν καινὴν γράφων σοι) in NA27. The awkward disjoining of the noun ἐντολὴν and its modifier (i.e., καινὴν) by the word group γράφων σοι in v. 5a has probably prompted some copyists to smooth the grammar by transposing the adjective καινὴν to follow immediately the word ἐντολὴν in a number of manuscripts including codices Sinaiticus (ℵ or 01), Alexandrinus (A or 02), Athous Lavrensis (Ψ or 044), and Vaticanus Graecus (048). Thus, the textual reading adopted in NA 28 is likely to be original because it best explains the rise of other variants and is supported by codex Vaticanus (B or 03), several minuscules, and the Byzantine witnesses.[5] While the object of the participle γράφων is the word group ἐντολὴν καινὴν, the Elder places only the accusative singular feminine noun ἐντολὴν in the emphatic position subsequent to the comparative conjunction ὡς to stress the notion of "commandment" in the adjunctive construction above in v. 5a (cf. 1 John 2:7–8). The second part of this adjunctive construction above comprises the elliptical clause ἀλλ᾽ ἣν εἴχομεν ἀπ᾽ ἀρχῆς. Following the elided adversative conjunction ἀλλ᾽, the feminine singular accusative relative pronoun ἣν does not have a specified antecedent but rather refers to the implicit ἐντολήν that is presumed in this elliptical clause in v. 5a.[6] In contrast to the idea that the Elder writes a novel commandment to his audience, he avers that both of them (cf. the inclusive

---

4. Aside from the present active subjunctive verb ἀγαπῶμεν, the imperfect active indicative verb εἴχομεν is also in the first-person plural in v. 5a.

5. See Yarbrough, *1–3 John*, 347.

6. Culy, *1, 2, 3 John*, 145.

"we") have had the commandment at the time when they came to know Jesus and became part of the God's family.[7]

The Elder deals with the two notions of "love" and "commandment" again in v. 6a and v. 6c, respectively, in reverse sequence as compared to their preceding occurrences in v. 5a and v. 5b. The demonstrative pronoun αὕτη (v. 6a) is cataphoric and points forward to the epexegetical ἵνα-clause in v. 6b, in which the Elder explicates that love is that we walk according to God's commandments. In view of the employment of the lexeme περιπατέω from semantic domain 41 ("behavior and related states"), it is evident that genuine love for one another entails the ethical aspect of living a life in congruence with the precepts of God in v. 6b. The Elder avails himself of the literary device of the inclusive 'we' (cf. the first-person plural present active subjunctive verb περιπατῶμεν) to enhance the solidarity with his audience in the respect of obeying what the Father commands. Rather than using a singular form of the lexeme ἐντολή (cf. vv. 4c, 5a, 6c), the accusative plural ἐντολάς is employed to underline the comprehensive range of the obedience to God's commandments required of the believers in v. 6b.

Each of the three clauses contains four words in v. 6c (i.e., αὕτη ἡ ἐντολή ἐστιν), v. 6d (i.e., καθὼς ἠκούσατε ἀπ' ἀρχῆς), or v. 6e (i.e., ἵνα ἐν αὐτῇ περιπατῆτε). It is possible to construe the demonstrative pronoun αὕτη (v. 6c) as anaphoric and pointing backward to either v. 6a–b as a whole or specifically the love commandment in v. 5b.[8] In either case, the antecedent of the subsequent feminine singular demonstrative pronoun αὐτῇ (v. 6e) is the nearest feminine singular noun ἐντολή that precedes in v. 6c. Thus, the Elder summons his audience to walk in the "commandment," which is presumably pertinent to the believers' mutual love in v. 6e. The weakness of the anaphoric reading of the demonstrative pronoun αὕτη (v. 6c) above is the redundancy caused by the repetition of the idea of walking in the commandment in 2 John 6 (i.e., "We walk according to his commandments [v. 6b]. This is the commandment [v. 6c] . . . that you walk in the commandment [v. 6e; cf. assuming the antecedent of αὐτῇ is ἡ ἐντολή]").[9] Alternatively, there is good reason to consider the demonstrative pronoun αὕτη (v. 6c) as cataphoric and pointing forward to the ensuing ἵνα-clause in v. 6e.[10] In this case, the "commandment" in v. 6c actually refers to that "you walk in it" in v. 6e. Furthermore, the antecedent of the feminine singular

---

7. The prepositional phrase ἀπ' ἀρχῆς is found twice in 2 John (vv. 5, 6; cf. 1 John 1:1; 2:7, 13, 14, 24 [2x]; 3:8, 11).

8. Brown, *Epistles of John*, 666–68.

9. Jobes, *1, 2, and 3 John*, 263.

10. Culy, *1, 2, 3 John*, 146.

demonstrative pronoun αὐτῇ (v. 6e) is not the nearest feminine singular noun ἐντολή (v. 6c), but rather the preceding feminine singular noun ἀγάπη (v. 6a) or even farther away another feminine singular noun ἀλήθεια (v. 4b).[11] On the whole, it is difficult to ascertain the antecedents of the two demonstrative pronouns αὕτη and αὐτῇ in v. 6c and v. 6e, respectively. Nevertheless, the cataphoric view of the demonstrative pronoun αὕτη in v. 6c is tentatively adopted in this commentary. Moreover, the subsequent demonstrative pronoun αὐτῇ (v. 6e) probably harks back to the noun ἀγάπη (v. 6a) because this noun is closer than another noun ἀλήθεια (v. 4b) to this demonstrative pronoun.[12] It follows that God's commandment is that the believers should "walk in love" (cf. NIV), just as they have heard about it from the beginning in 2 John 6. That said, whether the Elder specifies the commandment as walking in "love" or walking in "truth" in v. 6e does not have a significant difference in practical Christian living because the two notions of "love" and "truth" are intertwined in Johannine thinking.

The Elder explains to his audience why they should continue walking in love (or walking in truth) in v. 7a, in which the lexeme πλάνος occurs for the first time with reference to the deceivers who have gone out into the world in this letter. Rather than using the cognate verb πλανάω to implicate the process of deceiving (cf. 1 John 2:26; 3:7; 4:6), the Elder employs the subject phrase πολλοί πλάνοι in the nominative masculine plural to denote the false teachers in such a way that they are introduced as the active participant in v. 7a. The employment of the modifier πολλοί in this phrase above is telling of the large quantity of the "deceivers" and in effect heightens the danger facing the believers (cf. 1 John 2:18; 4:1). The Elder points out the deceivers' main error concerning Christology and specifically their refusal to acknowledge Jesus Christ as coming in the flesh via the elliptical clause (i.e., οἱ μὴ ὁμολογοῦντες Ἰησοῦν Χριστὸν ἐρχόμενον ἐν σαρκί) in v. 7b (cf. 1 John 4:2). Despite the omission of the finite verb, the message conveyed through this elliptical clause above is readily apparent. In fact, it is probable that the Elder tactfully uses the ellipsis to reduce redundancy and thereby focus attention on the deceivers' incorrect belief regarding the doctrine of incarnation.

Aside from the opening salutation (v. 3), the two lexemes Ἰησοῦς and Χριστός are found adjacent to each other only in v. 7b (cf. Χριστός in v.

---

11. Kruse and Campbell think that the antecedent of the demonstrative pronoun αὐτῇ is the preceding noun ἀγάπη in 2 John 6 (i.e., the commandment is that "you walk in love"). See Kruse, *Letters of John*, 208–9; Campbell, *1, 2, and 3 John*, 194. For the view that considers the commandment as walking in the "truth" in 2 John 6, see Jobes, *1, 2, and 3 John*, 263–64; Sherman and Tuggy, *Semantic and Structural Analysis*, 118.

12. See the relevant works in the prior note.

9a). It is possible to construe the accusative Χριστόν (v. 7b) as a title appositional to the proper noun Ἰησοῦν (v. 7b), which is also in the accusative case. On this reading, the name Ἰησοῦν alone is the object of the preceding nominative masculine plural present active participle ὁμολογοῦντες and the titular noun Χριστόν alone is modified by the following embedded participial clause ἐρχόμενον ἐν σαρκί. However, it is more probable that the word group Ἰησοῦν Χριστόν (v. 7b) in the accusative singular is used as a compound name given the Son's similar designation (cf. Ἰησοῦ Χριστοῦ) in v. 3.[13] Instead of the perfect active participle ἐληλυθότα in 1 John 4:2, the Elder avails himself of the present middle participle ἐρχόμενον with the imperfective aspect to portray the coming of Jesus Christ as in progress in v. 7b.[14] The Elder goes on to employ the singular masculine nominative demonstrative pronoun οὗτος to refer to an individual representative of the class of those denying Jesus Christ as coming in the flesh in v. 7c. Such an individual, who takes the doctrinal stance against the Son's incarnation, is further identified as the figure who beguiles the believers and opposes Christ. The lexeme ἀντίχριστος (v. 7c) is detected only once in this letter (cf. 1 John 2:18 [2x], 22; 4:3). Since the Elder speaks of the deceiver as the antichrist, he probably conceives of the damage to the church caused by the false teachers in light of the evil work of God's eschatological opponent in this age.[15]

In view of the threat posed by the deceivers, the Elder issues the command to his audience to be on their guard by employing the second-person plural present active imperative verb βλέπετε with the accusative plural reflexive pronoun ἑαυτούς in v. 8a. This is the first time the imperative occurs in this letter. Therefore, it is proper to consider the presence of the concluding climax of this section in v. 8a–c. The lexeme βλέπω literally means "see" but the imperative verb βλέπετε above is used to express the figurative meaning of self-alertness in v. 8a. Aside from this instance in 2 John, this imperative verb is present in the co-text in which Jesus exhorts his disciples to watch out for the counterfeit christs in the Synoptic Gospels (e.g., Matt 24:4–5; Mark 13:5–6; Luke 21:8) or Paul urges the Christians to be on guard against the false teachers in his epistles (e.g., Phil 3:2; Col 2:8). The Elder further uses the two contrastive clauses (cf. the adversative conjunction ἀλλά [v. 8c]) to evince that the believers' vigilance for the deceivers serves two interrelated purposes, which are in contradistinction to each other in

---

13. Brown, *Epistles of John*, 491–93, 669.

14. For a summary of the different understandings of the present middle accusative masculine singular participle ἐρχόμενον in 2 John 7, see Jensen, "Jesus 'Coming' in the Flesh."

15. Kruse, *Letters of John*, 209–10.

v. 8b and v. 8c. The first purpose, which is pertinent to the undesirable outcome that the audience should take heed to avoid, is articulated through the negative statement in v. 8b. There is an unexpected change from the use of the second-person plural (cf. βλέπετε [v. 8a] and ἀπολέσητε [v. 8b]) to the first-person plural aorist middle indicative verb εἰργασάμεθα in v. 8b. While the variant εἰργάσασθε (which is in the second-person plural) is found in a number of manuscripts including codices Sinaiticus and Alexandrinus, the first-person plural εἰργασάμεθα is the more difficult reading and thus is likely to be original in 2 John 8.[16] If the first-person plural εἰργασάμεθα bears an inclusive sense, the Elder intimates to his audience that they should be on their guard so that they will not lose what he and his audience have worked for. Alternatively, it is possible to construe the predicator εἰργασάμεθα with reference to exclusively the Elder and his associates and so the audience are not included as part of the referent in v. 8. That said, the former view is preferred because it accords with the predominance of the inclusive "we" or first-person plural in 2 John (cf. vv. 2 [2x], 3, 4, 5 [2x], 6, 12). In any case, it is probable that what the Elder and his audience (or his associates) have worked for is pertinent to the audience's faith in Jesus Christ, which leads to their possession of the eternal life (cf. John 6:27–29). As an antithesis to the negative purpose of not losing what we have worked for (v. 8b), the Elder utilizes the subsequent ἀλλά-clause to express the positive purpose of the believers' vigilance in v. 8c. It is affirmed that they may receive a full reward.[17] Following the adversative conjunction ἀλλά, the complement μισθὸν πλήρη in the accusative masculine singular is placed in the thematic position prior to the second-person plural aorist active subjunctive verb ἀπολάβητε to draw attention to the positive notion of the "full reward" in v. 8c. In short, the Elder puts forward the motivating factor to encourage his audience to stay on guard against the infiltration of the deceivers' erroneous Christology.

B. Prohibitions Against Welcoming the Deceivers (vv. 9–11)

The Elder draws on the semantic resource to utilize certain words or word groups (e.g., ἔρχεται πρὸς ὑμᾶς, λαμβάνετε αὐτὸν, εἰς οἰκίαν, χαίρειν, and κοινωνεῖ) in connection with each other to create the co-text concerning

---

16. Metzger, *Textual Commentary on the Greek New Testament*, 652–53.

17. Yarbrough notes that it is not uncommon to find the lexeme μισθός in the co-text regarding the promise of God's eschatological blessings to the faithful Christians in the NT (e.g., Matt 5:12; 10:41; Mark 9:41; Luke 6:23, 35; 1 Cor 3:8; 9:17–18; Rev 11:18; 22:12). See Yarbrough, *1–3 John*, 345.

the matter of hospitability in this section in 2 John 9–11. The pertinent statements are highlighted through the use of the present tense a total of thirteen times in vv. 9–11 (i.e., προάγων [v. 9a], μένων [2x; v. 9a, 9b], ἔχει [2x; v. 9a, 9c], ἔρχεται [v. 10a], φέρειν [v. 10b], λαμβάνετε [v. 10c], χαίρειν [v. 10d], λέγετε [v. 10d], λέγων [v. 11], χαίρειν [v. 11], κοινωνεῖ [v. 11]). The occurrences of the two second-person plural present active imperative verbs λαμβάνετε and λέγετε point to the presence of the climax or discourse peak in v. 10, in which the prohibitions against receiving the false teachers are set forth. There is a change in the participant references from the specific participants (i.e., the Elder or the lady) in the preceding co-text to mostly the generic participants in vv. 9–11 (see "Commentary on 2 John" above). The Elder is never the subject of the finite or non-finite verbs throughout this section. There is no first-person singular or plural pronoun with reference to him. Apart from the aforesaid two imperative verbs λαμβάνετε (v. 10c) and λέγετε (v. 10d) in the second-person plural and referring to the audience, the Elder primarily uses various generic or third-person singular expressions to depict certain kinds of individuals in this section. Furthermore, he indicates his negative or positive attitude towards the different behaviors of these individuals so as to influence his audience to align with his viewpoint.

The Elder portrays two classes of people in contradistinction to each other by means of the two antithetical statements in v. 9a and v. 9b–c. The entire construction πᾶς ὁ προάγων καὶ μὴ μένων ἐν τῇ διδαχῇ τοῦ Χριστοῦ constitutes the generic subject in v. 9a, in which the Elder intimates his disapproval of the first class of people with reference to the false teachers. The two nominative masculine singular present active participles προάγων and μένων share the article ὁ in this construction above. The Elder utilizes the lexeme προάγω, which is a *hapax legomenon* in the Johannine writings, to depict vividly a person who fails to obey and has gone beyond the boundary of the teaching of Christ in v. 9a. Depending on whether the genitive singular Χριστοῦ (v. 9a) is the subjective or objective genitive, this person does not remain in the sphere of what Christ taught (cf. John 7:16, 17; 18:19) or the teaching about him (specifically, the doctrine of incarnation), respectively.[18] In any case, the Elder says that this kind of individuals does not have God. Notably, the accusative masculine singular noun θεόν as the complement is placed prior to the predicator ἔχει to emphasize the lack of the relationship with the deity in v. 9a. In contrast to the first kind of individuals above, the person who abides in the teaching of Christ (cf. the

---

18. For the view that considers the genitive Χριστοῦ (v. 9) as the subjective objective, see Brown, *Epistles of John*, 673–75; Schnackenburg, *Johannine Epistles*, 286. For the view that the genitive Χριστοῦ is the objective genitive, see Marshall, *Epistles of John*, 72–73n13; Culy, *1, 2, 3 John*, 150.

anaphoric article τῇ) possesses both the Father and the Son (cf. καὶ . . . καί) in v. 9b-c. It deserves mention that the Elder uses the resumptive demonstrative pronoun οὗτος (v. 9c) to hark back to the participial clause ὁ μένων ἐν τῇ διδαχῇ (v. 9b) and thereby puts weight on the positive depiction of this person.[19] This demonstrative pronoun (i.e., οὗτος) above functions as the subject of the predicator ἔχει in v. 9c, in which the complement (i.e., the word group καὶ τὸν πατέρα καὶ τὸν υἱὸν) is marked to underline that this person have a relationship with "both the Father and the Son." By reason of the favorable portrayal of this latter kind of individuals, it is evident that the Elder endeavors to affect his audience to take a stance of remaining in Christ's teaching instead of succumbing to the false teaching that is at variance with it.

Building on what was said in v. 9, the Elder sets forth the two negative commands to forbid the audience to welcome anyone who comes to them but does not bring this teaching (i.e., the teaching of Christ) in v. 10. The first-class conditional sentence consists of four clauses in this latter verse. The first two clauses constitute the protasis beginning with the conditional conjunction εἰ in v. 10a-b. The subsequent two clauses, which pertain to the two negative commands, constitute the apodosis in v. 10c-d. The indefinite pronoun τις (v. 10a) in the nominative masculine singular is the generic subject of both of the two third-person singular present middle or active indicative verbs ἔρχεται (v. 10a) and φέρει (v. 10b) in the protasis clauses. Yet, the Elder indicates that the posited situation is relevant to his audience by using the prepositional phrase πρὸς ὑμᾶς, in which the second-person plural pronoun ὑμᾶς is with reference to them in v. 10a. Rather than employing the verb διδάσκω to express the experiential meaning of teaching, the Elder avails himself of the linguistic resource to formulate the noun phrase ταύτην τὴν διδαχὴν in the accusative singular and place it in the thematic position to highlight the notion of "this teaching (of Christ)" in v. 10b. The demonstrative pronoun ταύτην in this noun phrase above is anaphoric. It is noteworthy that the recurrence of the lexeme διδαχή (v. 10a) resonates with the preceding two occurrences of this lexeme pertaining to the two contrastive kinds of people in v. 9a-b. As an upshot, the audience are informed that any itinerant teacher who visits them and promulgates a belief out of step with Christ's teaching falls under the negative category of those who do not possess God (cf. v. 9a).

The peak of the Elder's hortatory discourse lies in the apodosis in v. 10c-d, in which both of the two second-person plural present active

---

19. The participial clause ὁ μένων ἐν τῇ διδαχῇ is treated as a minor clause and thus constituting a ranking clause in v. 9b in this commentary.

imperative verbs λαμβάνετε (v. 10c) and λέγετε (v. 10d) are found. The Elder employs these two imperative verbs above in connection with the negative polarity adjunct μή to realize the two prohibitions to his audience in case the posited situation as depicted in the protasis (cf. v. 10a–b) arises. He provides the circumstantial information regarding the location in a house through the prepositional phrase εἰς οἰκίαν in v. 10c. In addition, the present active infinitive χαίρειν is utilized to express the host's welcome greeting to the guest in v. 10d. The implication is that what the Elder forbids the audience to perform should be understood within the context of culture concerning the practice of hospitality in the first-century Greco-Roman society. It appears that there were certain deceivers traveling from place to place to promote their erroneous beliefs, which are in conflict with the teaching of Christ. Since receiving the deceivers has the ramification of offering support to them and associating with their false teaching, the Elder issues the two negative commands to his audience not to welcome them into the house or give them greetings in v. 10c–d. The reason why the believers should abstain from showing hospitality to such individuals is expressed through the generic statement in the conclusion of the body in v. 11, in which the postpositive conjunction γάρ is present. It is explained that the person who gives greeting to them shares in their wicked deeds in v. 11. That is to say, this person becomes a partner in doing the deceivers' wicked deeds, which are presumably pertinent to the furtherance of the false belief regarding the denial of Jesus Christ as coming in the flesh. Since the lexeme πονηρός is loaded with the negative overtone concerning ethics,[20] the Elder intimates his negative judgment of the deceivers' behavior related to their erroneous Christology by employing this lexeme to portray their deeds.[21] It should be remarked that the subject of the third-person singular present active indicative verb κοινωνεῖ is not actually the audience but rather the generic participant, who is encoded by the embedded participial clause ὁ λέγων αὐτῷ χαίρειν in v. 11. The rhetorical effect of pointing out a generic participant is to soften the negative commands so that the audience will be inclined to comply with the Elder's exhortation to abstain from welcoming the traveling deceivers. In summary, the Elder forbids his audience to welcome the deceivers because showing hospitality to them has the implication of becoming partners in doing their wicked works, which presumably include the promotion of the incorrect belief that Jesus Christ has not come in flesh.

20. Cf. the use of the lexeme πονηρός regarding Cain's "evil deeds" in 1 John 3:12 and Diotrephes's "evil words" in 3 John 10.

21. For the linguistic resource of appraisal and particularly the notion of "judgment" in the system of "attitude," see Martin and White, *Language of Evaluation*, 52–53 (esp. Table 2.3).

2 JOHN 12–13

OUTLINE:

I. Opening (vv. 1–4)
II. Body (vv. 5–11)
III. Closing (vv. 12–13)
    A. Desire to Visit (v. 12)
    B. Final Greeting (v. 13)

III. CLOSING (VV. 12–13)

There is a total of thirty-five words in the altogether four ranking clauses (vv. 12a, b, c, 13) in the closing of this letter. The occurrences of the lexeme γράφω (v. 12a), the second-person plural dative pronoun ὑμῖν (v. 12a), and the two indicative verbs in the first-person singular (i.e., ἐβουλήθην [v. 12a] and ἐλπίζω [v. 12b]) signal the beginning of this closing in 2 John 12. While the generic participants predominate in the prior section in vv. 9–11, the Elder and the lady are the two main participants in vv. 12–13. The Elder utilizes a total of four pronouns in the second-person plural (i.e., ὑμῖν [v. 12a], ὑμᾶς [v. 12b]) or singular [i.e., σε [v. 13], σου [v. 13]) to refer to the audience in this closing. In addition, he makes use of the device of the inclusive "we" to evoke a sense of togetherness with his audience in v. 12c. Furthermore, the Elder employs the lexeme χαρά from semantic domain 25 ("attitudes and emotions") and in connection with the inclusive first-person plural genitive pronoun ἡμῶν to evoke the positive emotion of shared happiness in v. 12c.[1] In contrast, there is no personal pronoun in the third person throughout vv. 12–13. Compared to the closing of 3 John, there are a few similar features including the Elder's indication of his hope to visit the addressee and the third-person type salutation in the closing of 2 John. Unlike 3 John 15, there is no peace benediction or second-person type greeting at the end of the closing of 2 John. It is noteworthy that the familial words (i.e., τέκνα, ἀδελφῆς) and the recurrence of the lexeme ἐκλεκτός in the final salutation to the audience in 2 John 13 hark back to the recipient's depiction in the prescript (v. 1a). The implication is that the Elder tactually uses the final greeting to close the frame that envelopes this letter.

A. Desire to Visit (v. 12)

This unit consists of the two independent clauses (v. 12a, b) and one dependent clause (v. 12c) in 2 John 12. These three independent or dependent clauses altogether take up approximately three-fourths (word count: twenty-six [74 percent]) of the total length of the closing of this letter. The Elder endeavors to enhance rapport with his audience by expressing his intention to communicate and meet with them. He firstly sets up an initial expectation by saying that he has much to write to the audience at the beginning of v. 12a. The embedded participial clause (i.e., πολλὰ ἔχων ὑμῖν γράφειν) is used to realize the concessive circumstance that contrasts with what will follow in v. 12a. Notice that the accusative neuter plural substantival adjective πολλά (cf. 3 John 13a), which functions as the object of either the masculine singular nominative present active participle ἔχων or the present active infinitive γράφειν, is fronted to underline that the Elder has "much" to write in v. 12.[2] Moreover, the second-person plural dative pronoun ὑμῖν is placed in the emphatic position prior to the infinitive γράφειν to denote the audience in this embedded participial clause above. Upon creating the initial expectation to communicate to the audience through letter writing, the Elder provides new information to counter this initial expectation in the remainder of v. 12a. This counter-expectation is set forth by way of negating the idea that the Elder wishes to communicate through paper and ink. As a rhetorical outcome of using the literary device of counter-expectancy, the

---

1. The cognate verb ἐχάρην, which is lexically related to the noun χαρά, has occurred in 2 John 4.

2. Culy thinks that the substantival adjective πολλά is the complement of the present active infinitive γράφειν in 2 John 12. See Culy, *1, 2, 3 John*, 152.

Elder is able to engage with the audience in such a way that they will be prepared to listen to what he has to say about his projected visit.³

The Elder utilizes the second independent clause beginning with the adversative conjunction ἀλλά to put forward the assertive statement concerning his hope to be with the audience and talk to them in person in v. 12b. While the aorist tense with the perfective aspect (cf. ἐβουλήθην) is used to express the Elder's undesirable wish to communicate through paper and ink in v. 12a, the present tense with the imperfective aspect (cf. ἐλπίζω) is employed to foreground his hope for the projected visit and face-to-face (literally, mouth-to-mouth) conversation in the future in v. 12b. The entire construction γενέσθαι πρὸς ὑμᾶς καὶ στόμα πρὸς στόμα λαλῆσαι, which consists of two conjoined embedded infinitival clauses, is the complement of the first-person singular present active indicative verb ἐλπίζω in v. 12b. The Elder stresses his hope to meet his audience in person by placing the two adjunctive phrases, πρὸς ὑμᾶς and στόμα πρὸς στόμα, adjacent to each other in this construction above.

The dependent clause headed by the subordinating conjunction ἵνα is used to realize the purpose statement in v. 12c. The Elder says that the purpose of his projected visit to personally connect with the audience is that their shared joy may be complete. The nominative feminine singular perfect passive participle πεπληρωμένη alone constitutes the complement of the third-person singular subjunctive verb ᾖ (cf. John 16:24; 1 John 1:4), whose subject is the word group ἡ χαρὰ ἡμῶν that precedes in v. 12c. The first-person plural genitive pronoun ἡμῶν in this word group above is attested in codices Sinaiticus (ℵ or 01), Porphyrianus (P^{apr} or 025), and Athous Lavrensis (Ψ or 044), the Byzantine manuscripts, and all Syrian versions. However, the variant ὑμῶν in the second-person plural is supported by codices Alexandrinus (A or 02), Vaticanus (B or 03), minuscules 5 and 33, the Vulgate, and the Bohairic versions. These two different readings (i.e., ἡ χαρὰ ἡμῶν and ἡ χαρὰ ὑμῶν) are considered as equal to each other in 2 John 12c in NA28. Regarding the internal evidence, the textual reading (i.e., ἡ χαρὰ ἡμῶν) seems to be weightier because the scribes would have been likely to amend the text in v. 12c to assimilate to the occurrences of the two second-person plural pronouns ὑμῖν (v. 12a) and ὑμᾶς (v. 12b) in the preceding co-text.⁴ Assuming the authenticity of the first-person plural genitive pronoun ἡμῶν, its referent probably includes both the Elder and his audience. The lexeme χαρά appears for the first time in v. 12c in the

---

3. For the linguistic device of counter-expectancy, see Martin and Rose, *Working with Discourse*, 56–57.

4. Metzger, *Textual Commentary on the Greek New Testament*, 653.

letter closing. Yet, the Elder has previously employed the cognate lexeme χαίρω to intimate his rejoicing as a result of knowing some of the audience walking in the truth in v. 4a. In view of the lexical connection between the two related words (i.e., ἐχάρην [v. 4a] and χαρά [v. 12c]), it is likely that the Elder seeks to encourage his audience to continue living in the truth so that their meeting in the future will be a very happy occasion in v. 12c. In fact, the audience's adherence to the truth in daily lives requires them to love one another, uphold the doctrine of incarnation, remain in the teaching of Christ, and refuse to welcome the deceivers.

B. Final Greeting (v. 13)

Second John ends with the third-person type salutation (cf. the predicator ἀσπάζεταί) in v. 13, in which the children of the lady's chosen sister send their greetings to her. The shift from the second-person plural pronouns (e.g., ὑμῖν, ὑμᾶς) in v. 12a–b in the preceding co-text to the second-person singular pronouns (e.g., σε, σου) has the effect of focusing attention on the lady (who figuratively denotes a church) as the recipient of the final salutation in v. 13. It was customary to find the lexeme ἀσπάζομαι in the closing greetings in the familial letters or the correspondences between friends beginning the reign of Augustus.[5] Although the predicator ἀσπάζεταί above is in the third-person singular, the subject is constitutive of the word group (i.e., τὰ τέκνα τῆς ἀδελφῆς σου τῆς ἐκλεκτῆς) in which the articular head noun τέκνα is in the neuter plural in v. 13.[6] Akin to the use of the feminine and kinship terms to denote a church and her members (v. 1a), respectively, in the prescript, it is likely that the "children of the lady's chosen sister" are cryptic references to the believers of the congregation that the Elder was belonged to at the time of writing in v. 13.[7] In other words, the Elder passes the greetings from these believers to the audience at the end of this letter. Furthermore, he enhances the Christian solidarity and close bonding between the two congregations through the use of the family metaphors and the theologically loaded word ἐκλεκτός in v. 13 (cf. 1 Pet 5:13).

---

5. White, "Greek Documentary Letter Tradition," 95.

6. It is not uncommon to find neuter plural subject using a singular verb in Greek. Mathewson and Emig, *Intermediate Greek Grammar*, 156.

7. Jobes, *1, 2, and 3 John*, 278; Kruse, *Letters of John*, 217.

COMMENTARY ON
3 JOHN

THIS BRIEF LETTER IS MADE UP of the opening (vv. 1-4), the body (vv. 5-12), and the closing (vv. 13-15). Three individuals are mentioned by name. They are Gaius (v. 1), who is the recipient of the letter, Diotrephes (v. 9), and Demetrius (v. 12). The Elder and Gaius are the two main participants, who are referred to directly or indirectly twenty-seven times and thirty-one times, respectively.[1] The next two participants referred to most frequently are the traveling Christian workers (14x) and Diotrephes (11x),[2]

---

1. The direct or indirect participant references to the Elder or Gaius include the direct addresses (e.g., the vocative), the relevant pronouns (e.g., the inclusive first-person plural pronouns), and the finite or non-finite verbs with the Elder or Gaius as the subject. There are altogether twenty-seven explicit or implicit participant references to the Elder. The reference chain of the Elder is as follows: πρεσβύτερος (v. 1); ἐγὼ (v. 1); ἀγαπῶ (v. 1); εὔχομαί (v. 2); ἐχάρην (v. 3); ἔχω (v. 4); ἀκούω (v. 4); ἐμὰ (v. 4); ἡμεῖς (v. 8); ὀφείλομεν (v. 8); ὑπολαμβάνειν (v. 8); γινώμεθα (v. 8); Ἔγραψά (v. 9); ἡμᾶς (v. 9); ἔλθω (v. 10); ὑπομνήσω (v. 10); ἡμᾶς (v. 10); ἡμεῖς (v. 12); μαρτυροῦμεν (v. 12); ἡμῶν (v. 12); εἶχον (v. 13); γράψαι (v. 13); θέλω (v. 13); γράφειν (v. 13); ἐλπίζω (v. 14); ἰδεῖν (v. 14); λαλήσομεν (v. 14).

There are altogether thirty-one explicit or implicit participant references to Gaius. The reference chain of Gaius is as follows: Γαΐῳ (v. 1) τῷ ἀγαπητῷ (v. 1); ὃν (v. 1); Ἀγαπητέ (v. 2); σε (v. 2); εὐοδοῦσθαι (v. 2); ὑγιαίνειν (v. 2); σου ἡ ψυχή (v. 2); σου (v. 3); σὺ (v. 3); περιπατεῖς (v. 3); Ἀγαπητέ (v. 5); ποιεῖς (v. 5); ἐργάσῃ (v. 5); σου (v. 6); ποιήσεις (v. 6); προπέμψας (v. 6); ἡμεῖς (v. 8); ὀφείλομεν (v. 8); ὑπολαμβάνειν (v. 8); γινώμεθα (v. 8); Ἀγαπητέ (v. 11); μιμοῦ (v. 11); οἶδας (v. 12); σοι (v. 13); σοι (v. 13); σε (v. 14); λαλήσομεν (v. 14); σοι (v. 15); σε (v. 15); ἀσπάζου (v. 15).

2. The total fourteen direct or indirect participant references to the itinerant missionaries do not include the specific references to Demetrius (v. 12), who is considered as an individual participant in 2 John in this commentary. The reference chain of the iterant missionaries is as follows: ἐρχομένων (v. 3); ἀδελφῶν (v. 3); μαρτυρούντων (v. 3); εἰς τοὺς ἀδελφοὺς (v. 5); ξένους (v. 5); οἳ (v. 6); ἐμαρτύρησάν (v. 6); οὓς (v. 6); ἐξῆλθον (v. 7); λαμβάνοντες (v. 7); τοὺς τοιούτους (v. 8); ἡμᾶς (v. 9); ἡμᾶς (v. 10); τοὺς ἀδελφοὺς (v. 10).

Diotrephes is referred to only in 3 John 9-10. The reference chain of Diotrephes (cf. total eleven participant references) is as follows: ὁ φιλοπρωτεύων (v. 9); Διοτρέφης (v. 9);

the former being the Elder's associates in ministry and the latter being his opponent. Compared with Diotrephes, the relatively high number of these Christian workers' participant references and their wide distribution in the letter's opening and body (vv. 3, 5–6, 7–10) suggest that the matter concerning these missionaries, not Diotrephes, is of a greater weight in 3 John. It is noteworthy that Gaius is never referred to in the unit in which Diotrephes comes on scene in vv. 9–10, despite that Gaius enjoys the highest number of the participant references in this epistle.[3] First and foremost, the Elder undertakes to influence Gaius to remain in cooperation with him and continue providing aid to his envoys for the sake of the spreading of the gospel. Secondarily, and in contribution to this foremost purpose, the Elder relays information regarding Diotrephes's bad behaviors to pre-empt the unfortunate happening that Gaius may be negatively affected by his misdeeds and accordingly refuse to welcome the itinerant evangelists sent by the Elder in the future. It is likely that Demetrius was a traveling Christian worker belonged to the Elder's band of associates. Thus, the immediate and favorable response that the Elder seeks to elicit from Gaius is his willing reception of Demetrius, who was probably responsible of delivering 3 John to him.

In terms of word count, 3 John is the shortest book in the NT. There is a total of 218 words in altogether thirty-eight ranking clauses in this letter,[4] twenty-seven words short of the length of 2 John. The average number of words in each ranking clause is approximately 5.7 words in 3 John. Apart from several exceptions (e.g., vv. 3a, 5, 7), the clauses tend to be concise (e.g., the chain of the elliptical clauses in v. 10e–f), straightforward, and not loaded with word groups or embedded clauses. As will be seen below, the Elder tactfully draws upon the lexico-grammatical or discourse resources to affect Gaius's behavior to achieve his communicative aims in this brief letter.

ἐπιδέχεται (v. 9); αὐτοῦ (v. 10); ποιεῖ (v. 10); φλυαρῶν (v. 10); ἀρκούμενος (v. 10); αὐτὸς (v. 10); ἐπιδέχεται (v. 10); κωλύει (v. 10); ἐκβάλλει (v. 10).

3. O'Donnell and Smith, "Discourse Analysis of 3 John," 134, 136.

4. The altogether thirty-eight ranking clauses are present in 3 John 1a, 1b, 2a, 2b, 3a, 3b, 4a, 4b, 5, 6a, 6b, 7, 8a, 8b, 9a, 9b, 10a, 10b, 10c, 10d, 10e, 10f, 11a, 11b, 11c, 11d, 12a, 12b, 12c, 12d, 12e, 13a, 13b, 14a, 14b, 15a, 15b, 15c.

3 JOHN 1–4

OUTLINE:

I. Opening (vv. 1–4)
    A. The Prescript (v. 1)
    B. The Health Wish (v. 2)
    C. An Expression of Rejoicing (vv. 3–4)
II. Body (vv. 5–12)
III. Closing (vv. 13–15)

I. OPENING (VV. 1–4)

The opening of 3 John is divided into three sections (i.e., v. 1, v. 2 and vv. 3–4), in which altogether four clause complexes are present in v. 1a–b, v. 2a–b, v. 3a–b, and v. 4a–b. Each of these four clause complexes is made up of the main clause (vv. 1a, 2a, 3a, 4a) followed by the subordinate clause (vv. 1b, 2b, 3b, 4b). The Elder primarily uses all the clauses in this opening to establish rapport with and give information to Gaius. Depending on the meaning of the first-person singular present active indicative verb εὔχομαί (v. 2a; more on this below), there is a concentration of six (or five) words that fall into semantic domain 25 ("attitudes and emotions") and carry an affective or positive connotation in vv. 1–4 (cf. ἀγαπητῷ [v. 1a], ἀγαπῶ [v. 1b], ἀγαπητέ [v. 2a], possibly εὔχομαί [v. 2a],[1] ἐχάρην [v. 3a], χαράν [v. 4a]). In addition, the lexeme ἀλήθεια from semantic domain 72 ("true, false") occurs a total of four times in the letter opening (vv. 1a, 3a, 3b, 4b; cf. vv. 8b, 12b, 12e). The recurrences of the cognate words from these two semantic

---

1. If the verb εὔχομαί (v. 2a) is meant "I wish," it falls into semantic domain 25 ("attitudes and emotions"). See the commentary on 3 John 2 below.

domains above have the effect of increasing the coherence of the opening of this epistle.

A. The Prescript (v. 1)

The first section of the opening is the prescript (v. 1), which consists of altogether ten words in the main clause (containing five words) in v. 1a and the subclause (containing five words) in v. 1b. The Elder adopts the standard convention, "A (the addresser) to B (the addressee)," commonly found in the opening of most Greek letters, albeit without the epistolary salutation. His self-designation (i.e., ὁ πρεσβύτερος) appears in the nominative case and prior to the recipient's name (i.e., Γαΐῳ), which is presented in the dative case in v. 1a. Akin to the opening prescript of 2 John, "the Elder" as the sender's self-designation should be taken as a title that is indicative of his respectable and authoritative status in the Christian community. In other words, the Elder writes in the position of a superior in regard to his social relationship to Gaius. The Elder employs a lexeme of affective meaning (cf. the dative phrase τῷ ἀγαπητῷ) to modify the preceding dative proper noun Γαΐῳ (v. 1a), thus striking a warm note at the onset of this letter. The earliest attestation of the word group ἀγαπητὸς ἀδελφός is present in Tobit 10:13 in extant Greek literature.[2] However, the lexeme ἀγαπητός often occurs to describe the early Christians as loved by the addresser or God in the NT and particularly in the salutatory addresses in the Pauline epistles (e.g., Rom 1:7; 2 Tim 1:2; Phlm 1).[3] In view of this, the Elder probably utilizes the lexeme ἀγαπητός to denote Gaius as a believer in v. 1a.[4] We know very little about Gaius and his relation to the Elder except that Gaius was probably a wealthy Christian and had offered hospitality to the traveling Christian workers before the composition of 3 John (cf. vv. 3, 5–8).

The wording of the subordinate clause (i.e., ὃν ἐγὼ ἀγαπῶ ἐν ἀληθείᾳ) in v. 1b bears a resemblance to the prescript of 2 John (cf. οὓς ἐγὼ ἀγαπῶ ἐν ἀληθείᾳ in 2 John 1b). This subordinate clause, which is used to expand the main clause that precedes in v. 1a, serves to enhance the correspondents' relationship by providing additional information regarding the Elder's endearment towards Gaius. It merits mention that the two important notions of "love" and "truth" appear in connection with each other for the first time

---

2. ἄδελφε ἀγαπητέ (Tob 10:13). See Blumell, *Lettered Christians*, 69.

3. Cf. Rom 12:19; 1 Cor 10:14; 15:58; Phil 2:12; 4:1; Col 1:7; 4:7, 9, 14; Jas 1:16, 19; 2:5.

4. The phrase ἀγαπητὸς ἀδελφός is a "distinctively Christian salutation" in early Christianity. See Blumell, *Lettered Christians*, 69–70.

in v. 1b.[5] While the prior clause is articulated in the third person and without a verb in v. 1a, the Elder employs the first-person singular present active indicative verb ἀγαπῶ with the expressed subject ἐγώ to indicate explicitly his loving affection towards Gaius in v. 1b.[6] This indicative verb (i.e., ἀγαπῶ) is related lexically to the preceding adjective ἀγαπητός and detected only once in 3 John 1. The prepositional phrase ἐν ἀληθείᾳ is found three times and always anarthrous in this letter (vv. 1b, 3b, 4b; cf. 2 John 1b, 3, 4b). In the present instance, this prepositional phrase is used to specify the Elder's love towards Gaius in v. 1b. While it is possible to construe the first occurrence of the prepositional phrase ἐν ἀληθείᾳ as expressing the idea of veracity,[7] the Elder probably uses this prepositional phrase above to assert that his love for Gaius is based on and motivated by their common identity as believers in 3 John 1b (cf. 2 John 1b).[8] It should be remarked that the information regarding the Christian faith shared by the Elder and Gaius is presupposed and not open to negotiation. The corollary is that Gaius should read the rest of this letter from the perspective of his Christian solidarity with the Elder.

B. The Health Wish (v. 2)

The Elder is the subject of the independent clause and continues to be the active participant in v. 2a (cf. vv. 3a, 4a). It was customary to find a wish for good health and fortune in the opening of ancient Greek letters (e.g., P.Oxy. XII 1422; 2 Macc 11:28),[9] though this epistolary feature may sometimes be found before the farewell in the closing. That said, 3 John is the only NT epistle that consists of a health wish. The Elder employs the vocative singular ἀγαπητέ to address Gaius affectionately to grab his attention before offering the good wishes to him at the beginning of v. 2a. The lexeme ἀγαπητός

---

5. Klauck, *Ancient Letters and the New Testament*, 31.

6. The Elder's self-references are expressed by the first-person singular a total of thirteen times (vv. 1b [2x], 2a, 3a, 4a, 4b [2x], 9a, 10a, 10b, 13a, 13b, 14a) and the exclusive or inclusive first-person plural a total of nine times (vv. 8a [2x], 8b, 9b, 10b, 12c [2x], 12e, 14b) in 3 John.

7. Bultmann, *Johannine Epistles*, 96.

8. Jobes, *1, 2, and 3 John*, 288; Brown, *Epistles of John*, 703.

9. See the following two wishes for good health in the Hellenistic letters: ἐρρῶσθαι σε εὔχομαι φίλατε in Demetrius's letter to Agathodaemon (P.Oxy. XII 1422), and εἰ ἔρρωσθε εἴη ἂν ὡς βουλόμεθα καὶ αὐτοὶ δὲ ὑγιαίνομεν in King Antiochus V's letter to the Jewish people (2 Macc 11:28). For more examples of the health wish, see Adams, "Paul's Letter Opening and Greek Epistolography," 48–49; Tite, "How to Begin," 65; Klauck, *Ancient Letters and the New Testament*, 21–22n11; White, "Greek Documentary Letter Tradition," 92–94.

occurs in the vocative case a total of thirty times in the NT.[10] Almost all of the various vocative forms of this lexeme are in the plural, save the three instances of the substantival use of the vocative singular adjective ἀγαπητέ as the direct addresses to Gaius in 3 John (vv. 2a, 5a, 11a). Furthermore, this vocative singular adjective (i.e., ἀγαπητέ) is always used to signal the beginning of a new unit in these three instances in this letter.[11]

Following the vocative singular ἀγαπητέ, the prepositional phrase περὶ πάντων serves as the point of departure of the message and the marked topical theme of the clause in v. 2a. In the Hellenistic letters, the health wish typically begins with the wording πρὸ πάντων (literally means "before all") to underline what is hoped for is of primary importance. Nevertheless, the Elder uses the prepositional phrase περὶ πάντων to point out the comprehensiveness instead of the significance of what the good wishes are pertinent to.[12] It is difficult to decide whether the first-person singular present middle indicative verb εὔχομαι is meant "I pray" or "I wish" in v. 2a.[13] On the one hand, it can be argued that there is no crucial difference between a wish and a prayer in a Christian letter because the Elder would presumably pray for Gaius's welfare.[14] Moreover, the health wish and the prayer of supplication are often connected syntactically in the opening of ancient Greek letters and particularly the letters dated to the second and third centuries AD.[15] If the predicator εὔχομαί above is meant "I pray," it is a verb of saying from semantic domain 33 ("communication") and is utilized to encode the verbal process in regard to the experiential meaning in 3 John 2a. On the other hand, the way in which the Elder's good wishes are articulated sounds like his thought rather than an intercession to God.[16] It deserves notice that God is not mentioned explicitly whereas there are several words from semantic domain 25 ("attitudes and emotions") in the letter opening (e.g., ἀγαπητῷ

---

10. Rom 12:19; 1 Cor 10:14; 15:58; 2 Cor 7:1; 12:19; Phil 2:12; 4:1 (2x); Heb 6:9; Jas 1:16, 19; 2:5; 1 Pet 2:11; 4:12; 2 Pet 3:1, 8, 14, 17; 1 John 2:7; 3:2, 21; 4:1, 7, 11; 3 John 2, 5, 11; Jude 3, 17, 20.

11. The vocative plural ἀγαπητοί is used to signal the beginning of a unit in several NT epistles (e.g., 1 John 4:1, 7, 11; 1 Pet 2:11; 4:12; 2 Pet 3:1, 8, 14, 17; Jude 3, 17, 20). See Dubis, *1 Peter*, 59; Davids, *2 Peter and Jude*, 4, 28, 32, 100, 107–8.

12. Contra BDF 121 (§229.2), the prepositional phrase περὶ πάντων in 3 John 2 is not equivalent to the customary expression πρὸ πάντων that is commonly found in the Hellenistic letter.

13. The lexeme εὔχομαι occurs altogether seven times in the NT (Acts 26:29; 27:29; Rom 9:3; 2 Cor 13:7, 9; Jas 5:16; 3 John 2). Yarbrough notes that this lexeme "may connote 'to wish' in Acts 27:29; Rom 9:3; and here [3 John 2]" (*1–3 John*, 366n1).

14. Akin says that the Elder offers a "prayer-wish" for Gaius (*1, 2, 3 John*, 240).

15. White, "Greek Documentary Letter Tradition," 93.

16. Marshall, *Epistles of John*, 82, though he uses the rendering "I pray."

[v. 1a], ἀγαπῶ [v. 1b], ἀγαπητέ [v. 2a], ἐχάρην [v. 3a], χαράν [v. 4a]). The implication is that the predicator εὔχομαι is likely to be a desiderative or mental verb from this semantic domain and with respect to the Elder's wish for the welfare of his addressee (i.e., Gaius) in v. 2a. Given that there is no explicit reference to God in the health wish, the latter understanding (i.e., εὔχομαι is rendered "I wish") is preferred in this commentary.[17]

Subsequent to the predicator εὔχομαι, the content of the health wish is spelt out by the two conjoined embedded infinitival clauses (i.e., σε εὐοδοῦσθαι καὶ ὑγιαίνειν) in v. 2a.[18] The accusative second-person singular pronoun σε is the subject of both the present passive infinitive εὐοδοῦσθαι and present active infinitive ὑγιαίνειν above. It is likely that only the first infinitive εὐοδοῦσθαι is modified by the foregoing prepositional phrase περὶ πάντων and the second infinitive ὑγιαίνειν focuses specifically on the dimension of physical health in v. 2a.[19] Regarding the former infinitive (i.e., εὐοδοῦσθαι), the lexeme εὐοδόω literally means "to travel along a good road" but there is no example of using this lexeme to convey this literal meaning in the NT (cf. Rom 1:10; 1 Cor 16:2).[20] It is rather the case that the Elder uses the present passive infinitive εὐοδοῦσθαι to wish Gaius enjoying prosperity and favorable circumstances in all respects. Regarding the latter infinitive (i.e., ὑγιαίνειν) above, the lexeme ὑγιαίνω often occurs pertaining to the health wish in the Greek letters (e.g., 2 Macc 11:28) and especially the correspondences between family members.[21] This latter lexeme (i.e., ὑγιαίνω) is found only once in 3 John 2 in the Johannine writings but is used to describe a person's physical wellbeing (e.g., Luke 5:31; 7:10; 15:27), or in a figurative way sound doctrine (e.g., 1 Tim 1:10; 6:3; 2 Tim 1:13; 4:3; Titus 1:9, 13; 2:1, 2) in other NT documents. The Elder continues to expand the health wish by utilizing the comparative conjunction καθώς to relate correspondingly Gaius's physical health to the wellness of his spiritual life in v. 2b. While the present middle indicative verb εὐοδοῦταί is in the third-person singular, the subject (i.e., σου ἡ ψυχή) consists of the second-person singular pronoun σου to indicate Gaius as being the referent. The recurrence of the lexeme εὐοδόω (v. 2b) contributes to the lexical link in the health wish between the two

---

17. See Brown, *Epistles of John*, 703; Jobes, *1, 2, and 3 John*, 290; Yarbrough, *1–3 John*, 366.

18. If the verb εὔχομαί is meant "I pray," the two conjoined embedded infinitival clauses (i.e., σε εὐοδοῦσθαι καὶ ὑγιαίνειν) are utilized to express the content of the verbiage in 3 John 2.

19. Sherman and Tuggy, *Semantic and Structural Analysis*, 126.

20. *BDAG* 410.

21. White, "Greek Documentary Letter Tradition," 94; Adams, "Paul's Letter Opening and Greek Epistolography," 48.

clauses in v. 2a and v. 2b. Notice that the notion of prosperity or wellness, which has been previously presented as new information (i.e., εὐοδοῦσθαι) in the prior clause in v. 2a, is reiterated as given information (i.e., εὐοδοῦταί) and assigned the thematic position in the καθώς-clause to orient Gaius for what the Elder will talk about in v. 2b. As an outcome, the textual cohesion of the health wish is increased in 3 John 2.

C. An Expression of Rejoicing (vv. 3–4)

In addition to having the same two participants (i.e., the Elder and Gaius) and the employment of several words from semantic domain 25 ("attitudes and emotions"; cf. ἐχάρην [v. 3a] and χαράν [v. 4a]) and semantic domain 72 ("true, false"; cf. ἀληθείᾳ [vv. 3a, 3b, 4b]),[22] the postpositive conjunction γάρ (v. 3a) serves to connect the present unit in vv. 3–4 with the preceding co-text.[23] While all of the five finite or non-finite verbs (i.e., ἀγαπῶ, εὔχομαί, εὐοδοῦσθαι, ὑγιαίνειν, εὐοδοῦταί) are in the present tense in vv. 1–2 in the preceding co-text, the Elder shifts to use the aorist tense with the perfective aspect (cf. the predicator ἐχάρην) for the first time to usher in the supporting evidence to back up his foregoing affirmation as regards Gaius's spiritual health in v. 3a. Akin to the similar wording in 2 John 4, the Elder does not simply express his rejoicing but also amplifies this positive affect of happiness by employing the adverbial modifier λίαν. Following the adverb λίαν, the entire construction ἐρχομένων ἀδελφῶν καὶ μαρτυρούντων σου τῇ ἀληθείᾳ is utilized to supply the information pertaining to the situation that has given rise to the Elder's exceeding joy in v. 3a. This construction consists of two genitive absolute clauses,[24] which are joined by the conjunction καί. The genitive plural noun ἀδελφῶν serves as the subject of the two genitive absolutes ἐρχομένων and μαρτυρούντων above. The believers, who are referred to by the genitive plural noun ἀδελφῶν, are introduced as a new participant in v. 3a.[25] Rather than denoting the blood relations, the Elder avails himself of the familial language to speak of the believers as brothers and sisters in God's spiritual family. It is probable that both of the two masculine plural genitive present middle or active participles ἐρχομένων and μαρτυρούντων function temporally to

---

22. O'Donnell and Smith, "Discourse Analysis of 3 John," 132–33.

23. Funk believes that 3 John 3–4 (and 2 John 4) can be construed as "the functional equivalents" of the thanksgiving in the Pauline epistles ("Form and Structure," 426).

24. The genitive absolute construction is treated as an embedded clause and thus not counted as a ranking clause in this commentary.

25. O'Donnell and Smith, "Discourse Analysis of 3 John," 132.

express that the Elder was very glad when some believers came to him and bore a favorable testimony about Gaius in v. 3a.[26]

The lexeme ἔρχομαι is an intransitive verb of action from semantic domain 15 ("linear movement") in the first genitive absolute clause (i.e., ἐρχομένων ἀδελφῶν) above in v. 3a. The other lexeme μαρτυρέω is a verb of saying from semantic domain 33 ("communication") in the second genitive absolute clause (i.e., μαρτυρούντων σου τῇ ἀληθείᾳ) above. As for this latter genitive absolute clause, the Elder does not specify the verbiage with respect to the content of the believers' witness to Gaius. It is unlikely that the dative phrase (i.e., σου τῇ ἀληθείᾳ) denotes what is spoken well of Gaius by the believers in v. 3a. Rather, this dative phrase is probably used to express that they have given a favorable report to the Elder to the advantage of approving Gaius's commitment to the truth.[27] On syntactic grounds, it is possible to construe the function of the following conjunction καθώς (v. 3b) as introducing an indirect speech regarding the content of the believers' testimony. According to this understanding, what the believers have testified of Gaius's faithfulness to the truth is pertinent to the manner in which or "how" (cf. καθώς) he is walking in it in v. 3b (cf. NRSV).[28] However, the downside of this understanding is that the single participle μαρτυρούντων (v. 3a) has to be linked with both the succeeding modifier (i.e., σου τῇ ἀληθείᾳ) in v. 3a and the subsequent dependent clause (i.e., καθὼς σὺ ἐν ἀληθείᾳ περιπατεῖς) in v. 3b.[29] The alternative reading is that the comparative conjunction καθώς is used to introduce the statement with respect to the basis of the Elder's great happiness in v. 3b.[30] The strength of this latter reading is that the overall structures of the two clause complexes appear to be roughly parallel in v. 2 and v. 3.[31] That is to say, the independent clause in v. 2a or v. 3a is longer than and succeeded by the dependent clause beginning with the comparative conjunction καθώς in v. 2b or v. 3b, respectively. Both of the two understandings above concerning the function of the conjunction καθώς are possible in v. 3b. On the whole, the balance tips slightly towards the latter reading that considers the conjunction καθώς as implicating the idea of comparison in v. 3b. At any rate, the Elder employs the second-person singular nominative pronoun σύ to draw attention to the subject

---

26. Culy, *1, 2, 3 John*, 157–58.

27. Culy, *1, 2, 3 John*, 158.

28. Cf. Acts 15:14. See Yarbrough, *1–3 John*, 367–68; Marshall, *Epistles of John*, 84; Schnackenburg, *Johannine Epistles*, 293.

29. Culy, *1, 2, 3 John*, 158.

30. Smalley, *1, 2, 3 John*, 333; Marshall, *Epistles of John*, 84.

31. Culy, *1, 2, 3 John*, 158.

(namely, Gaius) of the predicator περιπατεῖς in v. 3b. While the lexeme περιπατέω literally means "walk," this predicator (i.e., περιπατεῖς) is used to connote the figurative sense in regard to Gaius's way of life (cf. 2 John 4). It seems that the Elder has already had some knowledge about Gaius's good behavior.[32] On the basis of this knowledge, the Elder was greatly delighted because what the believers reported to him was in accordance with (cf. the comparative conjunction καθώς) Gaius's virtuous life as a faithful adherent of the truth. In short, the Elder gives a positive appraisal of Gaius's character and his dealing with the traveling believers in 3 John 3.

The Elder concludes the opening of his letter with an elaboration of the cause of his greatest joy in v. 4. Similar to the foregoing three clause complexes (i.e., v. 1a–b, v. 2a–b, and v. 3a–b), the present clause complex is made up of the independent clause (v. 4a) followed by the dependent clause (v. 4b) in this verse. However, unlike these three preceding clause complexes above, this independent clause in v. 4a is shorter than this dependent clause in v. 4b.[33] There are altogether five words in v. 4a, compared with a total of eight words in v. 4b. The adjunctive phrase μειζοτέραν τούτων is marked in the clause-initial position in v. 4a. The feminine accusative singular adjective μειζοτέραν above, which is a comparative form of the adjective μέγας, modifies the feminine accusative singular noun χαράν at the end of v. 4a. While the variant χάριν is attested in codex Vaticanus (B or 03), several minuscules (e.g., 5, 57, 1243, 2492), and the Latin and Bohairic versions, the textual reading χαράν adopted in NA28 has a stronger external support from the manuscript tradition including codices Sinaiticus (ℵ or 01), Alexandrius (A or 02) and Ephraemi Rescriptus (C or 04), several minuscules (e.g., 81, 614, 1739), and the Syrian, Sahidic, and Armenian versions.[34] On the assumption that the feminine accusative singular noun χαράν (v. 4a) is original, the coherence is increased in vv. 3–4 because this noun is lexically related to the predicator ἐχάρην that precedes in v. 3a. It is worthy of mention that the Elder formulates a litotes in the form of the negative statement, "I have no greater joy than these things," in v. 4a. As a corollary, the Elder accentuates rhetorically the positive overtone of his unsurpassed happiness by putting forward the understatement that is realized by the negative clause (i.e., μειζοτέραν τούτων οὐκ ἔχω χαράν) in v. 4a.[35] The subsequent ἵνα-clause

---

32. Smalley, *1, 2, 3 John*, 333.

33. The word count of the independent or dependent clauses in the letter opening are as follows: v. 1a (5 words), v. 1b (5 words), v. 2a (8 words), v. 2b (5 words), v. 3a (10 words), v. 3b (5 words), v. 4a (5 words), v. 4b (8 words).

34. Metzger, *Textual Commentary on the Greek New Testament*, 654; Schnackenburg, *Johannine Epistles*, 293n109.

35. There are six negative polarity adjuncts (vv. 4a, 9b, 10d, 11a, 11d, 13b) and one negative conjunction (i.e., οὔτε [v. 10d]) in 3 John.

in v. 4b is epexegetical and appositional to the foregoing genitive plural demonstrative pronoun τούτων in this negative clause above as regards the Elder's exceptional joy in v. 4a. The embedded participial clause (i.e., τὰ ἐμὰ τέκνα ἐν ἀληθείᾳ περιπατοῦντα) constitutes the complement of the first-person singular present active subjunctive verb ἀκούω that precedes in this ἵνα-clause in v. 4b. The recurrence of the idea of "walking in the truth" (vv. 3b, 4b) suggests an implicit correlation between Gaius and the Elder's "children" and in effect associates Gaius with the latter group. The Elder's "children" are not of kinship relations but rather refer to the believers who are members of the local churches under his pastoral care and oversight. Since the Elder assumes the role of the spiritual "father" of these believers as his children, he has the interpersonal power in relation to them.

3 JOHN 5–12

OUTLINE:

I. Opening (vv. 1–4)

II. Body (vv. 5–12)

    A. Gentle Demand for Gaius's Support (vv. 5–8)

    B. Opposition from Diotrephes (vv. 9–10)

    C. Do Not Imitate the Bad Example (v. 11)

    D. Recommendation of Demetrius (v. 12)

III. Closing (vv. 13–15)

II. BODY (VV. 5–12)

The Elder makes clear his reason or purpose of writing in the body of 3 John. In addition to relaying information to Gaius, the Elder undertakes to exert an influence on his behavior in certain respects. The body of this letter contains a total of twenty-three ranking clauses (60.5 percent) and altogether 133 words (61 percent) including thirty-one verbs in vv. 5–12.[1] The opening boundary of the body is indicated by the occurrence of the vocative singular ἀγαπητέ and a change in the active participant from the Elder to Gaius in v. 5. While all the finite verbs (i.e., ἀγαπῶ [v. 1b], εὔχομαί [v. 2a], εὐοδοῦταί [v. 2b]) are in the first person with reference to the Elder in the epistolary opening, Gaius is the subject of the two indicative or subjunctive verbs (i.e., ποιεῖς and ἐργάσῃ) in the second-person singular in v. 5. Gaius and the

---

1. In the body of 3 John, the altogether twenty-three ranking clauses are present in vv. 5, 6a, b, 7, 8a, b, 9a, b, 10a, b, c, d, e, f, 11a, b, c, d, 12a, b, c, d, e.

traveling believers, who have been introduced in v. 3, are the two participants in vv. 5–8. The appearance of Diotrephes, who is a new participant, points to the beginning of a new section in v. 9. This section closes at the end of v. 10. The Elder subsequently utilizes the vocative singular ἀγαπητέ as a discourse marker to intimate the start of another unit in v. 11. The first mention of Demetrius, who is a new participant, suggests that a new unit commences in v. 12. There are altogether three occurrences of the cognate lexeme μαρτυρέω or μαρτυρία in this verse. It is noteworthy that the first occurrence of the imperative mood is present in v. 11a, in which the Elder issues the explicit command (i.e., "Do not imitate what is evil!") to Gaius. There are altogether two implicit directives that are expressed metaphorically (e.g., incongruent mood choices in grammar) by using the indicative verbs and via the statements in v. 6b and v. 8a. These direct or indirect commands above are crucial for the understanding of the hortatory nature and objectives of 3 John.

A. Gentle Demand for Gaius's Support (vv. 5–8)

The two main participants are Gaius and the itinerant missionaries. There are ten and eight direct or indirect references to each of these two participants in vv. 5–8, respectively (see "Commentary on 3 John" above). Aside from the frequent references to these two main participants, the coherence of the present unit is enhanced by the use of several pairs of cognate words including the following three pairs of lexically related words: (i) ποιεῖς (v. 5) and ποιήσεις (v. 6b); (ii) ἐργάσῃ (v. 5) and συνεργοί (v. 8b); and (iii) λαμβάνοντες (v. 7) and ὑπολαμβάνειν (v. 8a). The division of this unit in vv. 5–8 is hinged on how one construes the function of the postpositive conjunction γάρ in v. 7 (more on this below). This commentary assumes a two-part division (i.e., vv. 5–6 and vv. 7–8) of this unit, with the exhortation in v. 8a being a sub-peak in the body of 3 John. According to this structural division, the first section (vv. 5–6) is made up of twenty-six words in altogether three ranking clauses in v. 5, v. 6a, and v. 6b. The second section (vv. 7–8) is made up of twenty-one words in altogether three ranking clauses, the first two being independent clauses in v. 7 and v. 8a and the last one a dependent clause in v. 8b. Notably, the Elder employs the rhetorical device of the inclusive "we" to attempt influencing Gaius to align with his standpoint in v. 8a–b at the end of this unit.

Following the vocative singular ἀγαπητέ, the neuter singular accusative adjective πιστόν is the marked topical theme that serves as the point of departure of the message conveyed through the clause in v. 5. The implication is that the Elder commences the body of his letter with a positive appraisal to affirm Gaius's faithfulness. Since the neuter singular accusative adjective πιστόν is without a noun, it could be construed as a substantive (i.e., "a faithful thing") representing the object of the second-person singular present active indicative verb ποιεῖς.² In this case, the adjective πιστόν is the complement receiving the action of the predicator ποιεῖς in v. 5. Alternatively, it is probable that this adjective (i.e., πιστόν) above functions as an adverb of manner (i.e., "faithfully") and thus the adjunct in the clause.³ The latter view is preferred because it is not uncommon to find the accusative neuter adjective functioning adverbially in the NT.⁴ Furthermore, it is possible that the relative clause ὃ ἐὰν ἐργάσῃ εἰς τοὺς ἀδελφοὺς καὶ τοῦτο ξένους (cf. here ἐάν is a marker of contingency) serves as the complement of the predicator ποιεῖς in v. 5.⁵ In any event, the Elder utilizes the combination of the accusative neuter singular indefinite pronoun ὅ and the adjunct ἐάν to point out an unspecified number of occasions in which Gaius has done something for the benefit of the believers, who are actually "strangers" to him. Therefore, Gaius has performed good deeds in their favor even though he does not know them.

The Elder goes on to indicate what the itinerant missionaries testify of Gaius and tell him the proper way to deal with them through the two relative clauses in v. 6a–b. It is probable that the two relative pronouns οἵ (v. 6a) and οὕς (v. 6b) have the same antecedent (i.e., either ἀδελφούς or ξένους in v. 5), though the scope of the referent of the latter relative pronoun (i.e., οὕς) seems to be broader (more on this below). There is a shift in the active participant from the traveling Christian workers (v. 6a) to Gaius (v. 6b) in these two relative clauses in succession. The first relative pronoun οἵ is in the nominative case and is the subject of the third-person plural aorist active indicative verb ἐμαρτύρησάν in v. 6a. Yet the second relative pronoun οὕς is in the accusative case and is the object of the nominative masculine singular aorist active participle προπέμψας in v. 6b. Since Gaius is the actor of both of this participle (i.e., προπέμψας) and the preceding second-person singular future active form ποιήσεις, he comes to the fore as the active participant again in v. 6b.

The Elder uses the third-person plural aorist active indicative verb ἐμαρτύρησάν with the perfective aspect to realize the statement in v. 6a,

---

2. Jobes, *1, 2, and 3 John*, 299.

3. Culy, *1, 2, 3 John*, 160; Schnackenburg, *Johannine Epistles*, 294; Yarbrough, *1–3 John*, 370.

4. Wallace, *Greek Grammar*, 200–201, 293.

5. Culy, *1, 2, 3 John*, 160.

which contains the background information regarding the Christian workers' testimony given before the church. The lexeme μαρτυρέω has occurred in the prescript (v. 3a) and will recur twice in v. 12a and v. 12c in the letter body (cf. the cognate noun μαρτυρία in v. 12e). The first and second occurrences of this lexeme are pertinent to the missionaries' witness to Gaius's truth (cf. σου τῇ ἀληθείᾳ) in v. 3a and his love (cf. σου τῇ ἀγάπῃ) in v. 12a, respectively. In view of this, these itinerant workers have given a very favorable testimony to Gaius as a devoted follower of Christ. The prepositional phrase ἐνώπιον ἐκκλησίας (v. 6a) is used to indicate the circumstance of location, namely a local church. It is likely that the Elder attended this church and so he had the opportunity to hear the missionaries' report concerning Gaius's acts of love and generosity. The lexeme ἐκκλησία occurs a total of three times in the body of 3 John but is missing from 1 and 2 John. The first instance of this lexeme refers to the Elder's "church" (v. 6a) and the remaining two instances refer to the "church" of Diotrephes (vv. 9a, 10f).

Upon his commendation of Gaius's past behavior, the Elder undertakes to induce him to continue welcoming the Christian workers. This undertaking is carried out subtly through a covert directive, which is couched in the embedded participial clause προπέμψας ἀξίως τοῦ θεοῦ that is present in the relative clause beginning with the relative pronoun οὕς in v. 6b. The Elder avails himself of this embedded participial clause above instrumentally to describe how Gaius "will do well" (καλῶς ποιήσεις; cf. Jas 2:8, 19; 2 Pet 1:19) and attempt affecting him to perform the desirable act accordingly. Notably, a variation of the phrase καλῶς ποιεῖν was commonly used to introduce a request or soften a command in the Hellenistic letters.[6] The second-person singular future active verb ποιήσεις (v. 6b) is the first of the altogether three occurrences of the future form in this letter (cf. 3 John 6b, 10b, 14b). The Elder does not simply use the future form to portray an event that he expects to happen in the future time in v. 6b. Rather, he seeks to provide an incentive (i.e., "you will do well") to Gaius to accomplish what is suggested in the gentle directive to send the traveling missionaries in a manner worthy of God. The adverb καλῶς, which is loaded with the positive value of appreciation, is placed prior to the predicator ποιήσεις to attract attention in v. 6b. The Elder underlines that what he asks Gaius to perform is a noble task by employing the adjunctive phrase ἀξίως τοῦ θεοῦ to modify the participle προπέμψα that precedes in v. 6b. Within the setting of first-century Greco-Roman society, the lexeme προπέμπω (which occurs only once in the Johannine writings) most likely carries the connotation of providing financial aid to the Christian workers to help on their journey (cf.

---

6. White, "Greek Documentary Letter Tradition," 101; Brown, *Epistles of John*, 710.

Rom 15:24; Titus 3:13). In all likelihood, the Elder's intended beneficiaries are not limited to Gaius's previous visitors but rather include other itinerant believers or evangelists who will need his assistance in the future.

The statement in v. 7 is often regarded as providing the grounds to bolster the Elder's gentle exhortation to Gaius to aid the Christian workers in v. 6b.[7] On this reading, v. 8 recapitulates the thrust of the messages in vv. 5–7 by restating this exhortation above in different terms. The underlying assumption of this reading above is that v. 7 is part of the clause complex that starts from v. 5. Thus, vv. 5–7 altogether constitute a section of the broader unit in vv. 5–8. That said, it is debatable whether v. 7 is related hypotactically to the preceding v. 6b rather than paratactically to the ensuing v. 8a. The issue at stake is the grammatical function of the postpositive conjunction γάρ in v. 7. The common understanding is that this conjunction is a marker of the causal relation between v. 7 and the preceding co-text. Nevertheless, it is probable that the postpositive conjunction γάρ serves to signal the "transition to a new but related concept" in v. 7.[8] The corollary is that the Elder uses the statement in v. 7 to lay the basis for the modulated command to receive the itinerant missionaries that will be spelt out subsequently in v. 8a. The strength of this latter view is that this modulated command in v. 8a is given due weight within the immediate co-text.[9] Note that the participle λαμβάνοντες (v. 7) and the infinitive ὑπολαμβάνειν (v. 8a) are lexically related, thus strengthening the connection of these two verses. If this latter view above is accepted, the unit in vv. 5–8 is constitutive of the two sections in vv. 5–6 and vv. 7–8. Furthermore, each of these two sections concludes with the Elder's subtle directive to Gaius to show hospitality to the traveling missionaries in v. 6b or v. 8a. On account of the reasons laid out above, v. 7 is linked with v. 8 rather than vv. 5–6 in this commentary.

The Elder highlights the noble purpose of the journeys of the Christian workers by fronting the prepositional phrase ὑπὲρ τοῦ ὀνόματος at the onset of v. 7. In doing so, the circumstance of cause, namely "for the sake of the Name," is the marked topical theme of the clause in v. 7. The "Name" could refer to God but it in all likelihood denotes Jesus Christ, who is never explicitly mentioned by name in 3 John (cf. 1 John 2:12; 3:23; 5:13; Acts 5:41; 9:16; 15:26; 21:13; Rom 1:5). Thus, the Elder hints at that these Christian workers traveled from place to place to spread the gospel of Jesus Christ. Moreover, the Elder employs the embedded participial clause (i.e., μηδὲν λαμβάνοντες ἀπὸ τῶν ἐθνικῶν) to rule out the source from which these Christian workers

---

7. See, e.g., Jobes, *1, 2, and 3 John*, 298; Lieu, *I, II, & III John*, 271–73.
8. Sherman and Tuggy, *Semantic and Structural Analysis*, 130.
9. Sherman and Tuggy, *Semantic and Structural Analysis*, 130.

were funded to go on their journeys in v. 7. The negative accusative neuter singular indefinite pronoun μηδὲν, which is the object of the nominative masculine plural present active participle λαμβάνοντες, is marked in the initial position of this embedded participial clause above. Aside from 3 John 7, there are only three other occurrences of the lexeme ἐθνικός (literally "non-Jew" or "gentile") in the NT and all occur in Matthew's Gospel (Matt 5:47; 6:7; 18:17). It is probably because of the few occurrences of this lexeme (i.e., ἐθνικός) that the more common word ἐθνῶς is used instead in the texts in codex Porphyrianus (P^apr or 025), a number of minuscules (e.g., 5, 307, 642, 1175, 1448) and the Byzantine manuscripts.[10] Nevertheless, the reading ἐθνικῶν (v. 7) adopted in NA28 is likely to be authentic because this is the more difficult reading and is attested in codices Sinaiticus (ℵ or 01), Alexandrinus (A or 02), and Vaticanus (B or 03), to name several weighty textual witnesses.[11] Since the substantival adjective ἐθνικῶν (v. 7) in the genitive plural are in contrast with the emphatic "we" (i.e., ἡμεῖς) at the outset of v. 8a, this substantival adjective above is not utilized to encode the literal meaning (i.e., the gentiles), but rather denote the non-believers. Simply put, the Elder tells Gaius that the itinerant missionaries do not solicit financial assistance from the people outside the church to support their living during the journey.

The Elder draws on the resource of modality to put forward the inferential statement (cf. the postpositive conjunction οὖν) based on the reason just provided in the foregoing co-text in v. 8a. While this inferential statement is realized by the indicative mood, it is in effect a modulated command (i.e., "we ought to receive such people") given the employment of the verb of obligation ὀφείλομεν (v. 8a) in the first-person plural. The lexeme ὀφείλω is not found in 2 John but occurs to express a covert directive altogether three times in 1 John 2:6, 3:16, and 4:11. Although the Elder has subtly exhorted Gaius to welcome the missionaries (v. 6b), the modulated command that is realized by the verb of obligation ὀφείλομεν is less mitigated in v. 8a.[12] It can be presumed that the appropriate way of supporting the Christian workers includes showing hospitality and providing financial aid to them. Therefore, the Elder sets forth his gentle demand for Gaius's

---

10. The lexeme ἔθνος is found a total of 162 times in the NT including the 5 occurrences in the Fourth Gospel (cf. John 11:48, 50, 51, 52; 18:35).

11. Yarbrough, *1–3 John*, 376.

12. Sherman and Tuggy comment that the exhortation in v. 8a is "more prominent" than that in v. 6b. See Sherman and Tuggy, *Semantic and Structural Analysis*, 130. For the different degrees of mitigation regarding the covert commands in the Johannine letters, see Miehle, "Theme in Greek Hortatory Discourse," 156; Sherman and Tuggy, *Semantic and Structural Analysis*, 2.

support to the traveling missionaries again through the modulated command in v. 8a.

The intended purpose or result of supplying the needs of "such people" (cf. the substantival adjective τοιούτους) is spelt out through the ἵνα-clause in v. 8b, in which the first-person plural present middle subjunctive verb γινώμεθα implicates the relational process (i.e., the process type of being, becoming, or possessing; see "Field" in "Introduction"). The implied subject of this subjunctive verb above is the inclusive "we" (i.e., Gaius is included as part of the referent) and its complement is the substantival anarthrous adjective συνεργοί (v. 8b) in the nominative masculine plural. The lexeme συνεργός occurs frequently to denote Paul's coworkers including Timothy, Titus, Priscilla, and Aquila in the Pauline epistles (e.g., Rom 16:3, 9, 21; 2 Cor 8:23; Phil 2:25; 4:3). There is an ambiguity regarding the function of the adjunctive dative phrase τῇ ἀληθείᾳ that ensues the subjunctive verb γινώμεθα in v. 8b. This adjunctive phrase has been variedly construed as a circumstance of accompaniment (i.e., in cooperation with the truth),[13] location (i.e., in the sphere of the truth),[14] or cause (i.e., for the benefit of the [spreading of the] truth).[15] The first construal with respect to the circumstantial idea of accompaniment presupposes a certain degree of the personification of the word "truth" in v. 8b (cf. John 8:32; 14:6). Moreover, it is assumed that the Elder's use of the dative case (i.e., τῇ ἀληθείᾳ) is due to the prefix (i.e., συν-) contained in the preceding substantival anarthrous adjective συνεργοί in v. 8b. As for the other two understandings of the phrase τῇ ἀληθείᾳ above (i.e., a circumstance of location or cause), the unspecified accompanier (i.e., the itinerant missionaries) with whom the Elder and Gaius work together has to be implied from the surrounding co-text. While all of the three readings above are probable, the third reading is most fitting in the co-text of the body of 3 John. The reason why this reading is preferable is that it is in the same wavelength with the Elder's hortatory aim to urge Gaius to support and partner with the Christian workers to advance the gospel.[16] If this understanding is accepted, the Elder says that we ought to support the Christian workers so that we may work together with them for the benefit of the spreading of the truth in 3 John 8.

---

13. Thus, the phrase τῇ ἀληθείᾳ is "the dative of association." Brown, *Epistles of John*, 714–15; Schnackenburg, *Johannine Epistles*, 296; Lieu, *I, II, & III John*, 273.

14. Thus, the phrase τῇ ἀληθείᾳ is "the dative of sphere." Yarbrough, *1–3 John*, 375n8.

15. Thus, the phrase τῇ ἀληθείᾳ is "the dative of advantage." Marshall, *Epistles of John*, 87n16; Jobes, *1, 2, and 3 John*, 304.

16. Marshall, *Epistles of John*, 87n16.

B. Opposition from Diotrephes (vv. 9–10)

The Elder moves on to criticize a certain Christian named Diotrephes for his hostile acts against him and the traveling brothers and sisters. The present unit contains a total of forty-five words in altogether eight ranking clauses, six being the independent clauses (i.e., vv. 9a, 9b, 10b, 10d, 10e, 10f) and two being the dependent clauses (i.e., v. 10a, 10c). There are altogether twelve finite or non-finite verbs, including seven indicative verbs (i.e., ἔγραψά [v. 9a], ἐπιδέχεται [2x; vv. 9b, 10d], ὑπομνήσω [v. 10b], ποιεῖ [v. 10c], κωλύει [v. 10e], ἐκβάλλει [v. 10f]), one subjunctive verb (i.e., ἔλθω [v. 10a]), and four participles (i.e., φιλοπρωτεύων [v. 9b], φλυαρῶν [v. 10c], ἀρκούμενος [v. 10d], βουλομένους [v. 10e]) in this unit. Since approximately one in every four words is a verb (26.7 percent; cf. twelve verbs to forty-five words),[17] there is a rich tapestry of experiential meanings and primarily of the material process type (which usually involves a performative or action verb) in vv. 9–10. It should be noted that Gaius is never a participant or referred to throughout vv. 9–10.[18] None of the altogether eight indicative or subjunctive verbs above is in the second person. While the three finite verbs in the first-person singular with reference to the Elder are in either the aorist (cf. ἔγραψά [v. 9a] and ἔλθω [v. 10a]) or future form (cf. ὑπομνήσω [v. 10b]), all of the five indicative verbs that are in the third-person singular are in the present tense and have Diotrephes as the subject (cf. ἐπιδέχεται [2x; vv. 9b, 10d], ποιεῖ [v. 10c], κωλύει [v. 10e], ἐκβάλλει [v. 10f]). In addition, Diotrephes is the subject of the altogether three present participles in the singular (i.e., φιλοπρωτεύων [v. 9b], φλυαρῶν [v. 10c], ἀρκούμενος [v. 10d]), save the present participle βουλομένους in the plural in v. 10e. Therefore, it is evident that the Elder is fond of employing the imperfective aspect to foreground what Diotrephes has done to oppose the Elder and his envoys. Also noteworthy is the Elder's choice of several words weighted with a negative meaning (e.g., φιλοπρωτεύω [v. 9b], πονηρός [v. 10c], φλυαρέω [v. 10c]) to depict the events surrounding Diotrephes. In a nutshell, the Elder endeavors to set forth his unfavorable judgment of Diotrephes's character and conduct through the relevant statements in 3 John 9–10.

The first independent clause starts with the predicator ἔγραψά, which takes the accusative neuter singular indefinite pronoun τι as the object in v. 9a in this unit. It is likely that this indefinite pronoun denotes a previous letter written by the Elder, though it is uncertain whether this letter refers to

---

17. For the purpose of comparison, the ratio of the total number of verbs to words (31 verbs to 133 words) is approximately 23.3 percent in the letter body in 3 John 5–12.

18. O'Donnell and Smith, "Discourse Analysis of 3 John," 134, 136.

2 John or a lost epistle unknown to us.[19] The dative article τῇ with the noun ἐκκλησίᾳ (v. 9a) is not anaphoric because the only previous occurrence of the lexeme ἐκκλησία refers to the Elder's own congregation in v. 6a. This dative article (i.e., τῇ) above may point to the particular church which Diotrephes belongs to or even holds an authoritative position. Alternatively, the Elder might have written a circular letter to the Christian communities in general within his circle of influence and including Diotrephes's congregation. In any case, the elided contrastive conjunction ἀλλ' hints at that the Elder's previous correspondence met with Diotrephes's defiance at the outset of v. 9b. Since Diotrephes is mentioned only in 3 John in the NT, very little is known about this person. Subsequent to this elided contrastive conjunction (i.e., ἀλλ') above, the Elder utilizes the nominal group ὁ φιλοπρωτεύων αὐτῶν Διοτρέφη to be the subject of the third-person singular present active indicative verb ἐπιδέχεται in the negative clause in v. 6b. This nominal group is made up of an embedded participial clause (i.e., ὁ φιλοπρωτεύων αὐτῶν) followed by the proper noun Διοτρέφη in the nominative case. By placing this embedded participial clause prior to Diotrephes's name, the Elder calls attention to Diotrephes's aspiration to be first in rank or occupy the leading position among other church members (cf. αὐτῶν ["over them"]).[20] The Elder's problem with Diotrephes is that he does not "receive" the itinerant missionaries and, by extension, does not "receive" or acknowledge the Elder as he is their sender.[21] The lexeme ἐπιδέχομαι is detected only twice in 3 John (vv. 9b, 10d) and nowhere in other NT documents. The Elder creates the lexical link between these two verses by employing this lexeme twice and thereby enhances the unity in vv. 9–10.

The Elder uses a chain of six ranking clauses to provide adequate information to Gaius regarding what Diotrephes has done to obstruct the missionary work of the Elder's envoys in v. 10a–f. Following the prepositional phrase διὰ τοῦτο, the conjunction ἐάν can be construed as introducing either a temporal or third-class conditional clause in v. 10a. If this conjunction conveys a temporal meaning, the Elder does not merely speak of a hypothetical situation of his visitation but rather a future plan that is already in his mind (cf. v. 10b).[22] At any rate, the Elder says that he will call attention to Diotrephes's wicked deeds (cf. the neuter plural τὰ ἔργα) upon his arrival. Diotrephes's misbehavior is elaborated through the four consecutive

---

19. Some commentators believe that the indefinite pronoun τι in 3 John 9 refers to 2 John. See Yarbrough, *1–3 John*, 377. For the contrary view, see Lieu, *I, II, & III John*, 274n13.

20. O'Donnell and Smith, "Discourse Analysis of 3 John," 137.

21. Mitchell, "'Diotrephes Does Not Receive Us'"; Jobes, *1, 2, and 3 John*, 313.

22. Marshall, *Epistles of John*, 90–91.

statements in v. 10c-f. The first statement is realized by the relative clause beginning with the accusative neuter plural relative pronoun ἅ in v. 10c, but the subsequent three statements are realized by the three independent clauses in v. 10d-f.

As indicated in v. 10c, Diotrephes performed his bad deeds by talking nonsense (cf. φλυαρῶν is a participle of means) about the Elder and his envoys with wicked words. The subsequent prepositional phrase ἐπὶ τούτοις (cf. the dative plural demonstrative pronoun τούτοις should be masculine, not neuter) in v. 10d harks back to the phrase λόγοις πονηροῖς in the masculine dative plural that precedes in v. 10c. Since Diotrephes was not satisfied (cf. the causal participle ἀρκούμενος) with spreading these wicked words, he refused to welcome the Christian workers. The Elder draws attention to the actor (i.e., Diotrephes) by utilizing the pronoun αὐτός as the expressed subject of the predicator ἐπιδέχεται in v. 10d. Moreover, the negative polarity adjunct μή and the negative conjunction οὔτε (v. 10d) are employed to heighten Diotrephes's antagonism. The unspecified complement of the present middle accusative masculine plural participle βουλομένους (v. 10e) can be deduced from the content of the prior clauses. It is presumed that Diotrephes has hindered the believers who wanted to receive the Elder's envoys. Lastly, the Elder tells Gaius that Diotrephes even threw these believers (who are the implicit object of the predicator ἐκβάλλει) of his congregation out of the church in v. 10f. Regarding the experiential meaning, it is apparent that the material process type (i.e., the process of doing or acting) predominates in the Elder's unfolding of Diotrephes's misbehaviors in v. 10c-f. Aside from the four verbs of action (i.e., ποιεῖ [v. 10c], ἐπιδέχεται [v. 10d], κωλύει [v. 10e], ἐκβάλλει [v. 10f]), the present active nominative masculine singular participle φλυαρῶν (v. 10c) is employed to express the verbal process with respect to Diotrephes's false accusation against the Elder. On the whole, the Elder's negative judgment of Diotrephes is not primarily concerned with his doctrinal belief, but rather what he has done or said to impede the Elder's envoys from accomplishing their missionary tasks. Notably, the Elder places the object (i.e., ἅ [v. 10c] or τοὺς βουλομένους [v. 10e]) or the circumstantial element (i.e., μὴ ἀρκούμενος ἐπὶ τούτοις [v. 10d] or ἐκ τῆς ἐκκλησίας [v. 10f]) in the thematic position to give emphasis in all of the four clauses in v. 10c-f.[23] As an outcome, the Elder moves Gaius from one instance to another instance of Diotrephes's wicked deeds in succession and thereby augments the rhetorical impact of the portrayal of his misconduct in v. 10c-f.

---

23. Martin and Rose comment that the marked themes in general have the effect of creating a discontinuity in the flow of discourse and thus stressing the topics of the clauses. See Martin and Rose, *Working with Discourse*, 192.

C. Do Not Imitate the Bad Example (v. 11)

Coupled with Diotrephes's disappearance from the discourse, the return of Gaius as the main participant points to the beginning of a new section in v. 11. The Elder employs the vocative singular ἀγαπητέ (v. 11a) the third time to address Gaius directly, show affection, and attract attention (cf. 3 John 2, 5). There is no conjunction to connect v. 11 and v. 12, in which Demetrius will come on scene as a new participant. Despite the brevity of this section, v. 11 stands on its own as a semantically and structurally coherent unit. It is noteworthy that there is a clustering of several lexemes (e.g., κακός, κακοποιέω, ἀγαθός, ἀγαθοποιέω) from semantic domain 88 ("moral and ethical qualities and related behavior") in this verse. The two negative or positive clauses are contrastive to each other in v. 11a–b (cf. the adversative conjunction ἀλλά in v. 11b). Furthermore, the Elder uses the two subsequent positive or negative clauses beginning with either ὁ ἀγαθοποιῶν or ὁ κακοποιῶν to establish an antithesis in v. 11c–d. As a corollary, the structural unity is increased in 3 John 11.

The concentration of the semantically related lexemes above, which are loaded with ethical overtones, is suggestive of the Elder's agenda to give his judgement of what is good or evil in v. 11. There are only two instances of the imperative mood in 3 John (vv. 11, 15). The Elder employs the grammatical imperative (i.e., μιμοῦ [v. 11a]) and the perfect tense (i.e., ἑώρακεν [v. 11d]; cf. v. 12a) both for the first time to intimate the presence of a discourse peak in this unit. In view of the employment of the second-person singular present active imperative verb μιμοῦ (v. 11a) and the third-person singular perfect active indicative verb ἑώρακεν (v. 11d), the Elder gives prominence to the messages of avoiding what is evil that are conveyed through the two negative clauses in v. 11a and v. 11d. The lexeme μιμέομαι is found a total of four times in the NT and only once in 3 John 11 in the Johannine writings (cf. 2 Thess 3:7, 9; Heb 13:7). Since the imperative mood is typically used to demand goods-and-services in Halliday's systemic functional linguistics (see "Tenor" in "Introduction"), the Elder apparently seeks to evoke a response from Gaius and affect him by means of what is said in the present section. Moreover, the employment of the imperative mood to issue the prohibition to imitate what is evil is telling that the Elder has some power in relationship to Gaius. The elliptical clause (i.e., ἀλλὰ τὸ ἀγαθόν) is without a verb in v. 11b. Yet, the implicit second-person singular present middle imperative verb μιμοῦ can be inferred from the prior clause in v. 11a. Thus, the Elder firstly puts forward the negative command to exhort Gaius not to imitate what is evil in v. 11a and subsequently the positive command to imitate what is good in v. 11b. These two negative or positive commands above in effect invoke two different "voices," which represent two antithetical positions for enhancing the persuasive effect of the Elder's exhortation to Gaius in v. 11a–b.[24] By using the negative polarity adjunct μή, the unfavorable position that the Elder does not want Gaius to take side with is brought up first and then immediately set aside in v. 11a. It is likely that "the evil thing" (cf. τὸ κακόν [v. 11a]) that Gaius should not emulate is concerned with Diotrephes's hostile actions and disparaging words against the Elder and his envoys (cf. vv. 9–10). Conversely, "the good thing" (cf. τὸ ἀγαθόν) that Gaius should imitate is probably pertinent to showing hospitality and offering assistance to the traveling Christian workers in v. 11b. In other words, this is what Gaius has performed and should continue following suit.

In order to encourage Gaius to comply with his demand, the Elder portrays two different kinds of people in contradistinction to each other through the two generic positive or negative statements in v. 11c–d. The positive statement in v. 11c comes before the negative statement in v. 11d. The generic subject is constitutive of the embedded participial clause (i.e., ὁ ἀγαθοποιῶν or ὁ κακοποιῶν) and is the point of departure of the clause viewed as message in v. 11c or v. 11d. The occurrences of the two lexemes ἀγαθοποιέω and κακοποιέω from semantic domain 88 ("moral and ethical qualities and related behavior") point to an emphasis on the experiential meaning of doing the good or bad deeds in v. 11c–d. While the Elder utilizes the third-person singular indicative (i.e., ἐστιν [v. 11c] and ἑώρακεν [v. 11d]) with respect to the generic participant, it is likely that the two generic statements are directed towards Gaius subtly and in service of the Elder's hortatory purposes. The use of the generalization has the rhetorical implication of softening the exhortation by "hiding" the real addressee, namely Gaius. The Elder uses the relational process clause (i.e., ὁ ἀγαθοποιῶν ἐκ τοῦ θεοῦ ἐστιν) to ascribe the feature of being "from God" to the person who does what is good in v. 11c. The prepositional phrase ἐκ τοῦ θεοῦ is placed prior to the predicator ἐστιν to draw attention to this admirable feature. The Elder goes on to aver that the person who does what is evil "has not seen God" through the negative clause in v. 11d. As mentioned above, the perfect tense (cf. ἑώρακεν) is used to give prominence to the message expressed by this negative clause. There is little doubt that the representative example of such a person is Diotrephes in view of what was said in the foregoing co-text in vv. 9–10. Given the twofold employment of the lexeme θεός (v. 11c, d) from semantic domain 12 ("supernatural beings and powers"), the gravity of the

---

24. Martin and Rose, *Working with Discourse*, 53–55.

outcome of doing what is good or bad is underscored. Since the notion of "from God" or "seeing God" is tantamount to having a relationship with him in Johannine thinking (cf. John 14:7–9), the Elder actually hints at that whether one does what is good or evil bears on his or her relationship with the deity in v. 11c–d. As a corollary, Gaius should heed the Elder's preceding exhortation (i.e., "Do not imitate what is evil but [imitate] what is good!") that has been set forth by using the grammatical imperative in v. 11a–b.

D. Recommendation of Demetrius (v. 12)

This section starts with the dative singular proper noun Δημητρίῳ (v. 12a) with reference to Demetrius, whom the Elder commends as a Christian worker worthy of approval on all fronts. This is the first time Demetrius is referred to in this letter. The Elder makes mention of Demetrius's name to create an expectation that the message that will be unfolded is concerned with this person at the beginning of this section. In fact, the Elder utilizes all of the total five ranking clauses to realize different statements to give an affirmative appraisal of Demetrius's trustworthiness in v. 12a–e. There are altogether three occurrences of the two related lexemes, μαρτυρέω (v. 12a, c) and μαρτυρία (v. 12e), with respect to the idea of testimony or approval in this section. The elliptical clause (i.e., καὶ ὑπὸ αὐτῆς τῆς ἀληθείας) is without a verb in v. 12b. Nevertheless, the third-person singular perfect passive indicative verb μεμαρτύρηται can be inferred from the prior clause in v. 12a to serve as the implicit predicator in this elliptical clause above in v. 12b. The way in which the Elder repeatedly points out someone's approval of Demetrius is in accordance with the Jewish tradition that at least two or three witnesses are needed to establish conclusive evidence in a legal case (cf. Deut 17:6; 19:15; 1 John 5:8).[25] The Elder also uses the perfect tense twice (cf. the two predicators μεμαρτύρηται [v. 12a] and οἶδας [v. 12d]) to give prominence to the commendation of Demetrius.

The four clauses are joined by the coordinating conjunction καί (3x) and related to each other paratactically in v. 12a–d. The predicator μεμαρτύρηται with the passive voice is used in v. 12a–b, in which the agent or sayer in the communicative event is encoded by the prepositional phrase ὑπὸ πάντων (v. 12a) or ὑπὸ αὐτῆς τῆς ἀληθείας (v. 12b). The Elder indicates that Demetrius is well spoken of by everyone and by the truth itself. The intensive pronoun αὐτῆς in the feminine singular genitive is utilized to stress the referent, namely the truth, and accentuate the approval it gives to Demetrius accordingly in v. 12b. The Elder shifts to use the first-person

---

25. Marshall, *Epistles of John*, 93.

plural expressions (cf. the subject ἡμεῖς and the predicator μαρτυροῦμεν) and the active voice in v. 12c. If these first-person plural expressions above carry out the function of the editorial plural or what is called the "we of authoritative testimony," the Elder indicates unwaveringly that he himself also affirms Demetrius's good character.[26] The verbiage or what is uttered by everyone, the truth, or the Elder (who is assumed as the referent of "we") to bear witness to Demetrius is not specified in v. 12a–c. Nevertheless, it is reasonable to suppose that their compliments to Demetrius pertain to his devotion to the spreading of the gospel for Jesus' sake (cf. v. 7). The Elder further employs the second-person singular perfect active indicative verb οἶδας to indicate that Gaius knows that "our testimony" (cf. ἡ μαρτυρία ἡμῶν) is true in v. 12d–e. It is probable that the first-person plural genitive pronoun ἡμῶν is utilized to add weight to the testimony and denote only the Elder (cf. v. 12c).[27] On the assumption that Demetrius is the letter carrier of 3 John and belonged to the group of the Elder's envoys, he calls for Gaius to receive Demetrius based on Gaius's knowledge that what the Elder speaks of Demetrius is true. Therefore, whether or not Gaius provides aid to Demetrius will evidence Gaius's trust or distrust in the veracity of the Elder's testimony regarding Demetrius's character. Summing up, the Elder concludes the body of his letter with the intimation that Gaius should not make the wrong judgment to imitate Diotrephes's wicked deeds against the traveling missionaries. Rather, Gaius should continue to stand with the Elder and show himself to be in a good relationship to God by receiving these Christian workers.

---

26. Jobes, *1, 2, and 3 John*, 311. For the idea concerning "we of authoritative testimony," see Bauckham, *Jesus and the Eyewitnesses*, 372–73.

27. Jobes, *1, 2, and 3 John*, 311; Bauckham, *Jesus and the Eyewitnesses*, 372–73.

3 JOHN 13–15

OUTLINE:

I. Opening (vv. 1–4)

II. Body (vv. 5–12)

III. Closing (vv. 13–15)

    A. Desire to Visit (vv. 13–14)

    B. Peace Benediction and Final Greetings (v. 15)

III. CLOSING (VV. 13–15)

In many respects the closing of 3 John is resemblant of the closing of 2 John. In both epistles, the Elder expresses his desire to speak to the addressee in person rather than communicate through writing (vv. 13–14; cf. 2 John 12). In addition, the lengths of the closings of these two letters are approximately the same. There is a total of thirty-four words in the closing of 3 John, as compared to the presence of altogether thirty-five words in the closing of 2 John. Yet, there are altogether seven ranking clauses in 3 John 13–15 (vv. 13a, 13b, 14a, 14b, 15a, 15b, 15c), whereas four ranking clauses are counted in 2 John 12–13 (vv. 12a, 12b, 12c, 13). The average length of the ranking clauses is 4.85 words in the closing of 3 John, which fall short of that in the closing of 2 John (on average 8.75 words per ranking clause). Overall, the clauses tend to be relatively short, simple, and not lexically packed in the closing of 3 John. Aside from the epistolary features including the peace benediction (v. 15a) and the predominance of the verbs in the first-person singular (vv. 13a, 13b, 14a) or plural (v. 14b), the Elder increases the coherence of this closing by employing a number of words (e.g., γράψαι [v. 13a], γράφειν [v. 13b], λαλήσομεν [v. 14b], ἀσπάζονται [v. 15b], ἀσπάζου [v. 15c]) from semantic domain 33 ("communication"). In short, the closing of 3 John constitutes a unified whole.

A. Desire to Visit (vv. 13–14)

There is a concessive relation between the two clauses in v. 13a–b (cf. 2 John 12a–b). The Elder uses the concessive clause to engage Gaius by creating an expectation (i.e., the idea that the Elder has much to write) in v. 13a. This initial expectation above is expressed by the positive statement in v. 13a, in which the first-person singular imperfect active indicative verb εἶχον and the aorist active infinitive γράψαι are present. The Elder subsequently sets forth the counter-expectation (i.e., the idea that the Elder does not want to communicate with pen and ink) by way of the clause beginning with the elided contrastive conjunction ἀλλ' in v. 13b.[1] This counter-expectation, which is expressed through the negative statement, is highlighted by the twofold employment of the present tense in v. 13b (cf. the first-person singular present active indicative verb θέλω and the present active infinitive γράφειν). Furthermore, what is said in v. 13b paves the way for the Elder's ensuing announcement regarding a possible visit in the future. He explicitly expresses his hope to see Gaius soon so that they will talk to each other face to face in v. 14a–b. The implicit subject (i.e., "we") of the first-person plural future active verb λαλήσομεν includes both the Elder and Gaius. The word group εὐθέως σε ἰδεῖν constitutes an embedded infinitival clause in v. 14a. Notice that the placement of the temporal adjunct εὐθέως prior to the complement (i.e., σε) and the predicator (i.e., ἰδεῖν) in this embedded infinitival clause above is emphatic to underline the immediacy of the Elder's hope to visit Gaius. The experiential meaning of the succeeding clause involves the verbal process, which is realized by the saying verb (i.e., λαλήσομεν) in v. 14b. Following the conjunction καί, the adjunctive phrase στόμα πρὸς στόμα (literally meaning "mouth to mouth") is fronted and placed prior to this saying verb above to lay stress on a prospective meeting in person when possible (cf. 2 John 12).

---

1. For the notion of counter-expectancy, see Martin and Rose, *Working with Discourse*, 56–57.

B. Peace Benediction and Final Greetings (v. 15)

The Elder gives a peace benediction to Gaius through the verbless clause in v. 15a. There is no peace benediction in the closing of the other two Johannine epistles, but this epistolary feature is found in the farewell near the end of several Pauline epistles (e.g., Rom 15:33; 16:20; 2 Cor 13:11; Gal 6:16; Phil 4:9; 1 Thess 5:23; 2 Thess 3:16).[2] Compared to the Pauline letters, the peace benediction (i.e., εἰρήνη σοι) is relatively brief and made up of only the subject (i.e., εἰρήνη) and the complement (i.e., σοι) in 3 John 15. Although the Elder does not mention the giver of peace, his benediction most likely takes root in the Jewish concept of the covenantal God bestowing shalom upon his people (cf. the greetings in Ezra 4:17; 5:7).[3] It is also worth mentioning that the risen Jesus greeted his disciples with the blessing of peace three times in the Fourth Gospel (John 20:19, 21, 26; cf. Luke 24:36).[4]

The final greetings to Gaius and others are present in v. 15b–c, firstly in the form of the third-person type greeting (i.e., the present middle indicative ἀσπάζονταί) in v. 15b and subsequently the second-person type greeting (i.e., the present middle imperative ἀσπάζου) in v. 15c. The Elder tells Gaius that "the friends" send him greetings through the statement in v. 15b. These "friends" probably refer to the Christians who were with the Elder at the moment when he was writing this letter. The Elder puts forward the directive to ask Gaius to pass on his greetings to the other "friends" personally by name in v. 15c. In the latter instance, these "friends" are probably the believers of Gaius's congregation or those within his reach. At any rate, the repetition of the friendship term (i.e., οἱ φίλοι) in effect strikes an affectionate note and connects the two last clauses in v. 15b–c. Contrary to Diotrephes's opposition against the Elder and his associates, there is Christian solidarity and mutual "friendship" between the members of his congregation and Gaius's congregation. Thus, the closing of 3 John is not merely conventional but rather plays a part in accomplishing the Elder's hortatory aim to induce Gaius to support the itinerant missionaries for the spreading of the gospel.

---

2. Weima, "Sincerely, Paul," 311–12.
3. Brown, *Epistles of John*, 725–26; Adams, "Paul's Letter Opening and Greek Epistolography," 47.
4. Brown, *Epistles of John*, 725–26.

BIBLIOGRAPHY

Adams, Sean A. "Paul's Letter Opening and Greek Epistolography: A Matter of Relationship." In *Paul and the Ancient Letter Form*, edited by Stanley E. Porter and Sean A. Adams, 33–55. Leiden: Brill, 2010.
Akin, Daniel L. *1, 2, 3 John*. New American Commentary. Nashville: Broadman & Holman, 2001.
Augustine. *Homilies on the First Epistle of John*. Translated by Boniface Ramsey. New York: New City, 2008.
Aune, David E. *The New Testament and Its Literary Environment*. Philadelphia: Westminster, 1987.
Bauckham, Richard. *Jesus and the Eyewitnesses: The Gospels as Eyewitness Testimony*. 2nd ed. Grand Rapids: Eerdmans, 2017.
Bennema, Cornelis. *Mimesis in the Johannine Literature: A Study in Johannine Ethics*. London: Bloomsbury T&T Clark, 2017.
Blass, Friedrich W., et al. *A Greek Grammar of the New Testament and Other Early Christian Literature*. Rev. ed. Chicago: University of Chicago Press, 1961.
Blumell, Lincoln H. *Lettered Christians: Christians, Letters, and Late Antique Oxyrhynchus*. Leiden: Brill, 2012.
Brooke, A. E. *A Critical and Exegetical Commentary on the Johannine Epistles*. Edinburgh: T&T Clark, 1912.
Brown, Raymond E. *The Epistles of John*. New York: Doubleday, 1982.
Bultmann, Rudolf. *The Johannine Epistles: A Commentary on the Johannine Epistles*. Philadelphia: Fortress, 1973.
Burge, Gary M. *The Letters of John*. NIV Application Commentary. Grand Rapids: Zondervan, 1996.
Campbell, Constantine R. *1, 2, and 3 John*. Grand Rapids: Zondervan, 2017.
Carson, D. A. *The Gospel According to John*. Pillar New Testament Commentary. Grand Rapids: Eerdmans, 1990.
———. "'You Have No Need That Anyone Should Teach You' (1 John 2:27): An Old Testament Allusion That Determines the Interpretation." In *The New Testament in Its First Century Setting: Essays on Context and Background in Honour of B. W. Winter on His 65th Birthday*, edited by P. J. Williams et al., 269–80. Grand Rapids: Eerdmans, 2004.
Clement of Alexandria. *Stromateis*. Translated by John Ferguson. Washington, DC: Catholic University of America Press, 1992.
Culpepper, R. Alan. *The Gospel and Letters of John*. Nashville: Abingdon, 1998.

Culy, Martin M. *1, 2, 3 John: A Handbook on the Greek Text*. Waco, TX: Baylor University Press, 2004.

Davids, Peter H. *2 Peter and Jude: A Handbook on the Greek Text*. Waco, TX: Baylor University Press, 2011.

Dubis, Mark. *1 Peter: A Handbook on the Greek Text*. Waco, TX: Baylor University Press, 2010.

Eggins, Suzanne. *An Introduction to Systemic Functional Linguistics*. 2nd ed. New York: Continuum, 2004.

Eusebius. *Ecclesiastical History*. Translated by Krisopp Lake. Loeb Classical Library. Cambridge: Harvard University Press, 2014.

Fantin, Joseph D. *The Greek Imperative Mood in the New Testament: A Cognitive and Communicative Approach*. New York: Lang, 2010.

Funk, Robert W. "The Form and Structure of II and III John." *Journal of Biblical Literature* 86 (1967) 424–30.

Gee, James Paul, and Michael Handford, eds. *The Routledge Handbook of Discourse Analysis*. London: Routledge, 2012.

Graber, Philip L. "Context in Text: A Systemic Functional Analysis of the Parable of the Sower." PhD diss., Emory University, 2001.

Halliday, Michael A. K., and Christian M. I. M. Matthiessen. *Halliday's Introduction to Functional Grammar*. 4th ed. London: Routledge, 2014.

Huffman, Douglas S. *Verbal Aspect Theory and the Prohibitions in the Greek New Testament*. New York: Lang, 2014.

Jensen, Matthew D. "Jesus 'Coming' in the Flesh: 2 John 7 and Verbal Aspect." *Novum Testamentum* 56 (2014) 310–22.

Jobes, Karen H. *1, 2, and 3 John*. Zondervan Exegetical Commentary on the New Testament. Grand Rapids: Zondervan, 2014.

Johnson, Luke Timothy. *The Writings of the New Testament: An Interpretation*. 3rd ed. Minneapolis: Fortress, 2010.

Keener, Craig S. *The Gospel of John: A Commentary*. 2 vols. Grand Rapids: Baker Academic, 2003.

Klauck, Hans-Josef. *Ancient Letters and the New Testament: A Guide to Context and Exegesis*. Translated by Daniel P. Bailey. Waco, TX: Baylor University Press, 2006.

Klawans, Jonathan. *Impurity and Sin in Ancient Judaism*. Oxford: Oxford University Press, 2000.

———. "Moral and Ritual Purity." In *The Historical Jesus in Context*, edited by Amy-Jill Levine et al., 266–84. Princeton, NJ: Princeton University Press, 2006.

Köstenberger, Andreas J. *A Theology of John's Gospel and Letters*. Grand Rapids: Zondervan, 2009.

Kruse, Colin G. *The Letters of John*. Pillar New Testament Commentary. Grand Rapids: Eerdmans, 2020.

Lamb, David A. *Text, Context and the Johannine Community: A Sociolinguistic Analysis of the Johannine Writings*. London: Bloomsbury T&T Clark, 2014.

Leung, Mavis M. "Ethics and *Imitatio Christi* in 1 John: A Jewish Perspective." *Tyndale Bulletin* 69.1 (2018) 111–31.

———. *The Kingship–Cross Interplay in the Gospel of John: Jesus' Death as Corroboration of His Royal Messiahship*. Eugene, OR: Wipf & Stock, 2011.

———. "Language and Characterization in the Roman Trial Narrative: A Sociolinguistic Analysis of Pilate's Dialogues with the Jewish Leaders and Jesus in John 18:28–19:16a." *Bulletin for Biblical Research* 29.4 (2019) 511–34.

———. "The Narrative Function and Verbal Aspect of the Historical Present in the Fourth Gospel." *Journal of the Evangelical Theological Society* 51.4 (2008) 703–20.

———. "The Metaphorical Expressions of the Commands in 1 John as a Hortatory Discourse." In *Systemic-Functional Linguistic Interpretation of the New Testament: On Being Considerate Readers of the New Testament*, edited by James D. Dvorak. Eugene, OR: Wipf & Stock. (forthcoming)

Lieu, Judith. *I, II, & III John: A Commentary*. Louisville, KY: Westminster John Knox, 2008.

Longacre, Robert E. "Exhortation and Mitigation in First John." *Selected Technical Articles Related to Translation* 9 (1983) 3–44.

———. "Towards an Exegesis of 1 John Based on the Discourse Analysis of the Greek Text." In *Linguistics and New Testament Interpretation: Essays on Discourse Analysis*, edited by David A. Black, 271–86. Dallas: Summer Institute of Linguistics, 1992.

Louw, J. P., and Eugene A. Nida, eds. *Greek-English Lexicon of the New Testament: Based on Semantic Domains*. 2nd ed. 2 vols. New York: United Bible Societies, 1988.

Marshall, I. Howard. *The Epistles of John*. Grand Rapids: Eerdmans, 1978.

Martin, J. R. *English Text: System and Structure*. Philadelphia: Benjamins, 1992.

Martin, J. R., and David Rose. *Working with Discourse: Meaning Beyond the Clause*. 2nd ed. New York: Continuum, 2007.

Martin, J. R., and Peter R. R. White. *The Language of Evaluation: Appraisal in English*. New York: Palgrave Macmillan, 2005.

Mathewson, David L., and Elodie Ballantine Emig. *Intermediate Greek Grammar: Syntax for Students of the New Testament*. Grand Rapids: Baker Academic, 2016.

Matthiessen, Christian M. I. M., et al. *Key Terms in Systemic Functional Linguistics*. New York: Continuum, 2010.

Metzger, Bruce M. *A Textual Commentary on the Greek New Testament*. 2nd ed. Stuttgart: German Bible Society, 1994.

Miehle, Helen L. "Theme in Greek Hortatory Discourse: Van Dijk and Beekman-Callow Approaches Applied to 1 John." PhD diss., University of Texas at Arlington, 1981.

Mitchell, Margaret M. "'Diotrephes Does Not Receive Us': The Lexicographical and Social Context of 3 John 9–10." *Journal of Biblical Literature* 117 (1998) 299–320.

Novum Testamentum Graecum: Editio Critica Maior. Vol. 6.1. Catholic Epistles. Stuttgart: German Bible Society, 2003.

O'Donnell, Matthew Brook, and Catherine Smith. "A Discourse Analysis of 3 John." In *The Linguist as Pedagogue: Trends in the Teaching and Linguistic Analysis of the Greek New Testament*, edited by Stanley E. Porter and Matthew Brook O'Donnell, 127–45. Sheffield, UK: Sheffield Phoenix, 2009.

Painter, John. *1, 2, and 3 John*. Sacra Pagina. Collegeville, MN: Liturgical, 2002.

Porter, Stanley E. *Idioms of the Greek New Testament*. 2nd ed. Sheffield, UK: Sheffield Academic Press, 1994.

———. *The Letter to the Romans: A Linguistic and Literary Commentary*. Sheffield, UK: Sheffield Phoenix, 2015.

———. "Systemic Functional Linguistics and the Greek Language: The Need for Further Modeling." In *Modeling Biblical Language: Selected Papers from the*

McMaster Divinity College Linguistics Circle, edited by Stanley E. Porter et al., 9–47. Leiden: Brill, 2016.

———. *Verbal Aspect in the Greek of the New Testament, with Reference to Tense and Mood*. New York: Lang, 1989.

Porter, Stanley E., and Matthew Brook O'Donnell. *Discourse Analysis and the Greek New Testament: Text-Generating Resources*. Library of New Testament Greek 2. London: T&T Clark, 2024.

Porter, Stanley E., et al., eds. *The OpenText.Org Syntactically Annotated Greek New Testament*. N.p.: OpenText.org, 2006.

Potterie, Ignace de la. "The Impeccability of the Christian According to 1 Jn 3, 6-9." In *Christian Lives by the Spirit*, edited by Ignace de la Potterie and S. Lyonnet, 173–96. New York: Alba, 1971.

Reed, Jeffrey T. *A Discourse Analysis of Philippians: Method and Rhetoric in the Debate over Literary Integrity*. Sheffield, UK: Sheffield Academic Press, 1997.

Roberts, Alexander, and James Donaldson, eds. *The Ante-Nicene Fathers: Translations of the Writings of the Fathers down to AD 325*. Revised by Arthur C. Coxe. 10 vols. Buffalo, NY: Christian Literature, 1885–96.

Schnackenburg, Rudolf. *The Johannine Epistles: Introduction and Commentary*. Translated by Reginald Fuller and Ilse Fuller. New York: Crossroad, 1992.

Sherman, Grace E., and John C. Tuggy. *A Semantic and Structural Analysis of the Johannine Epistles*. Dallas: Summer Institute of Linguistics, 1994.

Smalley, Stephen S. *1, 2, 3 John*. Rev. ed. Nashville: Thomas Nelson, 2007.

Stott, John R. W. *The Letters of John: An Introduction and Commentary*. Tyndale New Testament Commentaries. Downers Grove, IL: InterVarsity, 1988.

Streett, Daniel R. *They Went Out from Us: The Identity of the Opponents in First John*. Berlin: de Gruyter, 2011.

Taverniers, Miriam. "Grammatical Metaphor." In *The Routledge Handbook of Systemic Functional Linguistics*, edited by Tom Bartlett and Gerard O'Grady, 354–71. London: Routledge, 2017.

———. "Grammatical Metaphor in SFL: A Historiography of the Introduction and Initial Study of the Concept." In *Grammatical Metaphor: Views from Systemic Functional Linguistics*, edited by Anne-Marie Simon-Vandenbergen et al., 5–33. Philadelphia: Benjamins, 2003.

Thomas, John Christopher. "The Literary Structure of 1 John." *Novum Testamentum* 40.4 (1998) 369–81.

Thompson, Marianne M. *1–3 John*. Downers Grove, IL: InterVarsity, 1992.

Tite, Philip L. "How to Begin, and Why? Diverse Functions of the Pauline Prescript Within a Greco-Roman Context." In *Paul and the Ancient Letter Form*, edited by Stanley E. Porter and Sean A. Adams, 57–99. Leiden: Brill, 2010.

Wahlde, Urban C. von. *The Three Johannine Letters*. Vol. 3 of *The Gospel and Letters of John*. Grand Rapids: Eerdmans, 2010.

Wallace, Daniel B. *Greek Grammar Beyond the Basics: An Exegetical Syntax of the New Testament*. Grand Rapids: Zondervan, 1997.

Watson, Duane F. "Amplification Techniques in 1 John: The Interaction of Rhetorical Style and Invention." *Journal for the Study of the New Testament* 51 (1993) 99–123.

Watt, Jan G. van der. "Reciprocity, Mimesis and Ethics in 1 John." In *Erzählung Und Briefe Im Johanneischen Kreis*, 257–76. Tübingen: Mohr Siebeck, 2016.

Weima, Jeffrey A. D. "Sincerely, Paul: The Significance of the Pauline Letter Closings." In *Paul and the Ancient Letter Form*, edited by Stanley E. Porter and Sean A. Adams, 307–45. Leiden: Brill, 2010.

White, John L. "The Greek Documentary Letter Tradition Third Century B.C.E. to Third Century C.E." *Semeia* 22 (1981) 89–106.

Yarbrough, Robert W. *1–3 John*. Baker Exegetical Commentary on the New Testament. Grand Rapids: Baker Academic, 2008.

MODERN AUTHORS INDEX

Adams, Sean A., 149n12, 149n15, 150n16, 173n9, 175n21, 196n3, 197, 200–201
Akin, Daniel L., 2n4, 6n18, 50n47, 63n14, 68n30, 81n12, 119n26, 132n4, 135n14, 136n18, 139n30, 174n14, 197
Aune, David E., 20n87, 197

Bauckham, Richard, 3n6, 28n4, 193nn26–27, 197
Bennema, Cornelis, 45n34, 46,n39, 89n9, 115n18, 197
Blumell, Lincoln H., 172n2, 172n4, 197
Brooke, A. E., 2, 3n7, 197
Brown, Raymond E., 2n2, 3n7, 27n2, 29n9, 30n11, 36n7, 37n9, 45n34, 48n42, 51n1, 54n8, 58n18, 60n1, 60nn3–4, 62n12, 63n17, 65n20, 67n24, 69n33, 72n5, 74n11, 74n13, 80n8, 81n11, 90n13, 91n15, 91nn19–20, 94nn7–8, 101nn5–6, 102n9, 103n11, 104n19, 108n3, 112n8, 113n12, 115nn15–16, 117n24, 120n28, 120nn30–31, 121n34, 125n10, 127n14, 128n17, 133n6, 134n9, 135n12, 136n16, 140nn34–35, 150n19, 152n23, 156n8, 158n13, 160n18, 173n8, 175n17, 183n6, 186n13, 196nn3–4, 197
Bultmann, Rudolf, 173n7, 197
Burge, Gary M., 55n11, 81n14, 197

Campbell, Constantine R., 4n11, 56n13, 88n4, 90n13, 96n12, 103n11, 103nn14–15, 125n9, 139n31, 140n35, 157n11, 197
Carson, D. A., 47n40, 63n16, 68n32, 197
Culpepper, R. Alan, 136n18, 197
Culy, Martin M., 27n1, 29n6, 31nn14–15, 37n10, 39n16, 41, 42n25, 43n29, 45n33, 54n8, 54n10, 58n18, 62n11, 63n17, 67n26, 71n3, 72n5, 74n14, 80n9, 83n20, 84n23, 85n25, 88n5, 89n7, 90n13, 96n13, 97n15, 98n17, 102n7, 112n8, 113n12, 120n30, 124nn2–3, 126n11–12, 133n5, 137n23, 148n7, 152n22, 154n1, 155n6, 156n10, 160n18, 164n2, 177nn26–27, 177n29, 177n31, 182n3, 182n5, 198

Davids, Peter H., 174n11, 198
Dubis, Mark, 174n11, 198

Eggins, Suzanne, 8n22, 9nn27–29, 10nn30–31, 13n52, 15n63, 16nn64–66, 16n69, 17nn72–73, 18n76, 143n2, 144n3, 198
Emig, Elodie Ballantine, 62n10, 82n19, 166n6, 199

Fantin, Joseph D., 14n56, 198
Funk, Robert W., 151n21, 154n2, 176n23, 198

Gee, James Paul, 8n23, 198
Graber, Philip L., 8n25, 198

Halliday, Michael A. K., 8, 9n26, 12, 13, 15n62, 16n66, 17, 18, 37n10, 152n24, 190, 198
Handford, Michael, 8n23, 198
Huffman, Douglas S., 56n12, 198

Jensen, Matthew D., 158n14, 198
Jobes, Karen H., 4n10, 5n13, 28n5, 29nn8–9, 31n16, 48n42, 50n47, 53n5, 60n2, 62n12, 63n17, 68n28, 81n11, 91n19, 92n1, 101n4, 103n12, 104n18, 107n2, 108n4, 112n9, 115n15, 119n26, 125n9, 127n15, 131nn2–3, 133n6, 135n12, 135n14, 136n16, 140n33, 140n35, 146n3, 148n9, 156n9, 157n11, 166n7, 173n8, 175n17, 182n2, 184n7, 186n15, 188n21, 193nn26–27, 198
Johnson, Luke Timothy, 5nn13–14, 198

Keener, Craig S., 47n40, 198
Klauck, Hans-Josef, 146n1, 149n13, 150n18, 173n5, 173n9, 198
Klawans, Jonathan, 38n11, 39n17, 135n15, 198
Köstenberger, Andreas J., 2n2, 4n10, 18n78, 18n80, 19n81, 56n13, 124n14, 148n8, 198
Kruse, Colin G., 3n7, 4n9, 5n15, 7n20, 18n79, 19n82, 28n4, 43n27, 48n42, 53n5, 55n11, 63n15, 63n17, 64n18, 68n30, 80n8, 81n11, 82n16, 87n2, 90n14, 91n18, 103n14, 104n18, 117n21, 117n23, 119n26, 125n9, 131n2, 133n6, 135n14, 136n16, 137n24, 138n28, 140n35, 157n11, 158n15, 166n7, 198

Lamb, David A., 4, 5n12, 5n16, 14n58, 198
Leung, Mavis M., 7n19, 14n57, 15n60, 45n34, 46n37, 75n16, 82n18, 89nn9–10, 111n6, 115n17, 198–99
Lieu, Judith, 18n79, 52n4, 53n5, 54n10, 60n2, 77nn2–3, 81n15, 91n21, 104n17, 115n15, 140n38, 154n3, 184n7, 186n13, 188n19, 199
Longacre, Robert E., 7n7, 14n57, 19, 37n10, 40n20, 52n3, 78n4, 81n10, 82n18, 97n14, 114n14, 199
Louw, J. P., 11, 30n12, 38n14, 48n41, 61n8, 62n9, 64n19, 65n21, 71n4, 84n23, 95n11, 103n16, 113n11, 123n1, 135n13, 138n25, 199

Marshall, I. Howard, 6n17, 19n82, 29n8, 45nn33–35, 52n4, 53n5, 60n1, 61n5, 78n4, 82n17, 94n5, 103n13, 104n17, 110n5, 112nn8–9, 113n12, 115n15, 119n27, 120n29, 125n9, 126n13, 128n16, 134n8, 134n11, 137n24, 140n32, 140nn35–37, 160n18, 174n16, 177n28, 177n30, 186nn15–16, 188n22, 192n25, 199
Martin, J. R., 12, 13n50, 17nn74–75, 18, 91n16, 152n24, 162n21, 165n3, 189n23, 191n24, 195n1, 199
Mathewson, David L., 62n10, 82n19, 166n6, 199
Matthiessen, Christian M. I. M., 8n21, 9n26, 12, 13n49, 13n52, 15n62, 16n66, 17, 37n10, 152n24, 198–99
Metzger, Bruce M., 31n15, 46n38, 63n15, 88nn5–6, 117n22, 120n32, 124n6, 126n11, 137n22, 138n27, 150n17, 159n16, 165n4, 178n34, 199
Miehle, Helen L., 7n19, 14n57, 15n59, 37n10, 97n16, 185n12, 199
Mitchell, Margaret M., 188n21, 199

MODERN AUTHORS INDEX

Nida, Eugene A., 11, 30n12, 38n14, 48n41, 61n8, 62n9, 64n19, 65n21, 71n4, 84n23, 95n11, 103n16, 113n11, 123n1, 135n13, 138n25, 199

O'Donnell, Matthew Brook, 16n66, 17n70, 170n3, 176n22, 176n25, 187n18, 188n20, 199–200

Painter, John, 68n29, 136n17, 199
Porter, Stanley E., 11n36, 11n38, 13, 16n66, 17n70, 27n2, 55n11, 57n14, 197, 199–201
Potterie, Ignace de la, 82n17, 200

Reed, Jeffrey T., 8n24, 200
Rose, David, 12, 17nn74–75, 18, 91n16, 152n24, 165n3, 189n23, 191n24, 195n1, 199

Schnackenburg, Rudolf, 43n27, 71n2, 72nn5–6, 82n17, 107n2, 112n9, 115n16, 117n21, 117n23, 120n29, 125n7, 127n15, 160n18, 177n28, 178n34, 182n3, 186n13, 200
Sherman, Grace E., 14n57, 15n59, 18n79, 19, 28nn4–5, 31n16, 37n10, 40n18, 43n29, 46n37, 60n1, 80n9, 81n12, 81n14, 97n16, 100n3, 104n17, 108n3, 114n14, 116n20, 129nn18–19, 135n13, 137n23, 147n6, 149n14, 151n20, 157n11, 175n19, 184nn8–9, 185n12, 200
Smalley, Stephen S., 18n78, 36n7, 45nn34–35, 67n24, 69n33, 81n15, 84n22, 84n24, 90n11, 94nn5–6, 95n9, 107n2, 113n12, 116n19, 117n24, 137n24, 139n29, 177n30, 178n32, 200
Smith, Catherine, 170n3, 176n22, 176n25, 187n18, 188n20, 199
Stott, John R. W., 2n1, 4n9, 5, 45n34, 90n13, 91n18, 94n6, 95n9, 102n10, 103n11, 104n17, 112n9, 117n21, 119n27, 133n6, 134n7, 147n4, 200
Streett, Daniel R., 6n17, 200

Taverniers, Miriam, 15n61, 37n10, 200
Thomas, John Christopher, 19n81, 200
Thompson, Marianne M., 35n5, 68n30, 136n18, 137n23, 200
Tite, Philip L., 20n87, 173n9, 200
Tuggy, John C., 14n57, 15n59, 18n79, 19, 28nn4–5, 31n16, 37n10, 40n18, 43n29, 46n37, 60n1, 80n9, 81n12, 81n14, 97n16, 100n3, 104n17, 108n3, 114n14, 116n20, 129nn18–19, 135n13, 137n23, 147n6, 149n14, 151n20, 157n11, 175n19, 184nn8–9, 185n12, 200

Wahlde, Urban C. von, 36n7, 95n10, 136n17, 200
Wallace, Daniel B., 182n4, 200
Watson, Duane F., 19, 200
Watt, Jan G. van der, 45n34, 200
Weima, Jeffrey A. D., 196n2, 201
White, John L., 130n1, 146n2, 149n10, 166n5, 173n9, 174n15, 175n21, 183n6, 201
White, Peter R. R., 13n50, 162n21, 199

Yarbrough, Robert W., 5n15, 28n4, 35n5, 38n15, 50n47, 53n5, 55n11, 68n29, 74n14, 81n15, 82n16, 83n21, 84n22, 90n11, 115n15, 116n19, 125n9, 126n11, 128n17, 137n22, 139n30, 147n5, 149n14, 155n5, 159n17, 174n13, 175n17, 177n28, 182n3, 185n11, 186n14, 188n19, 201

ANCIENT SOURCES INDEX

OLD TESTAMENT

Genesis
1:1	29
3:1–24	80
4:1–16	80, 84

Exodus
13:21–22	35

Leviticus
4:2	135
4:13	135
4:22	135
4:27	135
5:15–18	135

Numbers
15:30–31	135

Deuteronomy
4:28	140
15:7–9	90n14
17:6	126, 192
17:12	135
19:15	126, 192

Ezra
4:17	150n16, 196
5:7	150n16, 196

Psalms
18:28	35
27:1	35
36:9	35
115:3–8	140
135:15–18	140

Isaiah
2:12–22	115
44:9–20	140
54:1	5
54:4–6	5
61:10	146
62:5	146

Jeremiah
10:5	140
31:21	146
31:32	5, 146
31:34	63n16, 68

Ezekiel
16:7–14	146

Hosea
2:2	146
2:16–20	146

Joel

2:1–11	115
2:32	115

Amos

5:18–20	115

Zephaniah

1:14–18	115

Zechariah

13:2	140

APOCRYPHA

2 Maccabees

11:28	173, 175

Tobit

10:13	172

PSEUDEPIGRAPHA

Jubilees

5.10	115
24.30	115

Psalms of Solomon

15.13	115

4 Ezra

7.113	115

NEW TESTAMENT

Matthew

5:12	159n17
5:47	185
6:7	185
7:23	77n1
10:41	159n17
12:31–32	135
13:41	49, 77n1
16:23	49
18:7	49
18:17	185
23:28	77n1
24:4–5	158
24:5	61
24:11	61
24:12	77n1
24:24	61
25:46	116

Mark

3:28–30	135
9:41	159n17
13:5–6	158
13:22	61

Luke

5:31	175
6:23	159n17
6:35	159n17
7:10	175
7:47	84n23
12:10	135
12:15	140
15:12	57
15:27	175
15:30	57

21:4	57	8:44–45	2
21:8	158	8:44	88
24:36	196	9:5	48
		9:31	58
		10:11	89

John

1:1	2, 139	10:15	89
1:4–7	2	10:17	89
1:9	48, 124	10:18	89
1:10	74	11:27	124
1:12	73, 132	11:48	185n10
1:14	2, 109	11:50	185n10
1:15	124	11:51	185n10
1:18	2, 109, 139	11:52	73, 185n10
1:26	125	12:13	124
1:27	124	12:25	139
1:29	78	12:31	54, 80, 103, 137
1:30	124	12:47	139
1:31	125	13:10	38n12
1:33	125	13:11	38n12
3:16	2, 109	13:18	147
3:18	2, 109, 132	13:33–34	2
3:19–21	2	13:33	40, 102
3:21	37	13:34	83, 154
3:31	124	14:6	140, 148, 152, 186
4:25	124	14:7–9	192
4:34	58	14:16–17	68
4:42	112	14:16	2, 41, 98
5:24	87	14:17	104
5:30	58	14:20	2
5:33–36	127	14:26	2, 41, 68, 98
5:36–37	127	14:27	84
6:14	124	14:30	103, 137
6:27–29	159	15:1–17	2
6:38	58	15:2	38n12
6:40	58	15:3	38n12
6:58	84	15:9–25	2
6:69	63	15:9–10	114
6:70	147	15:12	2, 83
7:16	160	15:13	89
7:17	58, 160	15:16	104, 147
7:27	124	15:17	2, 83
7:31	124	15:19	147
7:41	124	15:26	2, 41, 68, 98, 126
7:42	124	15:32	154
8:12	48	16:7	2, 41, 68, 98
8:32	148, 186	16:11	103, 137
8:34	77	16:13	126
8:41–44	2	16:24	31, 165

16:33	54, 102–3
17:3	66, 138
17:12	137, 139
17:13	104
17:15	137
17:23	2
17:25	74
18:19	160
18:35	185n10
19:34	125
20:19	196
20:21	196
20:23	39
20:26	196
20:28	139
20:31	2, 131–32
21:5	55

Acts

2:17	60
5:41	184
9:16	184
14:23	146
15:14	177n28
15:23	149
15:26	184
19:29	6
20:4	6
20:17	146
21:13	184
23:26	149
26:29	174n13
27:29	174n13

Romans

1:5	184
1:7	149n12, 172
1:10	175
4:7	77n1
5:5	98
6:19	77n1
8:14–16	98
9:3	174n13
12:19	172n3, 174n10
15:24	184
15:33	196
16:3	186

16:9	186
16:20	196
16:21	186
16:23	6

1 Corinthians

1:3	149n12
1:14	6
3:8	159n17
9:17–18	159n17
10:14	172n3, 174n10
15:23	72n7
15:58	172n3, 174n10
16:2	175

2 Corinthians

1:2	149n12
6:14	77n1
7:1	174n10
8:23	186
11:2	5, 146
12:19	174n10
13:7	174n13
13:9	174n13
13:11	196

Galatians

1:3	149n12
2:11	95
3:19	84n23
4:25–26	5
6:16	196

Ephesians

1:2	149n12
3:1	84n23
3:14	84n23
5:25–27	146
5:32	5

Philippians

1:2	149n12
2:12	172n3, 174n10
2:25	186
3:2	158
4:1	172n3, 174n10

4:3	186	1:5	84n23
4:9	196	1:9	175
		1:11	84n23

Colossians

		1:13	175
1:2	149n12	2:1	175
1:7	172n3	2:2	175
2:8	158	2:14	77n1
4:7	172n3	3:13	184
4:9	172n3		
4:14	172n3		

Philemon

1	172
3	149n12

1 Thessalonians

1:1	149n12
2:19	72n7
3:13	72n7
4:15	72n7
5:23	72n7, 196

Hebrews

1:9	77n1
6:9	174n10
10:17	77n1
13:7	190

2 Thessalonians

James

1:2	149n12
2:1	72n7
2:3–8	77
2:3	77n1
2:7	77n1
2:8	72n7
3:3	140
3:7	190
3:9	190
3:16	196

1:16	172n3, 174n10
1:19	172n3, 174n10
2:5	172n3, 174n10
2:8	183
2:19	183
5:7	72n7
5:8	72n7
5:16	174n13

1 Peter

1:1	3, 147
1:20	60
2:11	174nn10–11
4:12	174nn10–11
5:1	3, 146
5:13	5, 147, 166

1 Timothy

1:2	149n12
1:10	175
3:16	101
5:14	84n23
6:3	175

2 Timothy

2 Peter

1:2	149n12, 172
1:3	175
3:1	61n5
4:3	175

1:16	72n7
1:19	183
3:1	174nn10–11
3:4	72n7
3:8	174nn10–11
3:14	174nn10–11
3:17	174nn10–11

Titus

1:4	149n12

1 John

1:1–5	3, 36
1:1–4	10, 13, 18, 20, 27–32
1:1	2, 18, 27–31, 54
1:2	27–30, 71, 88, 128, 139
1:3	27–31, 124, 138
1:4	18, 27–31, 40, 111, 131, 165
1:5—2:11	21, 33–50
1:5—2:2	21, 35–42
1:5–7	2, 33
1:5	28, 33–35, 37, 42, 48, 83, 109
1:6	2, 6, 30, 34–40, 118, 152
1:7	30, 34, 36–41, 54, 110, 125, 152
1:8	2, 6, 34–40
1:9	34, 36, 38–41, 54, 65, 72, 81, 85, 95, 110, 135
1:10	6, 34–40, 44, 64, 128
2:1	2–4, 7, 18, 30–31, 34–36, 39–41, 47, 53, 72, 79, 81, 85, 90, 124, 131
2:2	38, 40–41, 56, 110, 138
2:3–11	21, 34, 42–50, 52
2:3–6	21, 34, 42–46
2:3	4, 13, 16, 42–43, 53, 108, 120–21
2:4	2, 6, 16, 34, 37, 42–44, 49, 64, 118, 120, 128
2:5	4, 13, 16, 34, 42–45, 73, 116, 120
2:6	14–15, 34, 36, 42, 44–46, 49, 75, 111, 115, 152, 185
2:7–11	21, 34, 42, 46–50
2:7	3–4, 18, 29, 31, 34, 40, 42, 47–48, 107, 155, 174
2:8	3, 18, 31, 34, 40, 42, 47–48, 54, 58, 138, 155
2:9	6, 34, 42, 44, 48–49, 118
2:10	34, 42, 49–50, 83
2:11	34, 36, 42, 50, 118, 152
2:12–27	19
2:12–17	19, 21, 51–58
2:12–14	4, 6, 21, 51–56, 102–3
2:12	3–4, 18, 31, 38–40, 52–54, 90, 139, 184
2:13	3, 18, 29, 31, 40, 52–54, 84, 121, 137
2:14	3–4, 18, 29, 31, 52–56, 60, 67, 84, 121, 137
2:15–17	21, 51–52, 56–58
2:15	14, 41, 51, 56–57, 66, 73
2:16	56–58, 89
2:17	48, 56–58, 132
2:18–27	17, 19, 21, 59–69
2:18–19	21, 60–62
2:18	3–4, 6, 17, 53, 55, 60–61, 64, 77, 101–2, 157–58
2:19	6, 61–62
2:20–23	21, 62–65
2:20	17, 60, 62–63, 65, 67–68, 102
2:21	2–3, 18, 31, 37, 55, 63–64, 67
2:22–23	6
2:22	3, 6, 14, 37, 61, 64, 101–2, 123, 128, 158
2:23	7, 64–65,
2:24–26	21, 65–67
2:24	14, 17, 29, 56, 60, 65–67, 79, 102
2:25	4, 30, 66–67, 88
2:26	3, 7, 18, 31, 38, 55, 61, 67, 79, 104, 131, 157
2:27	14, 17, 37, 56, 59–60, 63, 67–69, 102
2:28—3:3	21, 70–75
2:28–29	21, 60, 71–73
2:28	4, 13–14, 40, 53, 56, 59–60, 70–72, 77, 90, 95, 115, 132, 139
2:29	14, 58, 70–73, 77, 79, 82, 85, 108, 119, 137
3:1–3	21, 71, 73–75
3:1–2	4, 6, 10, 13
3:1	14, 56, 73–74, 82, 87
3:2	4, 47, 73–75, 77, 82, 107, 174
3:3	46, 70, 75, 115–16
3:4–12	21, 76–85
3:4–6	21, 76–79
3:4	38, 58, 76–77
3:5	38, 46, 71, 75–76, 78, 115
3:6	76, 78–79, 81–82, 136

ANCIENT SOURCES INDEX

3:7–12	21, 76–77, 79–85	4:6	37–38, 99–100, 104–5, 157
3:7	4, 7, 14, 38, 41, 46, 53, 55–56, 58, 60, 67, 72–73, 75, 77, 79, 82, 85, 104, 115–16, 139, 157	4:7—5:4	22, 106–21
		4:7–21	19
		4:7–11	19
		4:7–10	21, 107–10
3:8	6, 29, 38, 58, 71, 77–80, 136	4:7	4, 7, 14, 47, 90, 107–8, 114, 119, 137, 154, 174
3:9	38, 73, 80–82, 108, 119, 136–37	4:8	108–9, 114
3:10	2, 6, 16, 43, 58, 73, 82–83, 108, 136	4:9	2, 16, 43, 109
		4:10	16, 38, 41, 43, 109–10, 117
3:11–15	2	4:11–16b	22, 107, 110–13
3:11	2, 4, 7, 14, 29, 35, 47, 83–84, 90, 154	4:11	2, 4, 14–15, 46–47, 107, 110–11, 114, 174, 185
3:12	14, 80, 84–85, 87–88, 137	4:12	45, 111, 114, 116
3:13–18	21, 86–91	4:13	2, 16, 43, 97, 111–13, 120, 138
3:13	4, 14, 56, 86–87		
3:14	4, 13, 86–88, 90, 108	4:14	109, 112–13, 116–17, 128
3:15	30, 88, 118, 135	4:15	2, 6–7, 44, 65, 103, 111, 113
3:16–18	7	4:16	97, 111, 113–14, 116, 119
3:16	4, 13–16, 43, 46, 75, 89, 111, 115, 120, 185	4:16c–18	22, 107, 114–16
		4:17	16, 43, 45–46, 71–72, 75, 95, 114–16, 132
3:17	14, 44, 57, 89–90, 94	4:18	45, 116
3:18	4, 14, 40, 53, 90–91, 139, 154	4:19–21	22, 107, 116–18
		4:19	116–17
3:19–24	4, 21, 92–98	4:20	37, 41, 64, 111, 117–18, 128
3:19	16, 37, 43, 92–94, 120	4:21	15, 118
3:20	94–95, 127	5:1–4	22, 107, 119–21
3:21	4, 47, 72, 94–95, 107, 132, 174	5:1	2, 6–7, 11, 97, 119, 123, 137
3:22	93–94, 96, 120–21, 133	5:2	16, 43, 73, 82, 107, 121
3:23	6–7, 12, 14, 30, 54, 96–97, 100, 108, 118–19, 124, 136, 138, 154, 184	5:3	107, 120–21
		5:4	13, 56, 121, 137
		5:5–12	22, 122–29
3:24	2, 16, 43, 96–98, 103, 111–13, 120, 138	5:5–8	22, 123–27
		5:5	6–7, 14, 56, 97, 113, 119, 123–24
4:1–21	19		
4:1–6	16, 19, 21, 99–105	5:6–8	6
4:1–3	6	5:6	30, 37, 104, 124–26, 128, 139
4:1–2	2		
4:1	4, 6, 14, 47, 56, 97, 99–101, 107, 119, 174, 157	5:7	126, 138
		5:8	125–27, 192
4:2	2–3, 14, 16, 30, 43, 65, 100–101, 113, 120, 124–25, 157–58	5:9–12	22, 123, 127–29
		5:9	127–29
		5:10	37, 64, 97, 119, 128–29, 136
4:3	3, 6, 61, 65, 101–2, 158	5:11	13, 30, 88, 129
4:4	4, 40, 53, 90, 102–3, 121, 127, 139	5:12	66, 129, 136, 139
		5:13–21	18, 22, 130–40
4:5	56, 103	5:13–17	22, 130–36

5:13	2–4, 6, 18, 30–31, 54–55, 67, 88, 97, 119, 130–32, 184
5:14	13, 58, 72, 95–96, 132–33
5:15	13, 132–33
5:16–17	2, 135
5:16	38, 41, 81, 133–36
5:17	38–39, 135–36
5:18–21	13, 22, 130–31, 136–40
5:18	80–81, 84, 119, 136–37
5:19–20	6
5:19	51, 56, 84, 137–38
5:20	30, 88, 124, 138–39
5:21	4, 14, 18, 40, 53, 56, 90, 132, 135, 139–40

2 John

1–4	22, 145–52
1–3	20, 22, 145–50
1	5, 13, 16, 143–48, 150, 166
2	143–48, 150–51, 159
3	30, 143–44, 149–51, 159
4	4–5, 16, 20, 22, 36, 143–44, 146, 148–52, 159
5–11	20, 22, 151, 153–62
5–8	20, 22, 154–59
5	3, 5, 16, 29, 47, 83, 134, 143–44, 146, 153–56, 159
6	5, 16, 29, 36, 47, 143–44, 147, 151–52, 156–57, 159
7	3, 6–7, 16, 30, 38, 61, 101–2, 125, 143–44, 153, 157–58
8	5, 16, 143–44, 147, 158–59
9–11	20, 22, 144, 159–62
9	7, 16, 78, 143–44, 160–61
10	5, 7, 16, 143–44, 147, 160–62
11	143–44, 160, 162
12–13	20, 22, 130, 163–66
12	4–5, 16, 31, 143–44, 147, 159, 163–66
13	5, 143–44, 146, 148, 163, 166

3 John

1–4	20, 23, 146–47, 169, 171–79
1	6, 13, 95, 169–70, 171–73, 175, 180
2	47, 95, 150, 169–71, 173–76, 180
3–4	23, 151, 176–79
3	36, 147, 151–52, 169–73, 174, 176–78, 183
4	4, 147, 169–71, 173, 175, 178–79
5–12	20, 23, 169, 180–93
5–8	6, 23, 172, 181–86
5	47, 95, 169–70, 174, 180–82
6	169–70, 181–84, 188
7–10	170
7	54, 169–70, 181, 184–85
8	46, 169–70, 181, 185–86
9–10	8, 11, 23, 16–17, 170, 187–89
9	11, 16, 169–70, 183, 187–88
10	11, 169–70, 183, 187–89
11	47, 95, 169–70, 174, 190–92
12	8, 169–70, 183, 190, 192–93
13–15	20, 23, 130, 169–70, 194–96
13–14	4, 20, 23, 195
13	164, 169–70, 194–95
14	169–70, 183, 194–95
15	20, 150, 164, 169–70, 190, 194–96

Jude

3	174nn10–11
7	174nn10–11
16	84n23
18	61n5
20	174nn10–11

Revelation

2:14	49
3:7	63
5:6	84
5:9	84
5:12	84
6:4	84
6:9	84
11:18	159n17
12:1	5
12:17	5, 81
13:3	84
13:8	84

18:24		84	22:12		159n17
19:6–8		146	22:17		146
19:7		5			

DEAD SEA SCROLLS

Damascus Document

XX, 9   140

Rule of the Community

II, 11–12   140
II, 17   140
IV, 5   140

GRECO-ROMAN WRITINGS

Oxyrhynchus papyri

XII 1422   173

EARLY CHRISTIAN WRITINGS

Clement of Alexandria, *Stromateis*

II.15.66   2

Eusebius, *Ecclesiastical History*

III.1.1   4
III.23.3–4   4
III.39.17   2
VI.25.10   2

Irenaeus, *Against Heresies*

I.16.3   2
III.1.1   4
III.3.4   4
III.16.5   2
III.16.8   2

www.ingramcontent.com/pod-product-compliance
Lightning Source LLC
Chambersburg PA
CBHW070606300426
44113CB00010B/1418